ADVENTURE
VACATIONS

From Trekking

in New G

to Swimm

in Siberia

Kebos/SOBEK photo file

EDITED BY
RICHARD BANGS

SOBEK'S INTERNATIONAL EXPLORERS SOCIETY

DIANA SAINT JAMES, PROJECT DIRECTOR
TRACY JOHNSON, ASSOCIATE EDITOR
DENISE FARIA, PRODUCTION ASSISTANT

John Muir Publications, P.O. Box 613, Santa Fe, NM 87504

First edition. First printing

Library of Congress Cataloging-in-Publication Data
Adventure vacations : from trekking in New Guinea to swimming in
    Siberia / edited by Richard Bangs. — 1st ed.
        p. cm.
    "Sobek's International Explorers Society."
    ISBN 0-945465-76-9
    1. Outdoor recreation—Directories.   2. Safaris—Directories.
  3. Voyages and travels—Directories.   4. Vacations—Directories.
  I. Bangs, Richard, 1950- . II. Sobek's International Explorers
  Society.
  GV191.35.A35   1990   90-40729
  790'.025—dc20   CIP

Designer: Sally Blakemore
Typeface: Galliard
Typesetter: Copygraphics, Santa Fe, New Mexico

Distributed to the book trade by:
W. W. Norton & Company, Inc.
New York, New York

Contents

Camel/SOBEK photo file

William Weber/SOBEK photo file

Michel Orivel/SOBEK photo file

South America

Europe

Renee Kramer/SOBEK photo file

Oceania

Kebos/SOBEK photo file

Asia

Richard Bangs/SOBEK photo file

North America

Kebos/SOBEK photo file

Del E. Webb/SOBEK photo file

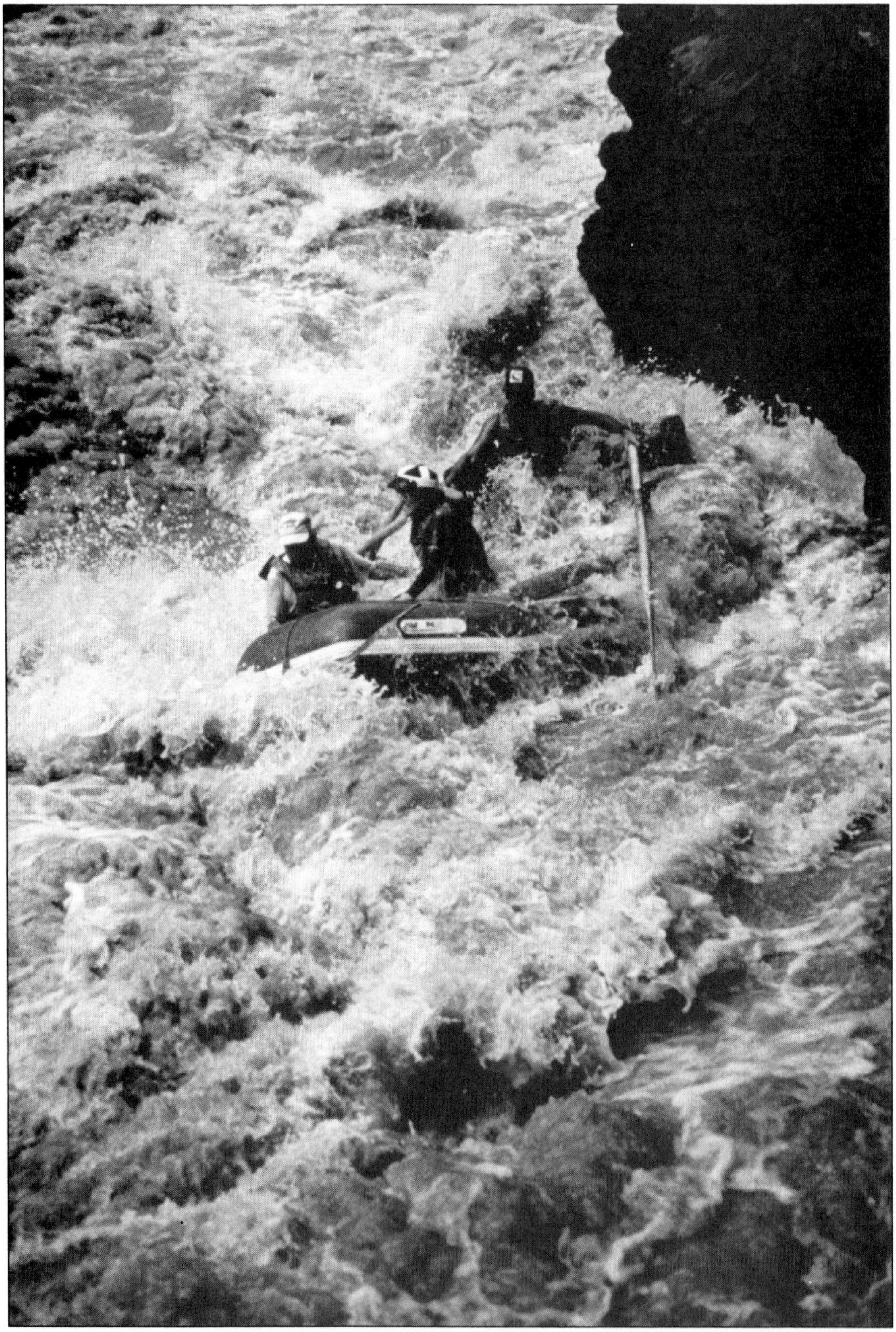

Bart Henderson/SOBEK photo file

PREFACE

Liquid names, improbable descriptions, real places; places that vibrate with a promise as true as the other side of your doorway. This book is the sinuous, shucked road that leads to those appointments with faraway feelings, the gladness of discovery. We invite you to explore the contours of the shorelines and mountains, to sharpen your senses in hot desert air, to succumb to the perfumes of the tropics, to indulge in the intemperate, keenly felt pursuit of adventure travel.

Adventure is a step down the overgrown path—a step that makes a difference, a world of difference. To push aside the tangle, venture beyond the mainstream, and taste heart in mouth is to vitalize the impulse of life, to reassert the play of passion, and to shed luster on the little gleam of time between two eternities. It is a grand difference.

Nothing Venture, Nothing Win is the title of Sir Edmund Hillary's autobiography. However trite this phrase may seem, the great majority of those capable of choice will never venture, never win. It is the first step, the follow-through on the impulse, that is the most difficult. It is as tough as climbing Hillary's Step, that last pitch up the South Face of Everest. It is harder than rowing the Colorado, ballooning over Kilimanjaro, sailing the Straits of Magellan. But it puts your feet on a path that is ultimately rewarding beyond your wildest dreams—the road to adventure. And, the irony is, anyone can do it. It can seem so impossible, beyond the limits of a normal body and mind, but it is as easy as stretching in the morning. It is nothing more than a stretch that goes just a little farther, one that snaps the limbs into a new state of good being, that allows a view just a little bit higher but with horizons that scratch the roof of the world.

Adventure travel can be defined as "active, participatory travel in remote locations," but it is more than that: it is the result of this travel, too. Adventure travel can provide in a week what some lifetimes never produce. It can validate existence, kindle passions, spark commitments, assert the life-force. Mrs. Malaprop might say that allegories should stay on the banks of the Nile—that each being has his assigned place, and to wander far afield is not a civilized pursuit. But it is. That's how we got this far. And we have far to go.

As the back streets of Kathmandu and Cuzco become as familiar as the lights of

Broadway, objections are sometimes voiced that we are losing the world even as we discover it. To a certain extent, this attitude is understandable, and we, the outfitters in this book, share it. Still, it is not the careful, softly stepping visits to Nature's prides that invite violation. With firsthand experience comes appreciation, acknowledgment of worth and respect, and a desire and a reason to preserve the treasure of the planet's bounty. The Colorado still flows through the Grand Canyon, and the Tuolumne still gushes and spills out of the Sierra. To know a special place is to love it, to be willing to work for its survival. Such is the moral imperative behind adventure travel.

Adventure travel is an endeavor that is good for many reasons. It is good for the self and good for the globe. It expands the mind. It tones the body, heightens awareness, promotes understanding. And, it is downright fun! At its least, it is a break from the workaday world, a weekend of exhilaration and good sensations. At its best, it is an exotic journey into a new world, our world.

For almost two decades, SOBEK Expeditions has been exploring the untried routes, the untrod trails, and the unrun rivers and has been sharing discoveries with friends. We have spanned the spectrum of adventure activities, from whitewater rafting to wilderness walking, and poked our paddles into the far corners from Alaska to Zambia. Along the way, we met and often worked with a raft of adventure outfitters whose offerings and outlooks complemented our own. It is the best of these offerings, by the outfitters proven and prime, that we have assembled in this book—a comprehensive compendium of international adventure tours and expeditions, the 200 best in the world. It is a reference book, yes, but also, we hope, a thing of art, a lasting collection of images and wonderfully evocative words by some of America's finest writers and of information on fantastic adventures from the seven lands and seas.

This book is for those who would as lief take the less traveled road, who would turn the unturned stone or seek the unclimbed summit. It is for those who are up before the day to try the fair adventure of tomorrow. Or for those willing to try. These adventures are the sprouts of a flowering spray of odysseys to the ends of the earth.

If the whiff of a wildflower, the cool caress of a wave or the gentle cuffing of flying snow incites your soul, we invite you to journey through this book. Or better yet, to join us on a road not yet taken.

RICHARD BANGS
Lake Merritt, California

INTRODUCTION

What Is Adventure Travel?

If you are in good health, have an open mind, enjoy the outdoors, and want to explore remote areas and meet our neighbors on Planet Earth, you qualify for our trips. Whitewater experience is required on only a few of our most demanding river trips; most trekkers are doing it for the first time, walking farther (and higher) than they ever thought possible. Of course, all participants should be aware of the stresses of climate, altitude, and remoteness, and in some cases, we request a medical certificate from your doctor certifying a clean bill of health. Age limits are generally up to the individual: certain exertions and activities are not appropriate for small children, but the top end of the age spectrum is highly flexible; if you have been living a life of action and curiosity, there is no reason to stop now. Adventure travel provides a safe opportunity for the traveler to step outside normal routines, to challenge expectations, and to test mettle. You don't have to be He-Man or Sheena: you just have to be yourself.

SOBEK and the selected adventure operators we work with are the elite worldwide. We have explored the remotest regions, worked out the logistics, found the best and most efficient ways of running our trips—and kept the motivation for being in the adventure travel business in the forefront of our minds. The job may be rugged and the hours long, but the rewards of doing something we like, and of introducing new people to the pleasures that spark their own enthusiasm, are many and intangible. "It's a tough job," you'll often hear, "but somebody's gotta do it." We do it because we want to.

The guides on adventure travel trips are frequently cited as the best part of the journey: as a rule, they are intelligent, respectful, witty, and tolerant. They may also be highly skilled at rafting, mountaineering, or other activities and trained in exotic languages and traditions, birding, geology, or the other aspects of travel that qualify them to make your trip safe, enjoyable, and educational. Nearly all have first aid training, and many have CPR or other advanced emergency medical qualifications. They are, in short, good company, and we are sure you will find traveling with them a real pleasure.

Meals on adventure trips also rank

high on passengers' evaluations—many meals cooked on the spot and consumed beneath a starry sky would tempt the palate of the most discriminating gourmet. In general, all meals on a trip are included in trip costs, except as stated in the detailed trip itinerary (often meals in larger cities are ''on your own''). Likewise, the equipment necessary for the journey—rafts or other transport, cookware, medical supplies, safety items, and other group camping gear—is provided by the trip operator. Participants are expected to bring their own clothing, sleeping bags and pads, favorite recreational beverages, and other items of a personal nature.

While adventure travel conjures up images of inflatable rafts plunging over waterfalls, pack-laden climbers leaning on their ice axes at the snowy summit, or perhaps, sore feet at the end of the day, we prefer to emphasize its emotional and spiritual rewards: the exhilaration of achievement, the thrill of discovery, the relaxation of rigid schedules, the satisfaction of a job well done. Adventure travel may not be for everyone, but we think it's for you.

Activities

The adventures listed herein reflect the great range and diversity of the modern adventure travel vacation. The 200 or so trips on every continent include activities from ballooning to skin diving and the entire world in between. However, while each trip may specialize in a particular activity—rafting, trekking, cycling, and the like—adventure travel is by its nature multifaceted. Most sailing trips include some diving; many overlanding trips feature hiking to scenic vistas or historic sites. Hence the activity listed just below the trip's title in the following pages is the primary activity but not the only one. Some trips pack so many different types of

adventure into their itinerary that they are just listed as variety. Read the trip description and itinerary, or write for a more complete day-by-day information packet on each trip. Then come along and leap into the world of adventure—with SOBEK.

Class Definitions

Every description in this book includes a grading for its level of difficulty. Since different people have different tolerances for altitude, duration, remoteness, and the like, this scale cannot be exact. It is intended for use in making general distinctions between the offerings in the following pages.

CLASS I — *Easy:* These trips emphasize the scenic or cultural value of a particular region, using hotel accommodations and travel by comfortable van or bus. Short hikes and gentle river floats may be included. These are trips suitable for all ages and inclinations.

CLASS II — *Moderate:* This class provides mild outdoor programs that immerse the participant a bit more fully in the world of adventure. Camping, longer day hikes, and/or whitewater river trips are usually included. The degree of exertion is optional, however, making these trips suitable for all ages as well.

CLASS III — *Average:* Camping is the normal means of sleeping overnight on a Class III trip; hikes and river trips may be longer and more difficult. However, some hotel or lodge nights are often included for convenience. Generally, treks are of a shorter duration (up to 10 days) and/or in lower altitudes (below 10,000 feet). Good health is the only physical requirement, though a minimum age of 12 is usually requested.

C L A S S I V — *Difficult:* Trips of longer duration, farther from population centers, involving physically demanding activity— such as trekking above 10,000 feet or rafting a Class IV-V river—are considered Class IV trips. Previous outdoor experience (camping, hiking, etc.) is often helpful, and a physician's certificate of health may be required. Age limits vary with individual trips, operators, and participants, but most Class IV trips have a minimum age of 18.

C L A S S V — *Strenuous:* When previous technical experience and skills are required, the trips are classed as strenuous. Generally, these trips are of an exploratory nature, in sparsely populated areas, and they may demand previous whitewater, rock climbing, or other technical skills. This category includes treks of long duration (a month or more) which reach an altitude of over 16,000 feet.

Code of Adventure Travel Ethics

The trips in this book will take you to uncommon places, to distinctive cultures, to exceptional yet fragile environments. We must always remember we are visitors on others' soil, and we must tread carefully. As adventure travelers we can do much for the world simply by understanding what we see and by learning to care about those whom we meet. In that spirit, SOBEK endorses the Ecumenical Coalition on Third World Tourism's Code of Ethics for Tourists. When you join an adventure travel trip, we request that you do the same:

1. Travel in a spirit of humility and with a genuine desire to learn more about the people of your host country. Be sensitively aware of the feelings of other people, thus preventing what might be offensive behavior on your part. This applies to photography.

2. Cultivate the habit for listening and observing, rather than merely hearing and seeing.

3. Realize that often the people in the country you visit have time concepts and thought patterns different from your own. This does not make them inferior, only different.

4. Instead of looking for the "beach paradise," discover the enrichment of seeing a different way of life, through other eyes.

5. Acquaint yourself with local customs. What is courteous in one country may be quite the reverse in another.

6. Instead of the Western practice of "knowing all the answers," cultivate the habit of asking questions.

7. Remember that you are only one of thousands of tourists visiting this country and do not expect special privileges.

8. If you really want your experience to be a "home away from home," it is foolish to waste money on traveling.

9. When you are shopping, remember that the "bargain" you obtained was possible because of the low wages paid to the maker.

10. Do not make promises to people in your host country unless you can carry them through.

11. Spend time reflecting on your daily experience in an attempt to deepen your understanding. It has been said that "what enriches you may rob and violate others."

Trip Codes

You'll notice that each tour in this book has a two-letter and then a numbered code, for example, AF 13 or OC 83. These are reference codes devised by SOBEK to facilitate the booking process. So when calling to inquire about or reserve a trip space, rather than go through the akward process of trying to describe a tour, you can use the shorthand codes. The letters correspond to continents with the exception of the Environmental category. The letter codes:

> EC: Environment
>
> AF: Africa
>
> SA: South America
>
> EU: Europe
>
> OC: Oceania
>
> AS: Asia
>
> NA: North America

The numbers that follow the letter codes are assigned to differentiate tours within the letter categories.

It should be noted that this coded system is a SOBEK-designed system and does not apply to other outfitters. When calling or writing SOBEK for any of the trips listed within this book, feel free to use the codes to facilitate the inquiry and booking processes.

SOBEK photo file

On Trip Pricing

An important consideration in choosing a trip from *Adventure Vacations* is its price. The land cost of an adventure trip—the cost of a trip excluding all air transportation, except where specified—can vary dramatically. Certain types of travel, or particular areas of the world, dictate high costs regardless of the level of service supplied. The Arctic regions are expensive, as are certain countries such as China and North Yemen. Cruise ships and hotel trips have high accommodation costs built in, reflecting the more comfortable features of these programs. These considerations can be the dominating factors in trip pricing, but they are not the only ones.

The single most important determinant of cost is still value: you get what you pay for. Features such as guide-to-client ratio, inclusion of hotels and in-city meals, domestic air transport or charter services, park and museum fees, the quality and amount of equipment used, and the use of nonlocal guide services can all explain the price tag of one trip relative to another.

International river trips tend to be more expensive than treks, for a variety of reasons. Inflatable rafts carry three or four passengers and a guide, dictating high per-person guide costs (and more guides per trip). The equipment itself is expensive, requires periodic repair and replacement, and is heavy and difficult to transport from trip to trip. Providing quality cuisine in remote river corridors, far from the local tienda or vineyard, necessitates heavier loads and more careful planning. The contrast with a trekking group of 15 to 20 people, led by a native guide, which buys much of its food along the way and carries little specialized equipment, explains why there are two ends to the price spectrum.

With this edition of *Adventure Vacations*, SOBEK's International Explorers Society uses Trip Value Coding, making it easy to compare trip costs and facilitating the selection of trips within certain price ranges. Each write-up herein is followed by a listing of the months of operation for that trip, and a one-word code indicative of the trip cost, based on a per-day price range:

MODERATE trips cost under $100/day

MEDIUM trips are between $100 and $150/day

PREMIUM trips cost more than $150/day

Adventure Vacations is designed to provide the widest possible selection of programs available in all areas—location, activity, and cost. Some trips are included which sacrifice comfort for cost and include few extra services; yet these are the very programs sought by some adventurous souls. The level of service and of trip value for the many excellent operators in this book is explained in detailed trip literature, available for each trip on request from SOBEK's International Explorers Society. The choice is yours.

Detailed information, including current dates and prices, equipment lists, health and travel advice, day-by-day itineraries, suggested reading, and much more, is available for the vast majority of trips.

Welcome to the World of Adventure

By electing to join an adventure tour, you will be opening yourself up to an unusual and memorable vacation. To assist you in planning your trip, we have collected this information about adventure travel, health, fitness, passports, insurance, photography—all matters relevant to going someplace new. This is, of course, just a guide, and the information herein may not answer all of your questions. So we urge you to contact SOBEK or the outfitter with your special questions about the trip once you have read this material.

MENTAL FITNESS

You may be traveling in an exotic and underdeveloped part of the world, where local people have a totally different outlook on life; but remember, that is often a chief reason for going! Do not always expect things to happen on time or as they might at home. In developing countries, transportation and other facilities are often strained and delays do occur. Just relax, take things in stride, and keep an open mind. Such attitudes will allow you to reap rewards in excess of your expectations. And remember, you are a guest in these countries, and aggressive tourists are not viewed favorably!

You will enjoy your trip more if you learn about the country or countries you are visiting before your departure. Our suggested reading list provides a good starting point.

PHYSICAL FITNESS

Since the theme of the trips herein is adventure, the healthier you are, the easier you will adjust to and enjoy your experience. We are not crusading for Olympic athletes. In fact, our clients regularly range from age 10 to 75. But the degree of difficulty does vary widely, and it is most important to select an appropriate level for you. Obviously, the degree of fitness needed for each trip varies according to the trips activity. On most rafting trips or a camel ride, for example, you need not be as fit as for a trek. Still, the better shape you are in, the more you will enjoy whatever adventure you take with SOBEK.

Fitness represents complete good health and must be planned and maintained. We recommend that for at least three months prior to departure, you do something strenuous every day, preferably related to the nature of your expedition—walking, hiking, cycling, and so forth. Because it is sometimes difficult to simulate the conditions you will encounter overseas, any active pursuit such as cycling, swimming, jogging, squash or tennis will help. A bit of gentle gardening or an occasional afternoon stroll is not enough. The idea is to get more oxygen flowing through your body, which requires sustained effort. On weekends, we urge you to try longer periods of the activity most related to your trip, so you can get a good notion of how your body copes with this activity over an extended period. The most important form of health for anyone is mental health: be confident and prepared, and your adventure will enrich your entire life.

ENVIRONMENT

We ask all participants to respect the natural and cultural environments of the area we visit. Our expeditions go into some of the remotest and most untouched areas of the world. In many cases, we are setting the pace for future tourism, so it is vitally important to start off on the right footing. The unspoiled areas of the world are already diminishing. Let us not hasten the process.

MONEY MATTERS

Costs are generally all-inclusive within the country of destination (with the exception of airfare), so little additional money is required. In the enclosed supplemental information, items not included in the land cost are specified.

We recommend that you bring enough money to buy local crafts and gifts. You know how much you like to spend on such things; use this knowledge as a guide.

Money should be converted to traveler's checks before departure. Upon arrival in foreign countries, you will be able to convert the checks to local currency. Buy checks of small denominations as these are more convenient to cash in places where you only need a little money at a time. Keep a separate record of the check numbers so you can replace them if lost or stolen. You may find it desirable to carry some cash with you, particularly one-dollar bills.

PASSPORTS

A valid passport is required for any international travel. If you do not already possess one, apply at the nearest passport issuing office (check your telephone book under U.S. Government, Passport Office). Passports are valid for ten years. Allow approximately six to eight weeks for preparation of the passport.

MEDICAL MATTERS

Good health makes for happy holidays. Often people on our trips tell us that they "have never felt better." Yet sometimes, problems can occur—most commonly, an occasional upset stomach or blisters on treks.

In the unlikely event of a serious illness, every effort will be made to take the necessary steps to preserve your well-being, up to and including evacuation. We advise all participants to take out a suitable travel insurance policy to assure the best possible care.

Good pretrip preparation and observance of the following basic rules should ensure your well-being throughout. Though these remarks may generally not be applicable in developed countries, use common sense and good judgment whenever and wherever you travel.

➤ If you feel unwell, inform your trip leader or local representative IMMEDIATELY.

➤ Be very particular about personal hygiene, making sure always to keep your hands and face clean. Hand-washing before meals is the most commonly overlooked health precaution. Bring alcohol hand-wipes ("wet ones"), if there may be a shortage of wash facilities.

➤ Do not drink water unless you know it has been purified or boiled or comes directly from a spring source. Even in city hotels and on houseboats, we recommend that you avoid drinking water from the tap. Use the flask in your room, or ask for some boiled or bottled water. This caution should prevent you from getting the dreaded "Delhi Belly."

➤ Do NOT eat uncooked vegetables or uncooked meat, and wash and peel all fruit before you eat it. Eat only food that has been recently cooked.

➤ Get all the vaccinations we recommend. Remember to regularly take your antimalaria tablets, if they are recommended. We suggest that everyone take them on Sundays so we will all be on the same schedule.

➤ In the cities, eat at reputable restaurants, or get tips from the guide on where to go to sample the local cuisine. If you've followed all these suggestions, don't be afraid to try something new!

TRAVEL INSURANCE

We strongly recommend a personal insurance policy against sickness, accident, loss of baggage, trip cancellation, and so forth, as you would for any overseas trip. You may want a policy that will cover you in the unlikely event that you need evacuation by plane or helicopter.

NOTES FOR PHOTOGRAPHERS

Many are already familiar with the basics of outdoor photography. For those who are not, we recommend a single-lens reflex (SLR) camera, which uses 35mm film. Since most SLRs take interchangeable

lenses, we suggest a three-lens system consisting of the normal 50mm lens; a 135mm telephoto or 80-200mm zoom for distance shots; and a wide-angle lens of 28 or 35mm for shooting in close situations such as aboard a raft or indoors. Leather cases for your camera and lenses help prevent jarring and internal damage.

Other accessories you might consider are ultraviolet or skylight filters for all your lenses, as they prevent damage to the lens surface and are considerably cheaper than a new lens. For color film, a polarizing filter for daylight use is an exceptional way to get the most out of your scenic shots.

You might also consider bringing films with different ASA ratings for different situations. The lower the ASA, the more light is necessary to properly expose the film—so Kodachrome 25 or 64 is best for exterior shots, while Ektachrome 200 or even 400 is better for low-light conditions. We do recommend slide film over print film for better color and flexibility.

For indoor photography, a flash attachment is recommended; or you could make use of the 1000 ASA and 1600 ASA films that have recently become available. One precaution about indoor photography: please be sure you have the permission of the household or keeper of the premises you wish to photograph.

You should be familiar with any camera equipment you have, and be certain it works well prior to your departure. Buy and develop all film at home, as film in most of the countries we visit tends to be expensive if it is available at all.

If you're already a photographer, we would like to invite you to contribute to the SOBEK PHOTO FILE. As one of adventure travel's leading outfitters, we have recurring requests for color slides of cultural interactions, wilderness activities, and outdoor adventures around the world. We would like to share these possibilities with you. Here is how it works. Send us as many slides as you wish. Label every slide clearly with your name, address, and a description of the slide's subject, including the location. Send only high-quality duplicates. If your slide is selected for publication it may be necessary to request the original from you.

As needs arise, we will send relevant slides to the editors. If your slide is published, we will deduct a 50 percent agent and handling fee and forward the rest of the payment to you. (Professional photo agents commonly take 60 percent or more of a sale, so we feel our arrangement is more than fair.) You retain all rights, unless a publication purchases them with your consent; and you have the final say over all sales.

Contacting the Outfitter

For specific rates and prices, complete itineraries and up-to-date information, you should contact SOBEK or the outfitters included in these pages. In the back of the book, there is a listing with addresses and telephone numbers of all the outfitters. You may contact them directly, or work through your local travel agent, or you may contact SOBEK, which, in addition to being an outfitter and a travel agency, acts as a clearinghouse for the vast majority of adventure travel firms.

You can contact SOBEK by calling toll-free 1-800-777-7939 or by writing to: SOBEK, P.O. Box 1089, Angels Camp, CA 95222.

Pamela Roberson/SOBEK photo file

With a Limp and a Grin

JON CARROLL

"The test of an adventure is that when you're in the middle of it, you say to your-self, 'Oh, now I've got myself in an awful mess: I wish I were sitting quietly at home.' And the sign that something's wrong with you is when you sit quietly at home wishing you were having lots of adventures."
—Thorton Wilder, "The Matchmaker"

An adventure, I learned very early, has to do with a group of guys trying to find something. It could be the secret of the old clock, or the lost treasure of the Incas, or even kindly Dr. Cooper who was being held against his will by Nazis. In between the goal and the guys were a series of obstacles; overcoming the obstacles constituted the adventure.

There was Tom, who was the leader; everybody liked Tom. Tom was friendly and brave and smart and humble and tall. Tom's best friend was Billy, who was almost as brave and almost as tall and even smarter, a real brain. Billy could some-times figure out things that stumped Tom. And there was Butch, who was very tall and very strong and didn't say much. Standing a little apart from the group was Eric, who was a little broody and was always getting into fights. It turned out that Eric's father had died in the war, the last one. And there was The Kid, who was younger and made silly mistakes early in the adventure, but when the chips were down, why, he saved the whole gang.

And then there was Wally. Or Chester. I identified with them both.

I didn't want to go on an adventure. Your Wallys and your Chesters would have to be real dumb to get involved in an adventure. If I did go off with Tom and his pals, through some misguided sense of wanting to belong, I'd be the one who got bumped off. I'd be the one who stepped on the dry stick that made the noise that alerted the Nazis. I'd be the one who dropped the ruby down the rat hole. There'd be a moment of silence for me, but I wouldn't be around to enjoy it.

The thought of humiliation and death can be a real factor in any career decision. When they came around looking for astronauts and Arctic explorers, I was tied up in meetings. I was unable to come to the phone. I was on the other coast.

So until I was 33, I pretty much watched television and took hot showers and played poker. I learned to drive a stan-dard transmission; that was about the apex of my adventure experience.

Then I met a girl. Not the first time that had happened, but this was different. There was a hormonal surge of tidal proportions; there was hopeless adoration mixed with wallowing devotion. This girl liked to backpack; I liked to backpack. I didn't, but I did. That's the glory of, that's the story of love.

Five years later, I was trekking in the

Himalayas. Somewhere west of Junbesi, three days into a 30-day experience, I said to myself: I am either committing suicide or having a midlife crisis. Either I am Wally and will die; or I'm not Wally and will live.

The truth turned out to be rather more complicated. That afternoon, we were standing on a ridge. We had just caught our first glimpse of the very high mountains. Around us, the dead green fields of millet arced in descending circles. A red-robed lama stood with us, beaming, leaning on a ski pole he used as a walking stick. We could see the dark outline of a wall of mani stones on the next ridge.

Not Wally, I decided. I began walking down the trail, faster and faster, then skipping, then running, leaping, whirling, laughing, waving to the girl of my dreams, now my wife, my honeymoon chum. Down the mountainside I rushed, happy to be me, happy not to be Wally.

At the bottom, I said to myself: Jeez, I think I've done something to my knee.

The next morning, in a room above a shop in Those, Nepal, my worst fears were confirmed. I had a real throbber. Every step hurt. Sahib's knee, my experienced companions called it, a name I instantly resented. A classic Wally ailment, sahib's knee. Serious jerk material.

I wallied on. I hung back from the group and squeezed tears of frustration down my cheeks. That night, at Bhandar in a huge hidden valley, I stood alone in the courtyard of a gompa and cursed everyone and everything. This was a completely stupid experience, a trashy and pathetic activity indulged in by spoiled, self-deluded Westerners. I didn't belong here; I belong in my own bed in my own room with the covers up to my neck. I wanted good wine and bad fiction, and I wanted it now.

Still, I continued. No choice. I gimped on, whining twice a day, feeling lumpy and lost. The landscape was eerie and odd; the teahouses friendly; the gompas serene. My knee did not feel better, but I learned to live with it. We walked up to Namche Bazar (they walked, I wallied) and beyond. Ama Dablam stood like a sentry, the crown of creation, as constantly amazing as any sight on earth.

By this time, I had developed a satisfying gait, swinging my right leg in a wide stiff semi circle as I walked, the foot grabbing gently in for a landing to minimize the shock. I was able to plant my walking stick at just the proper moment so that my weight was balanced just as my foot began its descent.

We got up to Loboche, just across the glacier from Everest Base Camp. The air was thin and fragile; it felt like glass in my lungs. We paused a day, then started back down the valley. At Namche, we reentered the world of traveler's checks and airplane reservations. If we make it back to Lukla in one day, we were told, we could make a morning flight.

(This turned out to be a classic Nepal fantasy—Lukla is an airport in the sense that ketchup is a food—but the point is that we trusted the timetable we were given. Lukla or bust.)

For complicated reasons, my wife started walking an hour before I left. When I finished my business in Namche and started down the trail, I got the notion to make up the hour's differential and catch her before she got to Lukla. The day was warm; the trail was crowded. I'd been hiking for a month; I was in good shape, skinny and brown and clear-eyed. With my swinging leg and my brandished walking stick, I cut a wide swath. I yielded only to yaks.

I caught up with my wife by the middle of the afternoon. "Hello," I said, pulling alongside, casual as all get-out. "Hello," she said, not as impressed as I'd hoped.

And that was, finally, it. A man nearing 40 and his wife, walking in the Himalayan twilight; a man with a limp and a grin pushing through the outskirts of town. Something that started badly had ended well; something that had started as

an obstacle had been redefined as a blessing. In the context of this book, I suppose, it was not much of an adventure. Death was not defied. But it had been for me a triumph, a talisman I could carry with me, a thought I could always think. Whatever I am, I am not Wally.

I think maybe that we do not climb a mountain because it is there. We climb it because we are here.

Skip
the Balloon

RITA MAE BROWN

"Nothing is impossible: I engage to be back here in London, in the card room of the Reform Club, on Saturday the 21st of December at a quarter before nine p.m. And now, Gentlemen, I believe diamonds are trumps?"

With that challenge begins the most famous traveling expedition know to the world. Jules Verne gave us Phileas Fogg who said he could go around the world in eighty days. When this adventure took place, the late nineteenth century, it wasn't always easy to go around the corner. Except in the wealthiest of cities the roads were unpaved, lorries were rough, and coaches, expensive. Penicillin lay mouldering on old bread undiscovered, and an illness, easily cured today, could end your days on Hotel Earth.

Phileas's wager, taken in the bosom of High Church abundance, an upper-class London club, was astonishing. Even in 1955 and 1956 when this delicious story was filmed with David Niven as Fogg, it remained astonishing. *Around the World in Eighty Days* shot 68,894 people, logged four million passenger miles, and used 140 actual locations plus interiors. David Niven was a latter-day Phileas Fogg.

When I picked up my copy of *Adven-*

ture Vacations, I kept thinking of Fogg. The more I read, the more I thought that these tours are our version of *Around the World in Eighty Days*. There are some big differences. For one thing, we can fly, so we can go around the world in a matter of hours assuming you can stand the food at 37,000 feet. The second big difference is that today you don't have to be upper class to travel for pleasure. A vacation is within reach of all but the poorest of people. The third thing is we have plastic money, which reduces the risk of winding up broke in the middle of Peru. And perhaps, best of all, our medical preparation is vastly superior to even twenty-five years ago, much less one hundred. Compared to Phileas, we ought to be able to do anything.

What if I discounted the airplane time and tried to go around the world on SOBEK's tours? Naturally, my starting point would be the United States. I'll try to stay on the up side of the equator. Can I do it? And more, can I do it and not teeter toward bankruptcy? Let's see.

Rafting down the Grand Canyon of the Colorado River seems a bracing place to start. This takes nine days at the cost of $125 per day. Granted, Miss Brown thinks

if she were supposed to be on the water she would have gills, but I've got to start somewhere and this tour is appealing. The kaleidoscope of colors, shifting with the light, as one hurtles over rushing waters is worth whatever discomfort I might feel at being on a liquid surface. A friend of mine took this trip a few years ago. This was a woman who would have a grand mal seizure if she broke a nail. I figured she'd finish this shoot down the river and wind up a basket case in the emergency room of her hairdresser. Wrong. She loved it. In fact, it changed her life. She takes one physically demanding vacation a year. She's also doing much better on the job. The two may or may not be connected, but the fingernail queen is a far more confident woman than the lady I used to know hanging over the L'oreal counter. She described going down the Colorado as flying. She knows she moves faster in an airplane, but it felt faster in the raft. What the hell, if she can do it, I can do it.

I keep heading north and west and wind up in Vancouver, Canada. Having been here three times before, I feel at home. The city, with the snowcapped mountains as a backstop, circles a deep body of water that is almost cobalt blue. Vancouver is clean and the natives are friendly. The temptation is to hang around town for a while because so much is going on. But looking across the Strait of Georgia that glistens between Vancouver Island and British Columbia, I want to get on the tour.

I get to sail through New World fjords, which is spectacular in itself, but one of the major reasons I like this tour is the smells. The Northwest pulsates with a scent unique in the world. The tonic odor of living evergreen is mixed with salt air and the faint hint of salmon. When you wake up in the morning you are instantly invigorated. The wildlife spills over even into the civilized parts of the area. Fraser Park is filled with black squirrels that brazenly scamper up to you for a handout. In American cities the only thing that scampers up to you is the local wino. If this glorious mixture of smells, sights, and sounds (the wind in the pines, the splash of a fish jumping toward sunlight) doesn't thrill you, then you're dead and too dumb to fall over. Nine days on a medium-priced tour, roughly $100 per day, is a bargain. You'll want to stay for months.

While I'm on the West Coast of North America, I'd certainly like to climb Mount McKinley up in Alaska. I've never seen the tundra. I've flown over it and I've been to Anchorage but that's not the same as actually trudging along hundreds of miles from a buzz saw.

Phileas Fogg had a sidekick, Passepartout. I've got Juts, my red chow. Granted she isn't as amusing a conversationalist, but she's fierce about guarding my person. And she loves me even when I'm most unlovable.

Some investigation before winging across the Pacific brings the bad news that while Juts is welcome in some countries, she is barred from others. Crestfallen, I'll have to pack off my buddy. She'll be home with the horses while I vault the ocean and land in Beijing, China.

The Tienshan Silk Route is a 21-day tour at $125 per day. From the capital city, Beijing, I head out like a great merchant from the thirteenth century pushing toward the rich inland markets. Pack animals sway on roads that are probably in a condition identical to that which greeted Marco Polo. Passing through ancient gates, I wonder is Asia really the key to the twenty-first century as economists predict or is it eternally locked in a timelessness removed from Western impulse? Guarding some of these ancient gates are huge, carved lions and in some instances, chow dogs. Juts would be right at home.

The Tienshe Lake and the mountains offer testimony to the variety of landscape, and our brush with the southernmost reaches of Siberia is a reminder of that still unsettled, ancient border dispute with the Russians. These people have been living with tensions for thousands of years. They have also responded by creating majestic

artifacts. The Ming Tombs greet us as a silent reminder of how new we Americans really are.

Here people live side by side with an unbroken chain that reaches into prehistory. There's probably no such thing as an identity crisis in China. If you don't know exactly who you are, you certainly know who came before you to infinity. The Chinese live without McDonald's, *The Wall Street Journal*, or Paula Abdul.

When at last I leave this provocative tour, I'm ready to keep heading west. This time I'll leap across to Pakistan. It takes 15 days and it costs $125 a day. This tour is of keen interest to me because I'll be riding across the landscape etched in popular minds by *The Jewel in the Crown* by Paul Scott. Lyrical names like Rawalpindi, Chitral, and Hindu Kush tantalize my ears even as the scenery greets my eyes. Pakistan unfolds before me like torn pages from the book of the British raj.

Before the split with India after World War II, Pakistan was part of the British Empire. Independence brought forth confusion, violence, and, inevitably, a separate state for the Moslem people. Americans think of rugs when they think of Pakistan, or the more athletic will think of squash because of the Khan dynasty in that sport. But bouncing along roads, peering over icy precipices into gorgeous valleys, I'm reminded that environment shapes people. These are rugged people and no foreign power is going to get satisfaction by pressuring them. Like mountain peoples everywhere, they are friendly. But don't ever try to tell them what to do. Since I live hard by the Blue Ridge Mountains I feel a kinship with these folks. I sure wish the jeep had better shocks though.

For the last eight weeks, I've been rafting, hiking, floating, and jeeping. I need a break. Luckily, SOBEK has 20 days in the Vale of Kashmir for $75 per day. I'm only going to stay for ten days but what a ten days. I get to dump my bones on a houseboat in Srinagar and watch the world go by. What a difference from Pakistan. Here life is positively indolent. The floating gardens of Dal Lake provide visual stimulus and mental relaxation. Transitory beauty fascinates me as much as it did my literary forbears. What is there about chance or even studied magnificence that provokes one to consider the meaning of life? Flowers, sumptuous and bright, die on the morrow. It may be a fitting metaphor for life. If so, then all the more reason to cram one's life with adventures both physical and intellectual.

As I observe the ebb and flow of this remarkable culture, the other SOBEK people start out for the Himalayas. I've got to move toward the setting sun and cross over into Europe. Like Hannibal, I'll go over the Alps.

There's a glorious eight days of powder along the spine of these mountains, so prominent in history and imagination. Emotionally, mountains, for me, are like magnets. I gravitate toward them and the people who cling amidst the narrow fingers of valleys. The Alps gave the Romans false confidence until Hannibal of Carthage crossed over them with a well-trained army and his famous elephants. The Punic Wars made Hannibal and the Alps famous, and time has embellished the luster of their names. These snowy sentinels faced Charlemagne, Roland, Napoleon, and Hitler. France, Austria, Italy, and Switzerland share these glorious mountains but they've sent spurs beyond those nations for millennia before the coming of humankind. If the gardens of Dal Lake call forth thoughts on the transience of life, then the Alps call forth the comfort of knowing they stand and they shall always stand no matter what foolishness we humans concoct. Small wonder that the Greeks put their gods and goddesses on mountaintops.

These eight days are roughly $100 per day—a real bargain. Aside from the scenery and the sensation of familiarity

(because you are now on European soil), the skiing is outstanding. One minute you are slashing into Italy and the next you've cut over into France here on top of the world. Skiing takes strong legs and quick reflexes and, up here in this rarefied atmosphere, good lungs. If you didn't have good lungs when you started, you will have them when you finish.

My finish leads me into Switzerland. There's a 15-day canoe trip for a mere $75 a day. I start in Zurich, a city of financial power and a nest for spies during the last world war. Like everything in Switzerland this city borders on perfection. Window boxes overflow with brilliant colors. Streets sparkle. The people are healthy, vigorous, and polite, not overfriendly, mind you, like, say, the beloved Australians, but correct and polite. Money burns a hole in your pocket in Zurich because there are attractive bargains in jewelry and those much sought after Swiss watches are far cheaper here than in Chicago or Atlanta.

I practice my paddling, shades of summer camp, and then I plunge into the Ardeche Gorge and into France, the France most Americans never see. The wild river has created sculptures dazzling and curious. I am very excited about seeing Avignon, the home of renegade popes. The Middle Ages are still accessible here and I begin to understand that the French Americans see in Paris are not the French of the provinces. These are sturdy people who don't much give a damn what St. Laurent is doing. The quiet faraway waters of the Gardon lull me even as I rhythmically stroke deeper into the Gaul of the Romans. While this is new to me, I remind myself that Julius Caesar got here first. "Gallis est dividsa in tres partes." Gaul is divided into three parts. I'm seeing the untamed side of France, the side first beheld by the Roman legions when they brought their eagles, unwanted, into this barbaric land. They were set upon by fierce tribes much like an American tourist is set upon by Parisian taxi drivers except that the warlike Gauls were more honest. Nearly two thousand years have passed since Caesar came here, and the French are supposed to be one of the world's most civilized peoples. Yet paddling on the Dronne and into the Tarn Gorge, I wonder if civilization isn't a slick veneer and the French have better paintbrushes than the rest of us?

After skiing and canoeing I'm ready for some walking. I hydroplane across the English Channel, that body of water that dashed the hopes of Phillip II of Spain. Once on English soil I am greeted by the world's most efficient and pleasant customs officials. This is not yet a skill mastered by American officials, but I suppose the trade-off is that many of the English have yet to learn about deodorant.

Stepping onto English soil I am reminded that once England and huge chunks of France were one. Brittany and the western regions of France were irretrievably lost as the Plantagenet, Richard III, went to his miserable, hushed-up death. Later kings dreamed about restoring France's duchies to the crown and probably about English real estate taxes but it never came to pass. Even the gargantuan ego of Henry VIII couldn't accomplish what geography, more than man, set asunder.

I am, at last, spiritually home. Everyone who speaks English should, at least once in their life, pay homage to this tiny, eccentric island. What better way to do it than to walk across the Lake Country for 7 days at $75 a day. Here amidst moor and mountain were nurtured some of the world's greatest poets. The Romans called this 35-mile square district Cumbria, from which we get "Cumberland." Here in astonishing beauty developed Wordsworth, Coleridge, and Southey, who lived in Grasmere, Keswick, and Ambleside, respectively. They represented new men and women bursting forth into the fledgling nineteenth century eager to cast off the literary conventions of the eighteenth century. Even before the Lake Poets fomented their rebellion, Thomas Gray (a pivotal poet for modern times in that he developed naturalism) recorded his impressions of this land.

So rich is this area in literary terms that for me this walking tour is a kind of heaven. After the rebels came Harriet Martineau, Matthew Arnold, John Ruskin, Sir Hugh Walpole, Beatrix Potter and Arthur Ransome. The latter two enriched children ever after with their stories and illustrations. Even as I write this I wonder what fresh English youth is trying verse for the first time as she or he watches the ground fog creep up over a field of fresh hay.

Rome left her fingerprint even on this distant soil. Fortresses stand as advertisements for the greatest empire the world has ever known. The roads on which we walk are Roman. They are better than anything being laid down today, and you can still walk these twelve-foot-thick roads to Spain, Italy, France—wherever the Romans trod.

As the empire receded after a thousand years of glory (and treachery and brilliance, etc.), England was left to herself. The Saxons, Jutes, and Norsemen came here to the Lake District after they pillaged the coasts. The Irish ever threatened from the west. Finally on October 14, 1066, William the Conqueror mounted the last successful invasion of England. Not even the might of the Luftwaffe was able to smash these individualistic, exasperating, droll people. To walk from Shap in the east to Ravenglass in the west is to walk the centuries and hear the murmur of Latin, Norse, French, and Anglo-Saxon—as well as the sharp tongue of today's residents.

Back in London after this emotionally important week, I confront chartreuse hair, Turnbull & Asser (where I get my shirts made and have done so for over a decade), traffic, and heathen hamburgers.

An American is as at home in London as he or she is in Kansas City, except Kansas City doesn't have the British Museum. The library is overwhelming. You must see it. Even if you don't much care about literature, see it anyway. Even Lenin worked there.

It's time to get back to the New World. Phileas Fogg could stop in London, but I've got the Atlantic to conquer. It's pretty easy with the help of Pan Am. I've got one last SOBEK adventure. This is a sentimental journey as important to me as was the walk in the Lake District. I'm going to kayak down the New River for 5 days at $100 a day.

This is the Grand Canyon of the East. It's also close to home for me. I'm about two hundred miles away in Charlottesville, Virginia. I want to have one last adventure among my own people, Virginians. West Virginians are simply Virginians gone to seed. It was very foolish of them to break off from the mother state and to join with the Union during the War of Northern Aggression, but I am prepared to let bygones be bygones.

Here, south of the Mason-Dixon line we are the direct descendants of the Cavaliers, those peacock followers of Charles I. North of the line are the people who descended from the Pilgrims, the followers of Cromwell. So the fate of America was set in 1640 and never the twain shall meet. A Cavalier and a roundhead possess two opposing views of nature, God, and humankind. We coexist but we don't agree.

Here on the oldest river in the New World I'm close to Stonewall Jackson's victories in the Shenandoah Valley. Victories so amazing that they are studied in war colleges throughout the world including those in the Soviet Union. The waterfall that drenches me probably drenched a Confederate scout one hundred twenty odd years ago.

Embraced by the green of the oaks, the maples, the sweet gum trees, I am in my element. Deer, owl, raccoons (tons of them), wildcats and cougars (more than you think), bear, pileated woodpeckers, and those yakkety blue jays fill my world. There are red fox and gray fox and even, rarely, a jet black fox. The same animals that traipse across my lands at home fill the forests here. Why does anyone want to live in a city, that honeycomb of smog, decadence, and alienation? Why does anyone sell their life on the installment plan to a large corporation? Better to have less money and more freedom. At least, that's the choice I made. I was offered $30,000 a week to take over as head writer on a dramatic series three days ago. God, I need the money. Who doesn't? But I said, "No." I can't live in Los Angeles much as I enjoy that city. I can't live in any city. I belong here on the New River or sitting in an inner tube on the Moorman's Branch in Albermarle County. I reckon I may not get disgusting/rich but I am so happy, so rooted in red Virginia clay.

Being on this river in what was once Virginia teaches me a lesson I think I knew but sometimes forget. There is no security on this earth, only opportunity.

Well, SOBEK gave me the opportunity to circle the globe. It cost me $9600. That doesn't count purchases or plane hops between tours but still, to go around the world for $9600. You can't beat it.

However, Phileas Fogg did it in 80 days and I confess I tarried at 107. Well, I just couldn't help it. There was so much to see and do, and even cutting back on the Kashmir trip didn't lop off enough days. So he's first but I'm satisfied at second.

In fact, I've got this great idea if I can just talk SOBEK into it. Let's go around the world on the Southern Hemisphere side. We could start in Argentina and then go over to New Guinea before touching down on Australian soil (I love the Aussies and the Kiwis. Best people on earth!) and then—

Romancing
the Swamp

Tom Robbins

So you tell your girlfriend you're going to take her on a holiday to one of the most romantic spots on earth, and after she has tastefully expressed her gratitude and delight, she asks how she should pack. For the mountains? For the samba clubs of Rio or the boulevards of Par-ee?

"Oh," you say, "just throw a few things together that will get you by in a swamp."

Naturally, she thinks you're kidding, even after she notices you laying in a supply of mosquito repellent and Aquasocks. And when you usher her into the Victoria Falls Hotel, following a numbing, 27-hour flight, she smiles simultaneously at the pleasing surroundings and at what she believes was your little joke. The Vic Falls, perhaps the lone 19th-century colonial hotel still operating in southern Africa, may have a run or two in its safari stockings, a few stains on its bush jacket, but it's as romantic as the last act of a bad operetta.

Seedily luxurious, the low, rambling wings of the Vic Falls are tickled by palm fronds, scampered over by monkeys, serviced by an attentive staff in starched white livery, and moistened by mists from cataracts so immense they make Niagara seem like a leaky faucet. Your girlfriend is really settling into the place, especially its spacious patio, but the ice has hardly melted in her second gin and tonic before you've booked passage on Air Botswana, and by the end of the next afternoon the two of you are flying over territory that decidedly resembles. . .swamp. You feel a trifle sad about the look she gives you.

The flight from Victoria Falls, Zimbabwe, to Main, Botswana, arrives nearly two hours late, and as you wait for your luggage, the guide who has met you in the yam-patch airport is nervously glancing from his watch to the sky and back again. "We have a ways to go and we've got to get there before dark," you explain to your companion. When she asks, "Suppose we don't?" you shrug. You're afraid of what she might answer if you inquire if she's ever spent the night with a crocodile.

Before long, you're motorboating up a reedy, sullen river, exchanging waves with folks who've never so much as heard of George Bush, even though their relatives are Bushmen. Before you can think to congratulate them, they, their huts, and their goats have vanished and your boat is alone on a waterway that twists through the aquatic flora like a spastic vegetarian through a salad bar, and whose banks are closing in on you from both sides. The river narrows into a channel. The channel into a hippopotamus path.

Meanwhile, the sun has slipped below the palm-fringed horizon and the temperature is dropping so fast you think it must have fallen over a cliff. It gets later and later, darker and darker, colder and colder, lonelier and lonelier, the route more and more crooked, the papyrus beds denser and denser, and your girlfriend has to pee so badly she must gnaw on her camera strap to stifle a howl.

Still, the emerging stars are flamboyant, the bird calls crystalline, the frog din hypnotic, and the situation really isn't all that horrifying considering how lost you appear to be in the African swamps. Then, you hit the WALL OF GNATS!

You call it a "wall" instead of a cloud because clouds don't usually give a person whiplash. You're talking about the force of trillions of tiny bugs per cubic foot here, gnat cheek to gnat jowl, and you're swallowing gnats and breathing gnats while *National Enquirer* headlines— Couple Drowns in Gnat Tsunami—dance before your gnat-blinded eyes. On you bore, meter after meter, into the LIVING WALL, certain you're within a gnat's hair of asphyxiation, until the wall suddenly crumbles away as inexplicably as it materialized, and in the distance you glimpse a flicker of light, that of apparent human fabrication. In ten minutes you're docked at Ntswi Island, a campfire and beefy meal in your immediate future. Ah, but any illusion that things are now hunky-dory disappears when you discover that your poor girlfriend couldn't quite hold it until she reached the thatched latrine. There's nothing like wet pants to throw a wet blanket on swampland romance.

Add to that some loud-mouthed hippos reciting the Hippocratic oath a few score yards from your tent, and the savage chill that is piercing your lightweight sleeping bag (in Botswana, mid-June has

James Pleute/SOBEK photo file

turned out to be midwinter: you'd think those people south of the equator could get their seasons straight), and you have a night that belongs to misery not to Michelob. You greet the dawn with no more than your significantly silent sweetie.

Gradually, however, you warm to the place and it to you. Before the afternoon is over, the temperature will have hit eighty— a fifty-degree swing that occurs each day—and the sky will have pinned blue ribbons to every lapel of the Okavango Delta, irrefutably a first-prize swamp.

The Okavango is the largest inland delta in the world. It's formed when the Okavango river, overfed by floodwaters from the rains of Angola, runs headlong into the Kalahari Desert and skids to a stop without ever reaching the sea. The result is twenty thousand square kilometers of channels, lagoons, reedbeds, grass, pans, and islands. The water is pure enough to drink, warm enough to bathe in, although if you splash for more than ten minutes, a huge, drooling crocodile will usually show up and demand a wine list. In a week, however, your party sees not one poisonous snake or one squadron of carnivorous mosquitoes, lest anyone think to compare it to the Everglades. As for the WALL OF GNATS!, it seems to have gone the way of the walls of Babylon.

What you do see in this glistening oasis of water lilies, phoenix palms, and melapo grass are storks and fish eagles, hornbills and bee-eaters, parrots, vultures, lilac-breasted rollers, and literally hundreds of other ornithological showpieces. Everywhere, great wings beat the air as if it were a drum, and when the day chorus of doves and cuckoos punch off duty, the more esoteric night birds come on line.

On the larger islands—and some are many times the size of Manhattan—there is game. Big game. Buffalo, giraffe, zebra, elephant, lion and leopard: most of the stereotypes of the African tableau, although they appear anything but stereotypical when you're stalking them on foot and worrying that they might be stalking you. Hiking unarmed through acacia thornbush, in fairly close proximity to the eldest of animals, gives you Okavango experience, that dark edge of danger without which romance is merely the sappy side of lust.

Tranquillity is also a necessary component of romantic adventure, and there's no shortage of peaceful epiphany in this watery Eden. Early each morning, your party rushes off in dugout canoes hollowed from the single trunks of sausage trees. Powered by a native guide with a twelve-foot pole, you glide noiselessly along the hippo paths, your bow knocking a shower of dew pearls from the papyrus tops, whiffs of nectar in the air, as all about you fin, fang, and feather receive the orange day-glo kiss of the slowly rising sun.

After a day of walking and marveling, you are poled back to tiny Ntswi Island, where, at a primitive open-air bar decorated with skulls, that same sun, setting now, is reflected off cold cans of local beer. The dusk belongs to Lion Lager.

And one evening, sure enough, beneath the gloriously exotic configuration of the Southern Cross—it happens to be the night after a bull elephant drank the sudsy water in which your girlfriend had just washed out her underthings, an act that filled you with a perverse mixture of revulsion and jealousy—your paramour interrupts the Okavango concert of cricket and ibis and mystery beast to whisper, "Honey, you were right. This ol' swamp *is* the most romantic spot on earth."

Life
Among the Ruins

DAVID RAINS WALLACE

The tropical dusk was fading quickly as I walked along a parapet above the Tomb of the Condor at Machu Picchu. It was spookily quiet. For a little while, flocks of swifts and swallows had circled the ancient stone terraces, feeding on flying insects that rose from the rich soil just as they must have fed when the Inca city's corn and potato crops grew there. Then even the swallows disappeared: I seemed alone in a landscape of stone blocks and distant peaks.

I turned a corner, and there, crouched on a low wall, was one of the strangest creatures I have ever seen. It was about the size of a hare, but its head was shaped more like a deer's, and its fur was softer and denser. It seemed unperturbed by my presence, eyeing me calmly as I stood watching it. After a minute or two, another appeared, but it was shier than the first and jumped out of sight when it became aware of me. The creatures were even odder than I'd thought: the second flourished a long, bushy tail as it jumped. They seemed to incorporate not only hare and deer but squirrel as well. Finally, when the first one had tired of eyeing me, it hopped off like a kangaroo.

The creatures seemed like ghosts in their noiseless appearance and disappearance, and in a sense they were. They were much more a part of the ancient Incan world than they are of the modern Peruvian one. Called mountain viscachas, they are native South American rodents closely related to the smaller chinchillas. Fossils show that creatures like them have inhabited South America since the Oligocene Epoch some thirty million years ago. Once an important source of meat and fur for pre-Columbian cultures, they are a dwindling species today, pushed into obscure corners of the Andes by the spread of Western civilization.

The viscachas were the first wild mammals I'd seen during a four-day trek on the Inca Trail that leads to Machu Picchu from farther up the Urubamba Valley. The squirrels, chipmunks, marmots, pikas, and other furry creatures that throng North American mountains are largely absent from South America because the continents' evolution has been so different. Originally part of a vast, ancient super-continent paleontologists call Gondwanaland, which included Africa, Antarctica, and Australia. South America began to drift apart about 200 million years ago. Thus its flora and fauna evolved in isolation for millions of years, and primitive mammals that had inhabited Gondwanaland evolved into creatures that had no counterparts elsewhere—sloths, armadillos, anteaters, and even stranger, now extinct, forms.

Although South America has drifted toward North America over the past fifty million years, its life has continued to evolve in isolation. Island chains arose between the continents, allowing some organisms to cross between them, but then the islands eroded or subsided back into the sea and the new immigrants began to evolve separately again. Viscachas and their relatives may have arrived in South America in this way. They are true rodents, like North American squirrels, but they are so different that they clearly have been evolving separately for a long time. Even today, when the two continents have been connected by the permanent land bridge of Central America for several million years, there remains something remote and isolated about creatures like viscachas. They seem somehow oblivious to contemporary things, which may be one reason they are becoming so rare. Their unwariness apparently makes them easy to shoot.

It seemed appropriate to encounter these creatures from another time in the ruins of an Incan city that escaped the notice of conquering Western civilization until Hiram Bingham hacked it out of the jungle in 1911. The rock-dwelling viscachas probably have been the main inhabitants of Machu Picchu since the Incas abandoned it in the sixteenth century. I could imagine them making kangaroo hops across the silent plazas and creeping through tombs full of golden finery as yet unviolated by grave robbers. By creating at Machu Picchu a monument to the native civilization it has destroyed, the modern world has also created a sanctuary for a native species that it is threatening. Machu Picchu is surrounded by an eighty-thousand-acre national park,

which contains not only some of the most stunning mountain scenery imaginable but the extraordinary diversity of habitats and organisms that one finds only in the tropics.

Our four-day walk to the ruins began among cactuses and scrubby, red-flowered "tara" trees at about ten thousand feet along the Urubamba River. On the second day, the path led steeply upward, beside glacier-fed cascades bordered with Andean alders, elderberries, and wild cherries, and on to swathes of mossy, evergreen cloud forest. Then it turned upward again to the grassy "puna" of a 13,700-foot pass, a realm of mist and icy winds. We camped in a cloud-forested high valley, crossed a craggy 13,400-foot pass the next morning, then followed a long ridgeline beside luxuriant bogs full of plants straight out of the dinosaur age: giant club mosses rearing snakelike out of the grass and feathery-fronded cycads, which look like small palm trees but are in fact gymnosperms, more closely related to redwoods than to palms. Other stretches of the trail, through scrubby, heath family plants resembling huckleberry and salal, might have been in Alaska or Oregon.

We camped the third night at the end of the high ridge, surrounded by white peaks that became even whiter during an afternoon thunder and hailstorm, and then we descended as steeply as we had climbed into the high jungle. Eight-foot wild begonias and four-foot, shocking pink "Winayhuayna" orchids grew beneath giant bamboos, tree ferns, and bromeliad- and liana-covered clusias and laurels. Iridescent Morpho butterflies seemed to change color in midair as the turquoise on top of their wings alternated with the fawn of the underside. Then a final short ascent (a sign warned of poisonous snakes, but we encountered none) led to a ridge overlooking eight-thousand-foot-high Machu Picchu.

Although I didn't happen to see much of it, Machu Picchu National Park does contain a lot of mammals. Two species of deer are fairly common according to our guide, George Fletcher, who also said he'd almost run into the endangered spectacled bear, South America's only bear, while jogging along a trail. Deer and bear are relatively recent immigrants from North America, but the opossum that Fletcher reportedly saw scurry across the path as our party crossed a pass is one of the oldest South Americans of all. As a marsupial, the opossum gives clear evidence that the continent was once linked to Australia. It is the most primitive living marsupial and hasn't changed significantly since the dinosaurs disappeared.

The birds were more conspicuous than the mammals. Every change of habitat along the trail produced new species, most of which I'd never seen. Black-and-white-headed torrent ducks and diminutive torrent tyrannulets frequented the Urubamba rapids. The flowery vegetation along its tributaries was full of hummingbirds, including one species as large as a sparrow. We kept seeing hummingbirds right up to the passes, where groups of black-and-white-crested caracaras (a kind of hawk) played on the wind and a pair of Andean condors circled for a few awesome moments before disappearing into a cloud. The cloud forest of high valleys was full of colorful, tanagerlike birds, including a flock of a purple-faced, red-eyed species whose plumage was the same deep blue as the berries they were eating. At dusk, as I walked along the still-intact stonework of the Inca road connecting Machu Picchu with the many smaller ruins in the park, owls and pauraques (a tropical relative of the whippoorwill) called in the forest.

Some of the birds were as odd as the viscachas. I was standing in the forest along the descent to Machu Picchu, watching tanagers feed in a tree full of fruit, when something larger landed in the tree. It appeared so abruptly, and remained so still thereafter, that it hardly seemed like a bird but more like a brightly painted volleyball. It looked almost spherical, with a bluish-black head, green back, red legs, and bright chartreuse breast barred with black. When it finally moved, it seemed to bounce rather than fly from branch to branch. Then it was gone, as suddenly as it had appeared, as though someone had punched it away and over the net.

A field guide informed me that the volleyball bird was a barred fruiteater, a member of a group called the cotingas. Found only in the American tropics, cotingas have such odd shapes, colors, and habits that ornithologists have trouble relating them to other birds. (There are species that make mating calls resembling church bells and others in which males attract females by displaying what appear to be miniature umbrellas above their heads.) Like viscachas, they may have evolved in South American isolation, although they presently range north to Mexico. Also, like viscachas, they are suffering from civilization's growth. Most are forest birds and disappear when forest is cleared.

There is a certain irony in the fact that ruins such as Machu Picchu have become refuges for otherwise disappearing flora and fauna. Only decades ago, explorers had to travel through vast wilderness areas just to reach, much less excavate, Incan ruins. Today, the remnants of that wilderness often survive only within the boundaries of parks created to protect the ruins. The Andes are heavily grazed and plowed right up to the borders of Machu Picchu Park, and this summer fires partly caused by farmers burning fields for crops leapt into the park and burned large stretches of native vegetation (a possible reason we saw no deer or bears). Peru can ill afford to pay for trail maintenance, law enforcement, and other conservation measures needed to protect its wilderness. But at least it is trying. After all, the Incas lived in a world of viscachas, condors, and cotingas as well as stone temples and terraced fields.

Trekking
in Soviet Georgia

✳

JOSH HAMMER

We were hunkered down in our campsite on the banks of the Nakra River, amidst a grove of spiny shrubbery and boulders, when the thunder began. Rumbles echoed through the canyon. A flash of lightning crashed against the darkening cliffs surrounding us, illuminating their intricate tapestry of moss, alpine scrub, and patches of snow and ice. It was a son et lumiere show in the heart of the Russian Caucasus, a thrilling display of natural fireworks. There was just one problem. Our tents, which were being carried over the pass by Russian Sherpas, were nowhere in sight. Huddled in the open, I winced as the wind whistled down the canyon and the first raindrops began to splatter across my windbreaker.

"Sasha!" cried Skip Horner, our leader, to his Russian counterpart. "Where the hell are they?"

Skip wasn't pleased. Sasha had no idea where they were. Laden down like pack animals with roped-together duffels, our four porters had been forced early that morning to divide the bags into two loads and to tackle the difficult pass in two trips. Which meant that, as we waited at camp, the men were probably lugging our gear across a steep snowfield two, perhaps three hours away.

"Get that tarp up!" Skip shouted. Lightning bolts were crashing around us, and sheets of rain were swelling the Nakra River and turning the campsite into a quagmire. Buttressing four ski poles with heavy rocks, we erected a lean-to and squeezed ourselves inside. Only Leonid, our 73-year-old guide from Leningrad, refused to come underneath the shelter. Shrouded in white plastic sheeting, he sat in the midst of the rainstorm with his head bowed, a paragon of self-sacrifice, looking like a mournful ghost.

"Leonid Alexandreyevich!" shouted Sasha. But Leonid refused to budge.

Our group of eight Americans and six Russians was hardly the only band of travelers to have run into snags climbing through the Caucasus. The range's rugged beauty and strategic location have attracted and thwarted military invaders and sportsmen for centuries. Sandwiched between the Black and Caspian seas, touching the Soviet republics of Georgia, Armenia, and Azerbaijan, the Caucasus is a 900-mile-long range of dead-end valleys, vast glacier fields, rocky gorges, broken spurs, and jagged peaks rising higher than the Alps. With only a handful of passes, most of them snow covered year-round, the range creates a nearly impassable barrier between Europe and Asia Minor.

The land's inhospitality has been the stuff of myth: the Amazons were said to roam here, killing any man who intruded into their kingdom. Amid the impenetrable canyons, the ancient Greeks believed that Prometheus was chained to a boulder here for eternity, his liver picked at by Caucasian ravens. And Jason and the Argonauts came through in pursuit of the Golden Fleece, only to be beaten back by fire-breathing warriors.

For American trekkers hoping to explore the Caucasus, the chief obstacle has been, until recently, Cold War politics. But now, thanks to the warming trend brought on by glasnost and perestroika, eight of us had gathered at the Rossiya Hotel on Red Square in Moscow in late June to rendezvous with Russian guides and launch the first joint Soviet-American Caucasus trek ever conducted as a commercial venture—a true sign of the changing times. Joining us in Moscow was a Russian who'd been recruited by Soviet Travel to shepherd us along: Sasha, a boyish-looking mountaineer and mechanical engineer who proudly announced in thickly accented English that he was "member of Communist party." "But don't be afraid!" Sasha said with a laugh. "It is family obligation."

Sasha, who was to be our leader and comrade for the next ten days, looked the part: tall and muscular, he wore a CCCP t-shirt, bright red sweatpants, a white windbreaker, and a Polish-made wristwatch he'd picked up in Warsaw which came with an alarm that played, inexplicably, "Stars and Stripes Forever." This fall, he would be joining a group of Bulgarians and East Germans in an ascent of 23,000-foot Mt. Lenin in the Pamirs of Central Asia. He saw our hike through the Caucasus as a chance to get in shape for the climb and also to mingle with Americans for the first time in his life. "To go to America—hike in Rockies—it has always been dream," he told us. But though glasnost and perestroika had permitted thousands of Soviet citizens to travel to the West, Sasha had been left behind, told by the government that his access to technological secrets made him a high risk. "Secret, secret, everything is secret in Russia," he said with exasperation. "This country—it has many problems."

We escaped Moscow by plane early in the morning. It was great to get out of this drab metropolis, with its Stalinesque towers and black marketeers, and head for the provinces. Our destination via Aeroflot: the spa-town of Mineralnye Vody ("Mineral Water"), 1,000 miles south, on the steppes north of the Caucasus Range. And then, suddenly, we were in the Baksan Valley of rural Russia: two-lane blacktop highways rolling past wheat and sunflower fields, pine forests, olive-drab lorries transporting produce and fuel, the occasional Volga sedan packed with families on holiday. The sense of being far from cosmopolitan Moscow and heading toward adventure was growing stronger by the minute.

So was the feeling that Soviet Travel had not exactly mastered the organization aspects of this trip.

"Skeep, there eeez problem," Sasha announced to Skip Horner, on the morning of the trek, as we sat at breakfast in the shabby Hotel Elbrus.

"What sort of problem, Sasha?"

"I am afraid . . .We have not enough porters."

"What?"

"Four men, who were come with us, they will not be coming with us."

"Why not?"

"I am afraid . . . they drink too much vodka. Last night."

"So how many do we have?"

"Four," said Sasha with a shrug. "One porter for two hiker. With this number, we will do best we can."

The porters whom Sasha had recruited were vacationing Soviets who had been planning a climb up 18,470-foot Mt. Elbrus, the grande dame of the range. But they'd happily put their plans on hold in exchange for a week's generous pay and the chance to mingle with Americans. They came from many corners of the Soviet Union: Nikolai, 30, was a handsome sunburned engineer from Moscow; Zhenya, 43, was a bearded, fierce-looking construction worker who lived in the southern port of Odessa, where he'd served for two decades in the Russian navy; Igor hailed from Kiev in the Ukraine; and Ivan (nicknamed "Vanya"), at 20, the baby of the group, was a medical student in Leningrad. The grand old man was Leonid, a pensioner from Leningrad and an avid hiker who spent each summer in a tiny, cell-like room behind the Hotel Elbrus. Sasha had encountered him dining alone in a corner of the cafeteria and had invited him to join us for a meal. Leonid had decided to stay on and guide us through the region, which he claimed to know as intimately as the Nevsky Prospekt in central Leningrad. With his addition, we now had five porters.

With our motley collection of Russians, we took a chair lift past the tree line and began walking through a notch in the mountains, across an alpine meadow carpeted with daisies, forget-me-nots (*nye zabutkas* in Russian), violets, and conelike bears' ears. The flowers presented myriad colors splashed across the tundra. As we hiked toward the Donguz Orun ("Pig Sty") Pass that leads south into Georgia, I could almost sense the ghosts of would-be conquerors trudging alongside us.

It was eerie. Thousands of Nazi troops had marched across this very meadow in the winter of 1942, intent on reaching Baku on the Caspian Sea. They were part of Hitler's grand plan to dominate the Caucasus, an ambition the Germans had entertained for centuries, from Attila the

Hun to Kaiser Wilhelm. The *New York Times* reported on November 16, 1941: "From the gridwork airdromes strewn across the marshy grounds of northern Crimea, German reconnaissance planes and bombers already are droning over the snow-capped peaks of the Western Caucasus. The distant rumble of artillery and the thud of bombs echo against the western fringe of the Caucasus Range. Is this campaign too colossal, fraught with too many difficulties even for the German army?"

It was. Thousands died on the frigid climb to Donguz Orun Pass, shot down by fur-clad Russian infantrymen poised atop the notch. Now we were following the tracks of the Germans. We camped that night in a muddy basin beneath the pass, beside an alluvial stream that snaked and divided around our tents. Sunset over the camp and the mountains was a glorious high, but it was soon followed by a night of torment: I huddled in my paper-thin "polyester fiber" sleeping bag, a relic from my summer-camp days which I'd accidentally brought instead of my down bag. Stripped to my underwear, I was too cold in the subfreezing night to get out and rummage through my duffel bag for long johns. So I curled into the fetal position, shivering and waiting for the gray light of dawn.

At last, the sun rose over Donguz Orun, bathing the dun-colored landscape and the turquoise glacial lake in a pinkish, ethereal light; copper deposits at the shore of the lake glowed a fiery red. I crawled out of my dome tent into the chill of the morning and angled myself into position so that the sun shone directly on my face. At last, warmth!

"Dobray ootra!" I shouted to our Russian porters, who'd been up since well before dawn.

That was Russian for "good morning." I've always made it a habit to attempt to learn the language of whatever country I am trekking through, and this time I'd brought along a couple of Russian tapes and a Walkman and had been borrowing a fellow American's Berlitz book, which was full of helpful phrases for subjects ranging from "Buying a Refrigerator" to "What to Say on a First Date." I'd mastered about a hundred words already, but my enthusiasm for Russian 101 was waning. With just a week to spend with these Russian guys, there really didn't seem to be much point trying to gain a degree of fluency.

Still, the Russians loved it. Igor, a Hobbit-like fellow with pointed ears and a wisp of a mustache, could hardly believe it when I told him, in Russian, that my great-grandparents had been born in the Ukraine. "Near Kiev?" he asked in English. "Da, near Kiev," I said. He embraced me as if he were greeting a long lost brother, then reached into his knapsack and pulled out a metal medallion, a souvenir of Kiev, which he stuck to my shirt. "Next time, you will come to Kiev!" I promised I'd do my best.

The Russians, none of whom beside Sasha spoke much comprehensible English, were our all-purpose Sherpas: They planned the route, cooked our meals (porridge and milk for breakfast, bologna-and-cheese sandwiches for lunch, Rice-a-Roni and what else for dinner), cleaned the dishes, packed and unpacked the duffels, and carted the 150-pound loads along impossibly steep trails for vast distances. It was painful to watch them stagger along, bent over like hunchbacks, yet they claimed they didn't mind. "Good training," Nikolai insisted. In camp, they went diligently about their business, jabbering to each other in rapid-fire Russian, pausing once in a while to admire the Americans' state-of-the-art camping equipment: North Face tents, Gore-tex ponchos, down sleeping bags. By comparison, the Russians were paupers. All of their gear was homemade. "Of course, in Russia, you cannot buy such things anywhere," said Sasha, staring longingly at my

green domed EMS tent, large enough to snugly fit a family of four.

This morning, as I stood in the chilly mountain air, uttering Russian phrases, it was clear that the Soviets had more important matters to think about than trying to decipher this Amerikanski's abysmal Russian—like the upcoming slog over Donguz Orun. It was going to be a hell of a climb. Before us to the south, the vale opened up into a perfect, snow-covered bowl, with Donguz Orun Pass high on the left and one of the world's ideal ski runs to the right. Several years earlier, some ingenious Russians had installed a generator and a T-bar lift in this remote spot. Now, six blue-jacketed members of a Latvian ski team were already on their third run of the morning, and they waved as we rounded the lake and began climbing to Donguz Orun.

We slogged over snow, slush, and ice that extended like a wet blanket to the pass. Why couldn't they have installed the lift on this side? As I dug my toes into notches in the snow, carrying nothing but a light day pack, my mood ranged between pure exhilaration and disgruntlement. At last, I hauled myself up to the narrow pass between the two valleys and gasped in astonishment as the entire Caucasus range spread before me. I felt as if I were floating above the earth. As if on cue, a lone, yellow-billed chough glided just above me. It rested on a pile of stones and stared, blinked a couple of times, then flapped its wings and dive-bombed into the valley. That's one way to get down, I thought. Now it's our turn. But where the hell was the trail?

I couldn't believe it. Nobody could believe it. All we could see was a wide snowfield that plunged precipitously into the Nakra Gorge, its blinding whiteness juxtaposed against cliffs of black basalt and the arrowhead peaks of the Great Caucasus. Sasha simply shrugged and grinned, exposing a nasty-looking, rotten front tooth. Methodically, we placed one boot after the other into the slushy footprints of the hikers ahead of us, slipping every few steps and landing painfully on our butts. Twice, I lost my footing trying to sidestep down the hill and crashed into Sasha, descending tentatively a few feet in front of me. "Stop! Stop!" he shouted. Instead we hurtled together, completely out of control, grasping each other in an embrace of terror. Somehow, Sasha was able to stop the momentum by digging into the snow with his poles, then brace me and help me get to my feet.

And so it went for three long hours: The grand views counterbalanced by the pain-in-the-ass slog over wet snow, followed by fancy footwork over jagged rocks and boulders and hops across treacherous streams capable of washing a person to an icy death. The sun was brutal, and the protection offered by my number-five skin cream couldn't prevent me from developing a painful sunburn on my hands, face, and neck. Still, I wasn't in as nearly bad shape as some of the trekkers we encountered: Lithuanians, Poles, Czechs, even an exotic contingent from Tashkent in Uzbekistan. Two teenage girls from the Ukraine who'd been using no screen at all had developed pustulating sores on their lips which had swelled to the size of golf balls. Sasha's nose had already begun to resemble an extra-mozzarella pizza.

But now that we'd climbed over Donguz Orun, we were rolling. The high alpine meadows of the Nakra Valley, marking the beginning of Soviet Georgia, narrowed into a boulder-strewn chasm, through which the Nakra River frothed and roared. The sun was shining in a cloudless sky, the air redolent with pine, and slender birch trees and towering pines clung at gravity-defying angles from the cliffs. I was in such a good mood that, in the middle of the afternoon, I took a few swigs of vodka from a group of swarthy Svan lumberjacks who were "picnicking" by the trail. We were now just an hour away from a dirt road that led to Svanetia, the northernmost inhabited region of Georgia.

While I was drinking, the men were reading my T-shirt, one that I'd bought at a New York clothing and trinket shop called Brand Glasnost. "Vodka is the enemy! If you drink it, you won't be able to work!" it said in bright red Cyrillic letters. It was a leftover phrase from one of Gorbachev's early antialcohol campaigns, and it drove the Russians wild with laughter. As the men gathered around me, gesticulating and jabbering in Georgian, I had an inspiration. I whipped out my Berlitz book and flipped it to the "First Date" section. Sasha explained that I'd been studying Russian and wanted to practice a few words on some locals. I cleared my throat and began:
"You're a very good dancer." The guys roared with laughter.

"May I light your cigarette?" More laughter.

"I had a wonderful time this evening. May I see you again?"

Now they all grabbed for the book, babbling to each other. "What the hell kind of book is this? Let us see more! More!" After this brief diversion, we reached a dirt road and boarded a school bus for the trip into the Inguru River valley, the first populated valley we'd encountered in three days.

This definitely wasn't the Russia that I'd read about. We could have set down in Shangri-La. The villages seemed frozen in time, Brothers Grimm fairylands of checkerboard fields, gingerbread houses, sheep, pigs, and goats ambling through cobblestone streets. Locals occasionally flagged down the bus and hopped aboard, the children staring in wonder at these Westerners laden with Japanese cameras, Ray-Bans, and bright-colored backpacks. Svanetia had the feel of some lost mountain kingdom untouched by politics, as connected to Moscow as, say, some lamasery in Tibet. In the Svan capital of Mestia, a farming town beneath the mountains, a fat woman wearing a purple babushka clutched a basket filled with apricots. She froze in the middle of Mestia's main street, studying us with puzzlement.

"Czech?"

I shook my head. "Nyet. Amerikanski."

"Amerikanski?!" And she went rushing off to tell her friends.

In Mestia, I had one prime goal in mind—to find some "fabled" Georgian mineral water. Friends of mine who'd journeyed to Georgia were planning to import bottles of the stuff, which supposedly bubbles out of springs all over Svanetia. I decided to sample some to determine if they could find a market.

And so we prowled through the town in search of a spring. Dozens of ancient towers, granite and brick turreted columns rose fifty, sixty feet into the sky. They stood like sentries, climbing up the hillsides one behind the other in perfect alignment. They were built "maybe 1,000 years ago," Sasha explained, for protection against invading Turks. Finally, outside town, I came upon a well with a small crowd of Georgians around it slurping mineral water with a wooden ladle. This was it! I grabbed a ladle and brought some of the frothy beverage to my lips. Awful! I spat the stuff out. It was salty, gassy, lukewarm. Swilling this stuff was like drinking from the Black Sea! I envisioned my friends heading straight for bankruptcy.

"Don't be afraid. It will not be so difficult" said Sasha, as we sat in the dirt beside our kerosene stove, heating a dinner of Rice-a-Roni, pasta, tuna, and cheese. It was the end of our penultimate day of trekking, an exhausting, 12-hour climb that had taken us from Svanetia north through the lush Dolra Gorge toward the 11,500-foot Becho Pass. Dense, sunless pine forests had changed gradually to verdant meadows brimming with wildflowers, then into bleak tundra peppered with rocks and boulders and crisscrossed by glacial streams. Finally, we had climbed high above the valley for four hours, past patches of ice and snow, sometimes pulling ourselves up over near vertical rock faces. Tomorrow morning we would pass into the Yusengi Valley, returning to the Russian Republic. Tonight we were camped within sight of the pass: five tents squeezed on an outcropping that fell away thousands of feet on either side to the gravel floor. The wind whipped viciously at the tents, which were battened down with rocks to prevent them from blowing away. Not a great place for sleepwalkers.

Across the valley, a glacier hung like a freeze-frame avalanche, rivulets of water dripping from its mouth. To the north lay the Akhsu Glacier, aquamarine and crevasse-ridden, which we would have to cross to get to Becho. It was a bleak, dramatic landscape, with our orange and green tents the only splashes of color. I felt lonely, insignificant, like an astronaut on some sun-deprived planet, an unwanted intruder in a place that had no use for man.

As always, the take-charge guy was Sasha, with his bright red sweatpants, "CCCP" T-shirt, and homemade orange backpack stuffed with 80 pounds of gear. By now, he and Skip had developed a rapport, although it had been constantly tested by logistical lapses. Porters hadn't materialized, pack donkeys had been hired, then fired because they couldn't navigate the narrow trails through the canyons. Yesterday, Sasha had negotiated a deal with a troika of Cossack horsemen to tote our bags up the Dolra Gorge, but halfway up the men decided the horses were too tired, dumped the loads, and galloped off. Sasha had handled this the way he handled all such inconveniences. "In Russia," he said with a shrug, "there are many problems."

The next morning, we were ready.

"Slowly, slowly," shouted Sasha, above the roar of water cascading from the

glaciers. We inched single file across a bridge of snow that led from our outcropping to the glacier field, careful to look only at our feet. On the right lay a drop of 300 feet to rocks and mud. On the left, a skid down the plunging snowfield and the Ahksu Glacier, then a long, fatal drop straight to the valley floor. The desolate majesty of the peaks around us was unparalleled, but I was terrified. My knees sagged and I wondered what the hell had led me to such extremes; above all, I couldn't understand why the Russians or Skip hadn't thought to rope us together here. As I was having these thoughts, one American, who'd been predicting that some terrible accident would take place on the way to the Becho Pass, began to lose her balance. Her feet slipped out from under her and she began to slide. Skip grabbed her, steadied her back on the narrow path, and we continued to climb.

"Slowly, slowly," Sasha repeated.

It seemed to take us hours to reach the

Becho Pass, a near vertical slog over snow, muddy moraine, and more snow, but when it was over, and we stood atop wind-whipped Becho, adorned with monuments to the Russian defenders against the German fashistiki, I felt giddy with satisfaction. The terror was behind us. We began our steep descent into the lush Yusengi Gorge and homeward to the Baksan Valley where we'd begun.

At the Hotel Elbrus two mornings later, the mood was both celebratory and melancholy. We gathered around a picnic table for our farewell banquet—vodka, Georgian champagne, and a nasty pile of sheep innards—and Sasha rose to offer a toast. "We are joined by our terribles," he said, as the group exploded in laughter. Tonight, Sasha would return to Moscow to the one-bedroom apartment he shared with his wife, baby daughter and in-laws. The other Soviets would also go their separate ways. Only Leonid was staying on-moving back into the dimly lit cell he shared with another pensioner in back of the hotel.

Later, in a room that reeked of dirty laundry, I sat across from Leonid as he reached beneath his cot and pulled out a wedge of mouldy cheese and gray-brown halvah. Chewing the stuff in the murky darkness, watching Leonid as he boiled some water on a hot plate for tea, my eyes drifted to a tattered poster of Mt. Elbrus scotch-taped to the wall. Suddenly, I understood the power that the Caucasus Mountains, with their beauty and limitlessness, must exert on Soviets like Leonid and Sasha. Leonid must have read my thoughts. "Chorosha," he said, nodding at the poster. "Excellent." I swallowed a bit of cheese and tea, shook the old man's hand, and made plans to head back home.

Into the Yalimo

JAMES POLSTER

Somewhere in the western half of the island of New Guinea, someplace near the middle of one of the largest blank spots that still exist on maps of the world, sometime around 3:00 p.m., Jungle Tim sat on a rock. A dozen Neolithic warriors lounged about the flora watching him scrape ribbons of mud from his pants, his shirt, his ears, his nose, and incredibly, from under his hat.

Behind Jungle Tim: a day's worth of steep, treacherous climbs, two or three crossings of the requisite raging rivers, and one particularly slippery, nine-thousand-foot descent consisting largely of tangled tree roots. Strange noises escaped his throat, sounds that, when considered as a whole, were something like laughter.

"You know," said Tim, waving a grimy finger back in the general direction of Jenggo Mountain, "calling that a trail gives God less and man more credit than is justified."

This, of course, made no sense at all, but I knew exactly what he meant. We were on the first leg of a trek from the teeny village of Kosarek to the tiny village of Anggruk, a trek where smashing rainstorms and near vertical slopes had made many stretches of trail merely the trail du

jour, a trek where, as Jungle Tim put it, "If you slipped you would have been dead real easy, or wished you were."

Irian Jaya, as Dutch West New Guinea is now known, may be the wildest land left on the planet, its people the farthest back in time. It officially became an Indonesian province in 1969 as a result of Sukarno's carefully orchestrated referendum in which 1,025 Irianese voted against their own independence by a curious total of 1,025 to 0. But there are still roving bands of guerrillas, who, never invited to the ballot box, seem intent on uniting Irian Jaya with its eastern half, Papua New Guinea, and erasing that incongruous straight line that politically bisects the island.

Roughly the size of California, and consisting mainly of mountains and jungle, Irian Jaya is the least developed, least populated, and least visited of any part of Indonesia. One of the few travel books I could find that had anything to say about Irian Jaya wasn't exactly rhapsodic about its charms. On the capital city, Jayapura: "THINGS TO SEE—There's not a great deal to see." On Biak: "Not much of a town." On Wamena: "Not much in the town." And finally this: "You could make your way by air or sea to Fak Fak, Manok-wari, or Sorong on the 'bird's head,' but why bother."

The reason to go to Irian Jaya at all, of course is to penetrate the interior, much of which is still populated by "former" cannibals and headhunters. Jungle Tim and I were to visit the most untouched part, taking advantage of a pair of little used air-strips in the lands held by the Yali tribe, or the Yalimo as it is called by its neighbors. These two isolated landing fields would save us, round trip, six or eight torturous months on foot. An overland journey no one ever takes.

We came into the Yalimo after four numbing days of air travel, Los Angeles to Honolulu to Bak to Jayapura to Wamena, and finally to an aging, frail craft I could have probably folded into my backpack. The plane puttered between, not over, the mountains of the Central Highlands and on to the cluster of thatched huts that was Kosarek.

There had been a small problem with our Jayapura-Wamena connection. It didn't exist. The plane from Wamena was sixteen hours late and presumed crashed in the jungle. Attempts were being made to find it including, as I was to discover later in the *Indonesian Observer*, "a bid to encourage the public to search for the missing aircraft" by offering rewards. "It is said," the article stated, "that the prizes include a Johnson outboard motor." On the strength of this reward, the air search was scaled down, a substitute plane was dusted off, and those of us who sub-scribed to the "Lightning doesn't strike twice" theory got where we wanted to go.

I'd signed on as a writer for SOBEK's International Explorers Society Expedi-tion 129 because I knew our way led through the Stone Age. In fact, I'd found an Irian Jaya book in my local library called *I Come from the Stone Age* which fea-tured the most unique author's photo I've ever seen, a rather miserable, band-aged, and bewildered Heinrich Harrer, "a

fabulous athlete given to amazing feats of strength and endurance" being carried out of a place called the "Ya-li-me" on a crude, makeshift stretcher. But, as I had been informed that this was a trip of "average" difficulty ("Good health is the only physical requirement"), I'd taken the matter pretty lightly. In preparation, two or three times a week, I'd stuff my twenty-pound son Nick, into his baby pack and we'd hike our neighborhood mountain.

Having done this sort of backwoods travel before, I thought it best to review a worst case scenario and did so at the last minute, over cocktails at the Los Angeles airport International Departure Lounge. Difficulties seemed unlikely (the cocktails no doubt coming into play here), and all potential problems involved two improba-ble possibilities. What if, somehow, the trip was fifty times harder than I'd been led to believe? And what if the guy they're pairing me up with turns out to be a mara-thon runner?

Now, in Kosarek, I watched Tim repack his t-shirt collection—Twin Cities Marathon, Richfield 4th of July Run, The Corporate Marathon, The some-other-place-Marathon, The such-and-such-so-many-kilometer Run. But this seemed unimportant as it had become clear that we were onto something extraordinary.

Fifty Yali tribesmen shouldering time-less weapons of wood and stone had sur-rounded us and a number of women and children were swarming in their wake. The pull of curiosity was equally strong on both sides of the culture line and we all smiled and spoke continually though we didn't share a single word in common. Most of the men were there in hopes of being selected as porters—we were to take a dozen in all—and everyone else came because Jungle Tim and I were clearly the best entertainment in town.

The Yali make only the most minimal attempts at clothing, the women wear small bunches of rushes over the genitals, the men penis sheaths and perhaps a bone through the nose, the children usually nothing. Men begin to wear penis sheaths around the time of puberty. Fashioned from long, hollowed out gourds, some stretching over two feet, the sheaths are a mix of protection, modesty, and style. Each man has several, one to fit any occasion, the bright orange calabashes a contrast against his brown-black skin.

At the southern reaches of the Yalimo, warriors also wear coils of vines around their stomachs and chests. The layers of thick hoops can measure over a hundred feet end-to-end can serve as armor, and again, can represent a sort of personal style.

Small in stature—the man just over five feet, the women a few inches less—the Yali nonetheless have a reputation as fierce and dangerous fighters. Partly for this reason, the government allows neither guns nor alcohol. The Yali's tools are much as they must have been thousands of years ago, stone axes made from a heavy, pointed shard wrapped tightly onto a wooden stick; net carrying bags supported from the forehead; thick bows, five or six feet long with the patina of bittersweet chocolate; and arrowheads carved to a purpose, broad and flat for large game, a triple barb for birds, and a notched and tapered black version for settling disputes with finality.

As a rule, when men of the tribe walk about armed and in groups, it's an indication that something may be in the air. If the rule holds, Jungle Tim and I saw few days of calm. In fact, a month and a half before our arrival, two nearby villages had disagreed over with the ownership of a pig or the honor of an ancestor (these carry equal weight) to the tune of eighteen casualties.

Though the official Indonesian line is that the interior has been pacified, small, distant villages are obviously difficult to control. When the government does happen to learn of a trivial battle, they'll fly in a patrol and impress the warring factions into a peace ceremony—a feast in which each side roasts a pig and sweet potatoes for its enemies. If either party, or both parties, feels the matter has been resolved prematurely, they send their message past the nervous, benign smiles of the unsuspecting government envoys by simply undercooking the pork so that the blood still runs from its flesh.

Apparently, somebody kills someone in the Yalimo every week, but, according to our Indonesian guide, Bob, as long as Tim and I made no moves toward their women or their pig herds, had previously murdered no relatives, and refrained from making the often fatal missionary mistake of pushing them a little too hard to do something they didn't want to do, we'd be okay. He also delighted in pointing out that even though the Yali men smiled at us a lot, they were "killing smiles."

I came to look upon Bob Palege as a truly great guide, one of the few people I'd trust to escort me into parts unknown. I might never have had the chance to form this opinion, however, if we had strangled him that first day as planned.

Picture the well-known, classic shot of Machu Picchu, a lush green peak rising up through the clouds. Replace the Inca ruins with a village of ten or twenty domed huts and now picture a land full of nothing but Machu Picchus, and you have the Yalimo.

Towering jungle, thin bridges of lashed logs swinging at nosebleed heights, wild orchids, cassowaries and birds of paradise flitting about, and mountain after mountain packed so closely together that traveling across a valley to a point a few hundred yards as the crow flies may take hours of scrambling down, then up precipitous trails often narrower than the sole of your boot.

Tim had been told by SOBEK that he might find his first day "a bit strenuous," perhaps six or seven hours of hiking, but this was getting out of hand. Since we had been really pushing it for more than eight miles and were not likely to be stopping for long, on the trail in the middle of nowhere, these possibilities occurred to me: (1) the average American was in better shape than most people think; (2) the average SOBEK client was in better shape than I thought; (3) I was in worse shape than I thought; (4) something funny was going on.

The Yali porters had repeatedly proven themselves to be good fellows and I had passed out cigarettes, which turned this "breather" into a somewhat longer smoke break (a stalling tactic I was to employ many times before the end of the journey). To say I was beat is to criminally understate the facts. Jungle Tim, who earlier confessed to running fifty-five miles a week, had been reduced to a noodle. Still on his rock, muttering about God and man, he was now looking skyward. It had begun to rain.

"What do you think, Tim? Pretty steep back there, hmmm?"

"No," and then, with real feeling, "Merely calling that steep does not do justice to what we've just done."

"Ah hah. A bit strenuous then?"

"No. A bit hellacious."

At this point Bob sauntered over. He was wearing his standard guide outfit, Rambo headband, Harvard T-shirt, camouflage cutoffs, and the largest knife in the South Pacific. "Lunch?"

"Well, sure (it was, remember, three in the afternoon), but I was just wondering, uh, exactly where do people usually camp the first night?"

"In Serekasi village."

"I see. And how much farther is that?"

"Five hours ago! Why didn't we stop?"

"I see you guys very tough so I think we can go faster."

Bob went on to elaborate on how impressed the Yali were with our abilities, which I received as the worst possible news. Within the first twenty minutes on the trail, I had realized I would not be able to carry my own pack. Twenty minutes after that, I realized I would not be able to carry my own camera. And twenty minutes after that, the hand-over-hand climbing made me forget about taking pictures altogether. Since noon, I'd merely been hanging onto that magic figure of seven hours that Tim had inserted into my head. Now that the Yali had misinterpreted my grim determination, I could never let up, else risk losing face in that brotherhood of intercultural, macho camaraderie so important to underdeveloped, nineteenth-century throwbacks such as myself.

My knees were like liquid, my hands rubbed raw after hanging from all those rocks, and I was starving. I said the only thing that came to mind. "Well, now what?"

"I thought we could stay in Pemohan village," said Bob.

"Where's that?"

"Just over the next mountain."

"Ahh."

"But we can't stay there."

"We can't?"

"No. Our porters are having a fight with Pemohan and they won't go there."

"They won't?"

"No."

"Where will they go?"

"Telam Belam."

"How far is that?"

"We climb up to Pemohan, then down, then one more mountain up to Telam Belam. Maybe four hours."

Tim and I had started to laugh uncontrollably. Some of the porters were unfurling an orange tarp against the rain and Tim went for that.

"Bob," I continued, "Have you ever guided for SOBEK before?"

"Yes. Two times."

"And everybody did what we just did?"

"Oh no. Everybody always turns back after a couple of hours."

I believed I was experiencing real pain. Yet photos of that first day, and every day, all show me smiling. I attribute that in no small part to the fact that I was deep in the Yalimo with no maps, outnumbered badly by semireformed headhunters and cannibals, and at the mercy of a guide whose greatest pleasure was "watching my clients fall down."

"In Kosarek," chuckled Bob, "they all look around and say, 'Wow, this beautiful. Which direction do we go? That way? We climb up? Wow. Steep.' then we start, and they say, 'All the trip like this? This is crazy. Save me. Is possible to go back? Yes? I think let's go back to Kosarek.' Some men look macho, but before they get to Serekasi, boom!"

Thinking back, I did sort of remember a "boom" on the way into Serekasi. At the time, I'd written it off as just a vein or something exploding in my head. The amazing part of the Kosarek turnaround stories, however, was that these previous trekkers had gotten close enough to Bob, or "Nature Man" as he sometimes called himself, to get him into any kind of conversation at all. As near as I could tell, the first day of a trek he is just plain so excited to be back in the jungle that he takes off like a rabbit, scampering barefoot through the undergrowth.

And, in truth, his love of the people and the countryside became so infectious that it actually offset the physical surprises that were continually heaped on Jungle Tim and myself. That, plus the fact that Bob turned out to be a formidable cook.

Typically, dinner would be a chicken procured en route, vegetable soup, and rice or potatoes, all of it liberally spiced and sauced from the collection of mysterious bottles and jars in Nature Man's portable kitchen. Then we'd unbend into conversation, Bob holding forth about himself: "I have four girlfriends back in Jayapura. If they ever all come on the same night, Casanova must die." On our porters: "They asked to up their price

today. They always ask. I always do it." And on the Yali in general: "If a man says he wants my bow and arrow, I can say, 'Okay, but first kill so-and-so.' If the man doesn't do it, he's now dangerous to me because he knows I want to kill so-and-so, so I must kill that man."

Next, Tim might throw out something like, "You know, I was really not prepared for how dangerous this is," and, in my professional capacity, I'd be forced to interview him.

"What exactly do you mean?" I'd say, balancing my miniature notebook on one knee. "Kind of dangerous? A little dangerous? Sometimes dangerous?"

"I would have to say, very dangerous," Tim would reply giving me the answer I was secretly hoping for. "When you're trying to cross a slippery rock face on the side of a mountain, grasping for rotting tree roots with no real place to put your feet and at least a five-hundred-foot drop below, what else would you call it?"

Then we'd laugh until Bob served up his usual goodnight closer: "Just wait till tomorrow."

Almost nothing has been written on the Yali, who have had contact with the outside world only since 1961. At that time, American missionaries forged an agreement to split up the interior, the Protestants winning the Yali district. What the missionaries did not know, however, is that prior to first contact, low-flying reconnaissance planes had already scared the bejesus out of the Yali, causing them to prepare for war by initiating underage boys, suspending farming activities, and slaughtering their sacred pigs en masse.

Since each Yali village is usually, even in the best of times, operating under some degree of undeclared war with every other Yali village, there were substantial communication problems in 1961, and most of the Yali were not involved in the initial encounter. After a few years, however, the missionaries finally got around to everybody and encouraged all to just talk, visit one another, do a little trading, be friends. As a result, a series of long-standing but dormant feuds were revived, culminating in the Jaxole Valley massacre where many of the losers were eaten. The Yali blamed the missionaries, the missionaries radioed for the police, and the Yali received their first "rifle shooting demonstration."

Over time, the Yali have come to understand that violent behavior on their part can result in punishment from the more powerful, "bum-bow"-carrying men who cannot speak their language. There have been incidents, though. One particularly famous one was the cannibal feast that had taken place not so long ago on the Anggruk airstrip, our final destination.

Anggruk had begun to assume mythical proportions—the end of the journey, the far-off village in the clouds across the mountains—and we began to chant as we walked: "Anggruk, Anggruk . . ." Having scaled walls of jungle rising sharply from riverbanks to mountaintops, and lowered ourselves along cracked slabs of limestone where our descent was little more than a controlled dive, slogging from Kosarek to Wasaltek to Serekasi to Pemohan to Telam Belam to Membohan to Konai to Helariki, it seemed unfair that, for Tim, the worst moments lay waiting in Anggruk.

He had finally taught himself not to look down from great heights ("It was always a mistake"), and he had mud-skied Hohi Mountain ("If we'd had to climb it the other way, I don't know how I would have made it—the water was running right over us the whole time"), Jungle Tim had finally conquered the Kosarek-Anggruk trail. So it was with a well-deserved sense of satisfaction that he savored his dinner, unrolled his camping mattress, unzipped his sleeping bag, and, unsuspectingly entered The Night of the Cockroaches.

"Jesus, what the hell is that?"

"What?"

"Coming out of the walls."

"Oh, it's cockroaches. Tuck in your mosquito net."

"Aaagh. They're all over the place. This is disgusting."

"Just take a Valium."

"I'm going back to Helariki."

"But Tim, it's dark out."

"I don't care. All the trail had was fear. This is revolting."

I took my own advice and bit off half a Valium. The last thing I remembered was Tim, twisting in his bedclothes, screaming and muttering at the same time, "Jesus! They're going to crawl all over me! Aaaaagh . . ."

Tim survived the night, eventually there was a plane, and Bob bid us farewell: "When you get home, say hello to everybody from Nature Man who lives in the last Stone Age."

And there was civilization. And cold beer. And another plane. And another, and another, and more beer. And somewhere over the Pacific, someplace past the International Date Line, sometime around 5:00 a.m., Irian Jaya time, Tim turned to me and said, "You know, that wasn't so tough."

Swimming in Siberia

SUSAN DWORSKI

There are no atheists in foxholes. Or under rubber rafts.

"Oh, God!"

My screams were drowned in thundering water as the raft buckled and flipped. Committing the cardinal whitewater sin, I let go of my paddle.

Under the raft, in roaring darkness, I fought for my life. Grappling for a handhold anywhere, *anywhere* underneath the heavily loaded Avon raft, I felt it plunge toward a massive pour-over, dragging me with it. I gasped blindly for air as my contact lenses went swimming. Ugly brown waves bludgeoned me like freight cars from hell. I strangled on a life preserver designed by cretins for the sole purpose of severing my nose from my face. Clearly, I was history; doomed to disappear in glacial Siberian whirlpools that sucked and snickered and yawned hydraulically in the hypothermic death-boils swirling below.

We thundered through the rapids, the Avon and me. My ears sang with blood, my mouth filled with water. Powerless. The word banged in my brain. You are POWERLESS. Give up. Let go. *Now*. Pushing off, I dove down deep into the maelstrom.

* * *

"Siberia! But . . . *why?*"

I went to Siberia looking for adventure. Instead, I found God, under a boat. I didn't just sort of *find* him. He kicked my ass. It took Him three tries before He got my attention. But then, I'm a mortally slow learner.

* * *

Shortly before midnight in July, we seven from SOBEK wrestled our deflated Avons onto a plane in Moscow and flew through four time zones to southeastern Siberia. We chomped on grizzled chicken wings and desiccated buns and sipped sugary, lukewarm lemon squash as the Aeroflot 737 ground steadily through the night toward Barnaul, near the Mongolian border. The gunner's emplacement to the right of the cockpit was filled with bags of mail and boxes of orange and magenta plastic sandals bound, no doubt, for the souks of Kazakhstan. Despite their egregious sartorial errors, the Soviets are a practical bunch. They don't bother to maintain a separate fleet of military planes for their air force. In an emergency they simply commandeer Aeroflot and swap sandals for an AK16.

Despite many hours spent poring over

a map of Siberia, I was still unprepared for its astonishing immensity. As we flew and flew over vast tracks of darkness, I gave up looking for any vestiges of humanity and surrendered to Aeroflot Muzak—crackling Soviet Stonesclones wanking away on ear-splitting electric guitars. Not a pinpoint of light intruded upon the eternal blackness below us.

We crossed the darkened Ural Mountains, the Great Wall of Europe, a 2,000-mile-long barrier stretching from the perpetual ice of the Arctic to the deserts of Kazakhstan. For thousands of years, this wall effectively separated Europe from Asia, civilization from anarchy. The Urals were not breached until the sixteenth century when an exploding, pillaging Cossack tide broke through, flooding the West. It was two hundred years later that the Great Wall took its other, more sinister connotation: it became a prison wall beyond which tens of thousands of Russians were exiled, many never to return.

We flew on toward the ever-reddening glow in the east, serenaded by a deafening Cyrillic version of "House of the Rising Sun." Below lay "Siber," the Sleeping Land, the Void of Darkness, a deep green world of bogs and marshes. Clusters of square log houses slumbered in tight knots on the fringe of nameless rivers meandering slowly through the somber taiga before joining that potbellied Amazon of the north, the mighty Ob.

In the spring, the Siberian forest is known as the Blue Taiga for the smoky blue-green hue of the larch trees, and in the fall, as the needles change to saffron and amber, the Russians call it the Golden Taiga. It is, in the words of a Siberian poet, a "universe without an end," where Altai bear hunters hunker around roaring fires in snowy clearings, roasting chunks of meat skewered on fresh-cut willow rods, sipping endless cups of hot *chai*; a land where the tracks of hungry wolves criss-cross midwinter meadows in search of a forgotten calf, or goat, their dainty pattern

marked by a lone eagle, drifting on an invisible ribbon of Arctic air.

The higher elevation of the Siberian taiga is punctuated by foaming white rivers tumbled with gold nuggets. It is a harsh yet seductive region, filled with hidden treasure. In addition to rich veins of gold ore, the sheen of sable and the flash of diamonds have lured adventurers to Siberia for centuries in search of fortune. Often this search has resulted in their untimely death.

"The power of Russia will grow as Siberia grows!" M. W. Lomonosov stated enthusiastically in 1736. These prophetic words have become a guiding principle in the Soviet Union.

Despite herculean attempts by the government to tame Siberia by building shiny, new, drawing-board cities and enticing the citizens of European Russia to relocate there with promises of higher wages and better housing, huge tracts of wilderness remain undeveloped. Thankfully so, for these government-created cities are stupefyingly ugly—vast technocratic achievements of the Soviet state presided over by looming concrete apartment complexes thrusting upward from the barren plains like bizarre, Tibetan lamaseries from which any Spirit has long since de-camped. Honeycombed with identical, boxlike hives, they command the steppes, dwarfing the surrounding taiga, shrouded by a pall of noxious industrial smoke belching from dozens of factory chimneys and steaming hydroelectric plants.

"We *do* like our apartments, yes!" says twenty-year-old Sonia, a Siberian student. We stopped in front of her home. It was a massive lump of rain-streaked concrete, a block of state housing, animated by clotheslines flapping with the popular, androgynous Soviet uniform: red and blue polyester jogging suits. "They are solid, no? And modern. Not like log houses. You see, we make powerful big progress, even here in Siberia."

* * *

Progress. Power. Big.

Three troublesome Soviet buzzwords. You hear them often in Moscow. *Pravda* headlines shout them. They're immortalized in hundreds of heroic bronze statues of soldiers, workers and pioneers with scythes, guns, and babies welded onto their muscular shoulders. The Russia Hotel is quintessentially big. A humongous, monolithic square city block, it contains 6,000 identical roomlets. You need a map and a compass to find your way home to bed.

"It is a big *lie*," whispered a babushka-ed woman with hairy calves, gaining the courage to speak to a foreigner after sharing forty minutes sardined against me in a bread queue. "They tell us we are Superpower, but is a fact we are Third World country!" She spat for emphasis, "No better than Afghani!"

Cynicism runs deep. Glasnost seems surreal for many, more to be feared than celebrated. In gray Moscow, faces are stony, eyes averted. Feet trudge, hands grip empty string shopping bags. Nobody smiles. Joy is at a premium, sensuality nonexistent.

"Please, Madam, do not smile at Russians," I was advised while asking directions. "They will think you are crazy. . .or a spy."

I stood at the top of an escalator in the sparkling crystal-chandeliered, graffiti-free Moscow underground. Muscovites poured past me; grim, sad, frustrated. Their anger was palpable. In Yiddish, there is a poignant, nearly untranslatable word, *Neshoma*. It means: an inner feeling of goodness. We call it heart and soul. I thought: they've lost their Neshoma, these people. It's been taken away. Their subway works, but their lives don't. The sense of melancholy desperation was overwhelming.

"It is a sinking feeling, almost a physical sensation of drowning. We have lost our faith, our trust in our government, to

Richard Bangs/SOBEK photo file

get us out of this." A Russian friend spread his hands helplessly as the lighted Ferris wheel in Gorky Park spun past overhead filled with shrieking children. "How will we feed them? You tell me. How?"

There are no old men in Russia, only old women. These black-clad widows guard the entrances to hotels, museums, and tombs like so many gnarled and abandoned crows. As self-appointed arbiters of public morality, they will brazenly scold and hiss at anyone foolish enough to appear to be enjoying life. They're catholic in their contumely, these crones; lovers, hippies, heavy-metalers, and perfumed Italians suffer equal opprobrium.

"Ted Turner should buy the country and colorize it," joked Billy Crystal during his recent Moscow concert. And, "I finally discovered what the Five-Year-Plan is. It's the wait for service in a restaurant."

When his Russian character, Misha, sighed, "I want to go to America to see those 24-hour grocery stores. And the food you make just for dogs," the Soviet audience howled.

Alongside the rainy highway leading into Moscow from the airport are flimsy stands selling shashlik. Blue smoke curls off the grills while the owners huddle under dripping plastic tarps. It seems a hard way to earn a ruble.

"One year ago or two, you don't see these. Something new! Soviet enterprise!" Michael Harshan, an entrepreneurial young Russian spoke proudly, and apologetically, as is so often the case whenever Soviets attempt to explain their country to foreigners. "Perestroika!" he snorted, then smiled ruefully, "You see, in Russia, we do not have so high an opinion of business. It is not our system."

"Why does it have to be this way?" my friend Tania shrugged despairingly. "No reason, I think. No reason."

She poured another round of vodka and raised her glass. The tiny apartment was crowded with fellow American and Soviet river rafters, the miraculous table groaned with black market delicacies: caviar, smoked fish, soft cheese, marzipan and chocolate pastries. Each item represented hours of secretive shopping and months of scrimped rubles.

"To our economy! To friendship! To Mickey Gorby!"

Everyone laughed and drained his glass.

* * *

The Katun River, shallow and sparkling gunmetal gray at our put-in in Ust'-Koksa, rapidly deepened to a fierce, transparent cerulean. Chuck O'Brien's boat led the way, laden with wet-packs and food for twelve days. It waddled rhythmically across the surface of the water like a pregnant water skater.

In the paddleboat, under the hot midsummer sun, we practiced our commands. For-WARD. Right TURN. Stop. Back PADDLE. Stop. We practiced Russian with Vanya and Misha, our guides

from Soviet Travel. Both were experienced kayakers, but I noticed that maneuvering our baloney-boat seemed to baffle them. It worried me.

In the Soviet Union, river running is a relatively new sport, but it has been embraced with true Slavic passion. An international whitewater rally in May 1989 on the Chuya River, a tributary of the Katun, drew participants from as far away as Canada and New Zealand. For the duration of our trip, we kept pace with several groups of ardent Soviet kayakers, feverishly paddling their homemade catamarans. They had strapped themselves to the stripped-log thwarts in a kneeling position, and they flashed us a silvery greeting with hand-wired, jury-rigged aluminum paddles as our high-tech inflatables slid past.

The Altai Mountains rose up around us, engulfing us in gloomy, granite gorges, a welcome respite from the sun's glare. As the days passed, tributaries joined us. The Cucherla dumped a load of lime and we lost the blue Katun forever in milky murk. We dozed, daydreamed, camped on sandy beaches, and tracked eagles. Living was easy. Then, without warning, the Katun took a dive downhill, rumbling toward rapids.

"There are three big rapids on the Katun: Ilgumeyn, Witches' Sabbath, and the Whirlpools," our math teacher, Vanya, ticked them off with precision. "Coming up now, these have no name."

For-WARD! Left TURN! *LEFTURN!* SWAPPP!!!

Patently, our team lacked Olympic finesse. Hit broadside, I was catapulted backward over the raft into No-Name rapids, my feet rudely ripped from the foot stirrups. I floundered wildly, rapping off boulders, spitting foam. Boatman Steve Jones hauled me in just as another wave crashed over us. Somehow we managed to haul down the remaining rapids to safety.

I shivered in fear's aftermath, secretly

exhilarated. I'd passed the exploratory dunk test with flying colors! Yost was right. Piece of cake. Ilgumeyn? Sabbath? Whirlpools? No sweat, Vanya. Got 'em wired. Under control. Right? Wrong. And to prove it, He turned the weather around and sent a grim omen: a bloated corpse with one hand missing. We watched in silence as it bobbed past us downstream, grateful it was not one of our Soviet counterparts. Or one of us.

* * *

Twelve hours of steady rain can change a river and humble a person, especially if one is camped above a set of rapids named Witches' Sabbath. Around 4 a.m. I gave up trying to calibrate the Katun's possible rise and moved my tent up the riverbank to safety. The voice of the witches had become a hellish roar. Logs worthy of Paul Bunyan powered past in the frothy shallows, sheets of rain crashed down. It was cold enough to snow.

My whole body/mind screamed one message: NO! I CAN'T DO IT. I CAN'T RUN THESE RAPIDS! I DON'T WANT TO DIE! I'd been under the boat twice already: No-Name and Ilgumeym. Three strikes and you're out. I had come to Siberia to escape reality. To live a little. Death was not on the agenda, not part of the plan.

Shivering, I fumbled in my wet-pack for something warm. My fingers touched a silky strap. . . my bikini!

My laugh sounded like a death rattle. Words like home, family, and responsibility slammed into other words like coward, quitter, and chicken. Questions like: Who am I? What am I doing here? Who needs me? Who is responsible for me if not me?

"Dammit, I'm in charge!" I shouted out loud.

A few yards away, the Katun thundered past, shaking the earth; hundreds of thousands of gallons per minute, heading for Sabbath.

I stared miserably at the sweating walls of my rented tent, terminally terrified, conjuring Siberian memories.

Ruddy-cheeked Asiatic women in flowered dresses walked hand in hand through the dust-clogged streets, their calloused feet jammed into delicate slippers. An Altai herder's hut crouched on a high mountain pass, sawed-off mutton shanks hanging over a smoky fire pit. The cracks between the logs were chinked with brindled moss to thwart the north winds, and the shepherd's wife smiled with two gold teeth.

The furious wind flung pinecones at my tent as I remembered the goat in the blue-linteled post office at Inye, contentedly munching the week's mail while the teenage postmistress flirted long-distance on a turquoise plastic telephone. I still ached from a ferocious volleyball game with a team of Soviet kayakers. We traded spikes in a dark forest glade, dodging giant tree ferns and falcon scat. Afterwards, leaning together over the dying embers of a shared campfire, we sang Russian love songs and gulped wild taiga tea as lightning flashed and thunder rolled down the steep canyons. Sweetest of all was the long afternoon when we crawled on all fours, like grazing bears, across a bee-loud meadow, picking miniature strawberries tiny as jujubes. Our hands and mouths were bright red for days afterwards.

* * *

A grisly dawn broke over Sabbath as we joined a team of Soviets kayakers to scout from a rock. Black clouds stormed down the valley, thunder grumbled.

I screwed up my courage and spoke to our leader, Chuck. "Please ask if one of them will paddle for me." My cheeks were red with shame, but I had said it: I was afraid. An eager Soviet kayaker took my paddle and clambered into the Avon, grinning from ear to ear with anticipation. A sense of relief spread over me like warm molasses. I was saved.

Perched on the bank, camera in hand,

I photographed the SOBEK paddleboat gruel through the rapids. They skirted the right side, missing the wave train, and eddied to the side.

With a light heart, I reclaimed by paddle, thanked my rescuer, hopped back in and we pushed off. We hadn't gone twenty feet when I heard something ominous. Something dark and full-throated. Something very nasty.

"Second stage of Sabbath!" Steve hollered, digging in furiously as we shot toward a churning slot between a jumble of boulders. "Let's go! For-WARD!"

Second what!!? What was this? Some kind of cosmic joke? Fear clogged my stomach, every mucous membrane shriveled and dried. Brown swells charged at us from all directions. One grabbed us and shook us and stood us on end, showed us a trough like a coffin. Our whirling paddles dug for river and ate air.

Too late! We were in it. And under it. We flipped. . .one more time.

*   *   *

Dusk seems to last forever in the Altai Mountains. The trail led upwards from camp. The stones underfoot flickered with mica in the growing starlight. They lighted a path worn smooth by eons of Asiatic traders transporting goods from China, Mongolia, and Afghanistan.

I sniffed the night wind, listening for the sounds of hidden animals. Siberian granite crunched beneath my feet. How big it all was, I thought, gazing over the immense valley spread out before me. Far below, the Katun was a minuscule silver thread, snaking its way through dusky nightfall. Ilgumeyn and Witches' Sabbath were nothing more than a crinkle of boulders, a pinch of foam.

In the Kremlin museum there is an enormous suit of chain mail flanked by halberds and a wicked-looking mace. It belonged to Boris Gudonov.

"You see there, on each little ring, is written the words 'In God We Trust.'"

Ludmilla, our guide, looked carefully over her shoulder for eavesdroppers before continuing. "I believe in God. Do you?"

I hadn't answered her then. Now, alone at night on the steppes of southern Siberia, I went down on my knees for the first time in my life, and I prayed.

I prayed for the wild animals I hadn't seen and the obscure native peoples I hadn't met, whose river we had shared and whose taiga had sheltered us on our journey. In the exquisite strangeness and familiarity of the Siberian twilight, I prayed for this unmanageable mess we call the world.

In life we are always under one boat or another. We are always walking through the valley of the shadow of death, whether we choose to admit it or not. In the wilderness, face-to-face with our limitations, we are forced to confront a Being higher than ourselves. We discover that the people and events that matter most in our lives are forever beyond our control. Like rivers, we do not own them. We merely flow through them, beside them. Before the rapids, we stand naked and trembling, powerless and alone, yet part of a Spirit much greater, the Tao, the Divine.

"Everywhere God reigns, just cast out your line and where you least expect it, there waits a fish in the swirling waters." Even, I thought, under a rubber raft.

A pair of owls floated overhead, nearly brushing my ear with their silent, pumping wings. At my knee, a cricket thrummed. Something scratched softly under a bush. Stars wheeled and brightened. The planet turned. Hey, I was still part of it all. . .the whole, amazing show! On my knees, in the middle of Siberia, I gave thanks.

Sealed
with a Kiss

✦

RICHARD BANGS

"If you're travelling in the North Country by canoe, you don't want to capsize, you don't want to find a bear in your camp, and you don't want to eat freeze dried food for more than a week. Those are the basics."
—*Bart Henderson, North Country Guide*

The primary response is one of exhilaration, the splendid frisson that comes with gliding by the edge. The river is fast here, and the paddles swallow yards with each stroke. We stretch to pull into the small eddy for a breather. We're halfway down Nine-Bar Rapid, named for the nine closely spaced bars on the 1:250,000 scale map indicating a rapid of consequence. Most rapids are rated three maybe four bars, so this was something special, a class five rapid that spits and fumes continuously for two miles. "Nice!" I yell to Pam in the bow of the canoe, then look behind to see how Ivor and Andy are faring. . . not well. Their paddles are wagging like semaphores. The water is up to the gunwales in their 17-foot Old Town, and the canoe is reeling, like a sailboat in a squall. "They're swamping!" screams Brad, our guide, who is pitching in the eddy in front of me. "Let's go help," I call to Pam, while pivoting the canoe downstream. We dig deep, but as we get close, something more distressing occurs: the white styrofoam cooler with the last of our fresh meat floats out of the swamped canoe and sails downstream, along with half a dozen different duffels, toward the next set of turbulence in Nine-Bar. "Pam,

Ivor and Andy can manage on their own; let's get the gear." I turn the canoe again, and shoot pell-mell into the next set of rapids, steering us toward the various duffels, so Pam can pluck them up and toss them in our canoe. One, two, three duffels she hooks like a bear scooping salmon, then the boat strikes a rock, rotates, and slides down a chute backwards. Water spills into the bilge, but I still have the boat under control, barely. Pam picks up Ivor's sleeping bag, the tent bag, and then just one piece of flotsam remains. . .the cooler. It is out ahead, cruising for the last and worst section of Nine-Bar. One side is shattered. Pieces of styrofoam fleck the surface, but the bulk of the precious $8 container appears intact. If we go for it, we risk running the worst of the rapids blind; if we don't, freeze-dried again for dinner. "Let's go for it, Pam," I scream, and we desperately sink our paddles into the spinning water. At the edge of the rapid, Pam, who heretofore had been wont to master the art of paddling, executes a perfect one-hand draw stroke, pirouetting us into shore, as she snags the cooler with the other hand. We check the contents. A tub of butter and some pepperoni gone. All else intact. Joy. Real chicken for dinner!

Thirty minutes later, all four canoes are collected at the cooler landing, and Pam and I are being lauded as heros. Even Andy, who has yet to say a word on the trip, says thanks, and Ivor, the closest living being to Bashful of Seven Dwarfs fame, is simply effusive in his praise. "My, you're such good canoeists; it was so wonderful of you to save our gear."

Feeling a bit heady with the praise, we steer into the last section of Nine-Bar, following the wake of Brad's canoe. Brad has been down the Seal just once before, two years previous, in September, when the water was low. He had to drag his canoe through many of the rapids, including Nine-Bar. Now, though, in mid-July, the water is high, a 15-year-high from a record snowfall and a late spring runoff, and the rapids are big. Brad doesn't know this water, I think to myself, and Pam and I had just proved our skills. And, I've always been tempted by waters of untested depth, by a dash of danger du jour. So, I steer the canoe down a course all my own, down the middle of the rapid. Sensing something amiss, Pam turns back at me and repeats her oft-said plea, "Don't let us capsize." "Trust me," I smile back. Yes, it had been more than twenty years since I had canoed competitively; ten since I'd been on a canoe trip. But, I'd been on scores of rafting trips, and, hey, whitewater is whitewater, no matter the craft.

We strike the center of the hydraulic at an angle, the worst way to hit a wave in a canoe, and water pours in. Miraculously, we are upright when we emerge on the other side, but water is swishing around at my belly, and the canoe is teetering. "Try to stay balanced," I screech at myself as much as Pam. And with one hand I grope behind me for the bailer. . . but it's gone, washed away. I try to keep the canoe straight as we head into the tail waves, but it's like steering an overflowing bathtub. Instead of riding over the crests, we plow through them. In the third rapid, we

slowly roll over, like a three-ton log.

Pam, worried more about her cameras than herself, howls for help from the canoes downstream, but they're filled with water from the rapid and can't negotiate back upstream to assist. So, we're on our own, at least for a while. I try to straddle the overturned canoe and paddle, but it's like riding a seal; I slide off with every second stroke. I attempt to muscle the canoe right side up, but the boat weighs tons. Finally, I just surrender, and hang on as the canoe washes down the middle of the river. Twenty minutes later, the other canoes reach us and tow us to dry land. As we drag the swamped canoe ashore, a dozen harbor seals pop up and down in a pool less than fifty yards from the bank, in a ballet that seems to mock our misfortune. But, it is great entertainment and a fitting way to end the day on the eponymous river, the Seal. We'd earned our Canadian Club.

The Seal is a wilderness river in the truest sense of the phrase. Running west to east in northernmost Manitoba, emptying its pebbly clear cargo in Hudson Bay, the course has no impoundments, no diversion projects, no bridges, no roads, no homes, no people, no pollution. The river flows, as it has since time immemorial, in balance with itself. The river and every rill that feeds it are in an unmodified natural state. If it belongs to anyone, it belongs to the wildlife, superbly adapted to this inimical region: moose, wolf, fox, barren-ground caribou, marten, beaver, snowshoe hare, lynx, otter, muskrat, black bear, and polar bear, and a multitude of waterfowl and songbirds. And the seals. Normally marine inhabitants, harbor seals can be found in the uppermost waters and throughout the course of the freshwater river that bears their name. The Seal's harsh environment and remoteness have allowed it to remain absolutely pristine into the late 20th century, one of the few survivors. Yet, its fate is coming to a bend in the river. An ambitious dam project has been in the planning stages for years, and mining companies are eager to secure rights to an area possibly rich in gold and other precious minerals. However, in June 1987, Manitoba environmentalists entrusted a 150-mile section of the river to the Canadian Heritage River System, a national recognition similar to the U.S. Wild and Scenic River System, that would be a step toward preserving the river from man-made development or interference. That was the reason I joined the expedition: to see one of the last, great North American wild and scenic rivers and to help in the campaign to secure its protective status.

SOBEK photo file

The river is so remote it doesn't appear on most maps, even the commercial maps of Manitoba. To reach our put-in, we first fly commercially to Thompson, the nickel capital of Canada, and then charter a Cessna 310 to shuttle us north over the Mystery Country wilderness to Tadoule, the largest lake on the Seal system and home to a resettlement of 300 Chippewa also known as the Caribou-eaters), moved in 1973 from Churchill to avoid the evil of drink and drugs. There another charter, a Cessna 206 floatplane, wings us farther north, over endless lakes, spots of water that look like human eyes glittering or brooding as the mood strikes. They seem to mirror the soul of the landscape. Finally we land at an unnamed island in the 25-mile-long Shethanei Lake, on a beach

backdropped by thickets of spruce thin as sharpened pencils. Here we will begin our ten-day adventure.

The air is usually the first sign you are someplace different, far away from the familiar. But here, as we step off the pontoons, it is the light, soft, diffuse, and intense at once. The air, too, makes its point but not as expected. It is hot, over 100 degrees, the sun so fierce I look away, to the north. It was cooler in California. There is another indicator this is not home—the Manitoba state bird, the red-beaked mosquito. A blizzard of mosquitoes swirls along our beach, mixed generously with horse flies and deerflies, flying in dense, whirling vertical columns, dark as the trunks of trees. While the mosquitoes suck our blood, the flies tear out minute chunks of flesh with saw-edged mandibles. Immediately we all pull on our bug jackets, pants, and headgear, necessary survival wear for the summer subarctic at the 59th parallel.

We are eight, including Brad Koop, our quarter-century-old stolid guide; Laurel Archer, his effervescent and equal-aged assistant; Ivor, a few months short of 60; electrical engineer Andy, 53; Alistair, 44, a Scot who immigrated to Canada when he was 19; and his brother-in-law, Bob, 56, a manufacturer who flew over from England just for the trip. Pam Roberson, the photographer, and I are the only Americans, or South Americans, as some Canadians consider anyone from south of the 53rd parallel.

The following day, the first downstream, we pass an enormous bald eagle, who whooshes by us like a prehistoric bird. We stop alongside a shallow kettle lake at a vacant trapper's cabin, where we pick through the owner's trash and wonder about his life and income trapping mink, otter, muskrat, and beaver. The real money is in illegal game, such as bear. Poachers sell the gall bladders to the Koreans as aphrodisiacs; the fur and claws are black-marketed to collectors in

Europe, the United States, and Japan. We camp just below the confluence of the colder Wolverine River, which as far as I can tell from the literature I'm carrying, may be the spot where Samuel Hearne, the first white man to see the Arctic Ocean, camped in 1771. A star explorer for the Hudson Bay Company, he was on his second of three great expeditions into the barren lands in search of legendary copper mines. My greatest curiosity is how in the world the man could survive eighteenth-century exploration in this area without mosquito netting.

I awoke the next morning to an unfamiliar, incessant hum. I look at the tent mosquito net and see thousands, no millions, of mosquitoes licking their chops, waiting for my emergence. It's like some Stephen King nightmare, smoky hordes of blood-sucking creatures all waiting for the inevitable call of nature.

Fully armored in the Bug Attire, I attend breakfast, strong coffee, powdered eggs, and the firm delicious flesh of fresh arctic grayling, the latter caught by Bob. Things move slowly; no need to rush on the Seal. I stash my watch, resolving not to look at it until trip's end.

As we're packing up camp, sometime midmorning I guess, Bob let out a squeal, and we all turn to see an arctic white wolf in summer pelage just a few feet from our firepit, staring at us. His eyes, accentuated by dark lines, are filled with curiosity, no fear. Bob steps toward the animal, and it stands its ground for long seconds, then moves like a shadow into a thicket of white spruce and willow. We're stunned with the moment passed, and stare at one another in silence. Then, the wolf appears again, poking his nose at us from another bush, firing a look as though we are invading his turf. Clearly, we are the intruders, and he makes it known, then saunters off over the loamy soil.

After Pam attaches a rack of caribou horns, festooned with Labrador tea blossoms, to the bow, we shove off for down-

stream under streaks of bone-colored clouds set like scratches on blue glass.

It's a short day. We come to a spectacular esker (a long ridge of sand and gravel deposited by the action of runoff water from receding glaciers), and climb 100 feet up its fine-grained banks to a camp with a view. It's early when we pull in, but Ivor thinks this is the ideal place for the Grand Ceremony. I have no idea what he's talking about, but then Alistair pulls out a book called *Path of the Paddle*, by Canadian canoeing guru Bill Mason and explains. As it turns out, Alistair, Ivor, Andy, and Brad were scheduled to run the Seal the previous summer with Bill Mason a hero to all these men, and canoeing partner to Pierre Trudeau. But, just before departure he fell ill, and the trip was cancelled. In November he died of stomach cancer. Now, a year after the originally scheduled trip, Ivor and his friends are paddling with the spirit of Bill Mason and have devised a tribute to the great man. Ivor, a plumber whose motto is "a flush is better than a full house," had created a metal plaque attached to four feet of plumbing pipe. He has us build a cairn of rocks around the pipe, and then using instant cement, we make the pile permanent. The plaque faces the river, for other travelers to see. It reads: "The River, The Canoe, The Paddle, The Man. Bill Mason. Seal River Trip 1988. His Spirit Will Come Through."

When we finish the deed, Ivor presides over a moment of silence. It seems an ancient silence, as unbroken as the flow of the river. Then, off to dinner. Over noodles, someone looks up past the memorial. A 300-pound black bear is poised above us, not twenty yards away. The bruin lifts his nose to the sky, then points it toward the monument, then trundles off down the sand and gravel esker. The spirit of Bill Mason, saying thanks, is my unspoken thought.

For the next several days, we descend the clear, clear river, running rapids, trying, in vain, to catch trout and northern pike, and admiring the osprey, plover, terns, eider, and geese. Each day the sun describes a horseshoe around the margins of the sky, and the sunsets, which begin about 10:00 p.m. and last an hour, are a haunting crimson and peach, so unnatural looking that Alistair guesses there must be a forest fire somewhere, the smoke filtering the end of our days.

The rapids get tougher with each day, the skies hazier, and the bugs thicker. I had read that a naked man on the tundra could receive more than 9,000 bites per minute, which would suck his body dry of blood in four hours. Ivor tells us that 170 moose and deer were found bitten to death last year in northern Manitoba, a comforting thought as we swat and scratch and hover over the smoke into the wee hours committing philosophy, becoming beasts of bourbon.

The day after Nine-Bar Rapid the weather turns cold and soggy, and a terrible headwind blows against us as we struggle to paddle. Clouds fill the sky and seal us off, enforcing a sense of claustrophobia. In some small rapids, if we stop paddling, we appear to be moving upstream, the wind is that strong. It's like paddling the North Sea, and blisters grow in my grip. A glint between a grove of pipe-cleaner trees on the south shore draws my attention, and we pull over to investigate. We had heard that a solo canoeist was on the river coincident with us and that we should look out for him. Perhaps this was his canoe. But, after wading across the soft, morassy mosquito muskeg to the source of the glint, Laurel looks at the twisted remains of an 18-foot aluminum Grumman and announces it was the infamous *Titantic*. Five Canadians had attempted the Seal two summers previous, three in the *Titantic*. The canoe had ripped apart in Nine-Bar, and the three had to wait for days until the rest of the party could paddle out and enlist a helicopter for a rescue.

The river gets bigger with each passing day and is now fatter than the Colorado through the Grand Canyon. I know because we stop on the north shore at an incongruous sight—solar panels above an aluminum shack. It turns out this is a gauging station operated by the Water Survey of Canada. A logbook inside makes references to a proposed bridge near here (called the Falcon 50) and a dam, just upstream on the north branch as it sweeps around the bedrock promontory of Great Island. The log also shows that a week before the river was flowing at 22,640 cubic feet per second, a huge volume for a canoeing river anywhere.

The nights, too bright for stars, are nevertheless filled with thunder and lightning (both the sky-splitting kind and Yukon Jack, the Black Sheep of Canadian Liquors), and the days continue to be hazy, the results we think of a remote fire, one probably so isolated nobody knows its existence save us.

By the sixth day, we're passing from boreal forest to heath to tundra desolate as the mare of the moon. From a distance, some of the raised peat plateau islands, bald except for a clump of black spruce, look like they're sporting punk haircuts. The natives call this area the "Land of Little Sticks." With the tundra, though, the wind shifts and is now behind us, galloping from the northwest, blowing us downstream. The air is as dank as an oyster, the tail winds so strong they create whitecaps and send us surfing through the waves. The few trees we do pass look like one half of a Christmas tree, naked on one side and branches on the other, all pointing to the southeast.

On Tuesday, July 25, we pack up and head downstream for the final stretch of rapids, including the last and most difficult of the entire river, Deaf Rapids, rated VI on a scale of VI. The wind is once again trumpeting, and Alistair reminds us that Bill Mason advised adding an extra point in the difficulty rating of a rapids for high winds. We had to add to this the knowledge that Brad didn't know these final rapids at all. On his previous trip, he had exited down the south channel, but the launch owner, who was scheduled to pick us up where the estuary meets Hudson Bay, said the south channel was too shallow for his boat; we had to exit out the north.

So, we fall through a land that looks nude, running several Class IV rapids, with the dark clouds pawing at our backs, and come close to capsizing several times but always sneak through. Finally we reach Deaf Rapids and park the canoes above the maelstrom on the north shore, near a nest of ptarmigans. We hike down to see an enormous 500-yard-long rapid that runs a course like a DNA helix, with holes that would swallow a boat whole and waves that would stop the USS *Enterprise*. The photocopied guide we're carrying states, "The chances of a canoe successfully running these rapids is slim." Yet, as I stare at the rapid I can see a clean cheat run that starts in the middle, and veers to the left bank, avoiding all the major turbulence. As I'm scouting the run, Pam, nervous as a snake, comes to me and says she thinks it would make a lot of sense for her to photograph this from the shore, a shot heretofore missing from her repertoire. I hesitate a second, then say. "Okay. I'll run this solo."

My throat is in my heart as I walk back upstream across the bleak moonscape of a felsenmeer, a glacially deposited boulder field. I had never canoed a rapid solo, and this is a world-class killer of a rapid. We have no radio, no contact with the outside world, so any injury must be treated on the spot. Still, I am excited, warmed by the little flame of risk. I remember from Bill Mason's book that he recommended kneeling in the center of the canoe for a solo run, so I rearrange the duffel to allow the proper positioning. I exchange my prescription sunglasses for my clear ones, so I can see better, especially with the darkening sky. Then, as I push out in the current, it starts to rain. I stop to look around. In the way that beach stones are more colorful when wet, the storm brings out the colors of the land, and for a second I'm entranced. Then I plunge into the reality pudding. This is a death-defying run, I think, as I paddle the canoe to the center of the river, then turn it downstream.

Immediately the current grabs at the canoe, which is unfamiliarly light without Pam in the bow. Still, I feel I'm in command, and I weave between the rocks and waves, over a washboard running with white ribs of foam, a controlled pinball, as I angle toward the shore. Halfway into the run I know I have it. Zen and the art of solo canoeing, I can feel my arms connected to the water and its currents and instinctively know what to do. As I ease by the shore I see the flash of a camera and hear Pam cheering, "Go, Richard, go," and I feel like Jerry Rice on an end run. Nothing can block my way.

At the bottom of the rapid, I pull over and see there is practically no water in the bilge. I gulp a deep breath of air, which feels like a dry and sparkling champagne. It had been a perfect run. I watch the others come through, hanging up on rocks, slowly crabbing down the left bank. They all make it, though, and we assemble at the rapid's end for a victory photo.

A few miles later, after a staircase of rapids, one of which almost fills the canoe to swamping level (too smug, once again), we steer through the final riffles, where the river makes its final adjustments, like a settling stomach. We take our last strokes on the fresh water of the Seal and meet the salt of Henry Hudson's Bay. Hundreds of arctic terns flap over our heads, and dozens of seals swim around us as we dock for the last time. We will camp above tidewater here for two days, waiting for the launch to pick us up and carry us forty miles south to the outpost of Churchill, also known as the Polar Bear Capital of the World.

The following day Pam and I take the canoe beyond the tidal flats out into the bay and drift among the pods of beluga whales. The Seal delta is possibly the area of highest concentration of belugas in the world, perhaps as many as 3,000. It was a perfect, still day, the Hudson Bay like glass, and all silent, except for the periodic whoosh of a whale surfacing and spouting water. It is a tremendous thrill to be quietly floating and see the white body of a beluga move toward the canoe like a gleaming underwater missile and then pass directly beneath us. Scores swim by us, and one stops to break the surface and blink an eye at Laurel, a hundred yards away in another canoe.

After a couple of hours of whale watching, we decide to head back for camp. But as we're paddling we see something odd. All the camp members are standing pressed together on a high rock and pointing animatedly into the middle distance. Something is up, and Pam and I paddle hard, dock the boat, and run up to the group. "Polar bear," Ivor whispers with all the drama he can muster, and he points. I hop onto the rock and see the monarch of the North lumbering through the tamaracks just beyond the perimeter of our camp, over where I had been collecting firewood a few hours earlier. With the Steiner binoculars I can see his white fur rippling like a field under wind. It speeds the blood to see a polar bear (*Thalarctos maritimus*) in the wild, but it is sobering as well; the beasts can run faster than a horse and can be swift and brutal in the kill. Brad pulls out his Remington Woodmaster 30.06 and tests it; and we shoot off three flares, to make sure they work. Ivor first sighted the bear poised on a rock in the bay. Slowly "Pihoqahiaq" (the ever-wandering one), as the Inuit call him, swam to shore just north of the Seal delta, then ambled around the fringe of camp to the west. After about forty-five minutes describing half the circumference of our encampment, he disappears. Will he return? Nobody knows, of course. I offer a piece of Eskimo advice, that most polar bears are left-pawed, so if one must leap in desperation from a charging bear, it should always be to the bear's right. And that night, under a heavy sky shot with color, Brad sleeps with his rifle. I tuck in with my Gerber knife, as if it could do any damage against a 1200-pound attacking bear. But, it's all I've got.

In the morning, no signs of our icy-haired visitor. And at the appointed hour, the launch shows up, ready to carry us back to Churchill and civilization. Our captain, an Inuk, also fills us in on the big news: that the smoke and haze we'd been seeing was not part of an isolated fire but rather a series of the worst fires in the history of Canada. Some three million acres were in flames, and nearly 25,000 people had been evacuated from their homes. The provincial premier had declared a state of emergency. The train we were to take back to Thompson was no longer running because a bridge had been burned out. Worse, since a number of dry Inuit communities had been evacuated to Churchill, all alcohol had been banned and it would be impossible for us to get a celebratory brew, even a light beer.

It was with some sadness that we motored across Hudson Bay back to reality. I thought the river's name stood for more than the marine mammals who played throughout its currents. To have been sealed off from the world of news and neon and concrete for near a fortnight allowed a sensation, an alertness, a freedom, a validation, that only a true wilderness can give. Looking back at the needles of light flashing off the mouth of the river, I wrote a mental missive of thanks and sealed it with a kiss.

Diving in the Dutch Antilles

RALPH GARDNER, JR.

Rain started to fall seconds after I'd finished dousing myself with sunscreen. Then the woman next to me told me the chair I was sitting in belonged to her friend in Room 113. This was not my idea of adventure travel. I had envisioned myself cavorting with penguins on Arctic ice floes, tracking mountain gorillas through the rain forests of Rwanda, or maybe sitting around a campfire with native tribesmen, the subject of much merriment and laughter as I tried to learn Swahili, Tagalog, or one of the glottal click languages. Instead, I was on a beach in St. Maarten where the furniture was assigned, and I was being dressed down by a lady in a mumu who came from the south shore of Long Island.

When she discovered I was also a New Yorker and morbidly began to grill me about the weather back home, I decided to go shopping in Philipsburg, St. Maarten's duty-free capital. Destiny, however, had other things in mind. The rain stopped, the sun reappeared, the lady, now complaining about the heat, went to the bar for a pina colada, and on the horizon I spotted an island shrouded in clouds that looked just like the one where they found King Kong. It had to be Saba, one of the most beautiful but eccentric islands in the Caribbean. People who had visited it described a volcano that soared out of the sea, populated by the fair-skinned descendants of the original Dutch settlers who had built little storybook villages on its steep slopes. Saba was also said to have some of the best scuba diving in the world. Its diving was to be my adventure, admittedly tame by the standards of some, but the reason I'd taken time off, two weeks before Christmas, from an article of dubious significance I was writing for a women's magazine.

My itinerary called for me to spend time on each of the three Dutch Antilles Windward Islands—St. Maarten, that ever-popular resort destination, Saba, and St. Eustatius, an island I'd never even heard of let alone harbored fantasies about visiting. But it was only the St. Maarten portion of my trip that caused me trepidation. I'd once spent twelve chaotic hours in its airport on my way home from St. Bart's, a competitively chic French colony where the women wear little and the men even less.

St. Maarten is what happens to an exquisite Caribbean island when it builds a runway to accommodate nonstop 747s from New York. It's urban sprawl gone Caribbean—a succession of casino hotels, time-share condos, and duty-free shops, separated only by the occasional palm tree and connected by inadequate roads. In fairness, I found white sand beaches just like the ones where leggy beauties sprawl and sip rum punch in the travel ads and food that is among the best in the Caribbean. At the West Indian Tavern in Philipsburg, I was introduced to *christophene*, a local vegetable that tastes like the offspring of a potato and a squash. Combined with snapper and thyme and deep fried, it's a dish I'll remember ten years from now. Also the relaxed scene in Philipsburg in the evening, when drivers stop their cars in the middle of the street to chat with neighbors and nobody ever honks his horn, is very different from the giant cruise ship's action in the day, when thousands of hyperventilating bargain hunters steam into Great Bay. Though each duty-free shop seems to carry almost identical merchandise—liquor, cigarettes, french perfume, and the full line of Sony Walkmans—the prospect of buying this stuff at 25 percent less then what you'd pay back home has a mood altering effect, and it isn't pretty.

In the departure lounge I sat across from a very self-conscious local couple who I am now convinced were on their way to St. Eustatius to have an affair. What one usually demands for such liaisons aren't beaches and waterfalls or even fine restaurants but seclusion. And in this respect St. Eustatius, commonly known as Statia, probably has no peer in the entire Caribbean. Though it's only seventeen minutes by plane from St. Maarten, it may as well be in another dimension: nature has thoughtfully conspired with the authorities to keep tourism at arm's length. The only beach is on the windswept Atlantic side and has a lethal undertow; the arid landscape seems barely able to support Statia's forlorn-looking livestock; and there are perilous few stores.

Still, there's a desolate beauty to the place. Maureen Rawlins of the Statia tourist office picked me up at President Roosevelt Airport (FDR visited in 1936) and drove me to my hotel along narrow roads through brambles of sea grapes and fields of high grass. The road ends at the ocean directly by my hotel, the Maison Sur La Plage. A cluster of bungalows maintained by Michelle Greca, a French woman and an excellent cook, and her two inseparable donkeys, the Maison is the perfect place to go if you want to read *War and Peace*. The view from the hotel, through veils of salt spray, is of an extinct volcano called "The Quill," judged by geologists to be the most perfectly formed volcano in the Western Hemisphere. It rises gently from the island's central plain and gives Statia a mythical quality.

Life was not always this unhurried on the island. In the seventeenth and eighteenth centuries, St. Eustatius was the port of choice for smugglers and pirates who trafficked in slaves, rum, sugar, and tobacco between the Old World and the New. Most of the muskets and gunpowder used by George Washington's army during the Revolution came through Statia. Benjamin Franklin had such faith in the island's post office that he had his mail shipped through here when he served as ambassador to France.

Statia became the first foreign government to recognize the newly united states when its commander, Johannes de Graaf, offered a thirteen-gun salute to the visiting American brigantine *Andrew Doria* on November 16, 1776—an action which so incensed the British they sacked the port in 1781, starting the decline in fortunes from which Statia has yet to recover. Today the unlucky boats that were in the port when the British arrived comprise a sort of underwater archaeological park. Divers regularly bring up shards of Delft pottery, bottles, pipes, and occasionally even anchors, cannons, and blue glass trading beads, of the kind the Dutch are thought to have used to purchase Manhattan Island. There's a roaring black market in the trading beads at the Cozy Corner bar in Oranjestad, Statia's capital, with single beads going for $35.00.

SOBEK thought that since I'd scuba dived only once before, and then in ten feet of water with an instructor who literally held my hand the entire time, I should take my first dive on Statia, where it's possible to wade into the water from shore. On Saba there's no shore to speak of and divers are compelled to roll backwards into the ocean from the boat, like Lloyd Bridges did on *Seahunt*. The most exciting moment came when my instructor, Dave Green, grabbed my regulator, that all-important piece of equipment that connects you to your air tank, and removed it. It was important, he said, to know how to respond in the unlikely event that some enthusiast's flipper accidentally knocked the thing out of my mouth in a hundred feet of water.

Dave coached me to blow a steady stream of air from my mouth while calmly replacing the regulator, and I complied, but not calmly and not without swallowing several quarts of seawater. After hitting the surface and exacting a promise from Dave not to teach me any other emergency procedures, we proceeded along an ancient seawall where Dave pointed out a coral-encrusted cannon that lay on the sandy bottom. Though my dive fell short of a spiritual awakening, it did give me the necessary confidence to believe my next dive could be off the back of a boat.

Dinner was at the Old Gin House, an eighteenth-century building that's been transformed into a luxury hotel by John May, a teacher from Connecticut, and Marty Scofield, who, according to them, won more awards and got more ulcers than any other creative director working in advertising in New York during the sixties. Neither time nor Statia have taken the edge off Marty's hyperactive personality. He attends to the kitchen, the house-keeping staff, and the interior decorating (a stark self-portrait, worthy of a Wyeth, hangs on one wall) while John attends to Marty.

Both men are inspired storytellers; they say they have no other choice if they hope to hold onto their guests since lonely expatriate Americans living in split-levels on the slopes of The Quill regularly swoop down on the Old Gin House and try to entice away guests by inviting them to have dinner.

Marty and John told me the story about the Texas doctor who disappeared into the crater of The Quill one day never to be seen again and another about the government-sanctioned whorehouse outside town where girls from the Dominican Republic decorate their rooms tastefully but are nonetheless expelled from the island after four months to discourage more permanent relationships developing between them and Statia's meager male population.

When I asked about violent crime on the island, they said it was nonexistent because of the rainwater the natives drink; it makes their bones so brittle they're afraid to fight. The only exceptions are in cases of voodoo murder, a subject rich in narrative possibilities but one that the men brushed over on their way to several charming anecdotes about Queen Beatrix of the Netherlands, who calls the Old Gin House home on her annual visits to Statia. Her majesty, they say, is a kick-off-your-heels type who takes her martinis very dry.

After dinner we retired to the inn's salon where, as ceiling fans turned slowly overhead, John told tales of his adventures as an educational advisor to the Ethiopian government, including a detailed description of one of Emperor Haile Selassie's ostentatious birthday parties and a story about the time John was ambushed by rifle-toting insurgents and made to strip bare. When I left the Gin House around midnight I felt as if I'd spent the evening at the British officers club in some forgotten outpost in the waning days of the empire.

The woman sitting in the row ahead of me on the Winair flight to Saba had the right idea. She buried her head in her boyfriend's lap and threw a raincoat over her head. Saba's airstrip, as short as an aircraft carrier's, is accessible only to specially designed planes that can takeoff and land in small spaces. The view of Saba out the plane window only compounds one's apprehension about being able to land safely. Saba soars directly out of the water to an altitude of 3,000 feet, with no signs of a valley, a plateau, or even a gorge. As we circled for a landing, it looked prehistoric in the twilight. I almost expected to see pterodactyl circling its towering summit.

Columbus spotted Saba in 1493 and decided to keep going. In the early seventeenth century, it was settled by Dutch criminals. They pelted unwanted visitors by throwing rocks down on them. Cut off from the world, there wasn't even a road on the island until the 1950s, and 24-hours-a-day electricity didn't come to the island until 1970.

If you throw your head back and look straight up while standing in the airport parking lot, you see Hell's Gate, the closest village, several miles away and 1,200 feet in the air. Josephus Lambert Hassell, the native engineer who built the serpentine, nine-mile road leading to Hell's Gate after the experts from St. Maarten said it couldn't be done, is understandably accorded the reverence the citizens of flatter nations shower on their founding fathers. Today, Japanese subcompacts sporting bumper stickers like ''You toucha my car, I breaka your face,'' and ''Vote for Hassell'' zip around the heart-pounding curves, somehow missing the roadside flowers: pink oleander and a dozen varieties of orchids.

Every house on Saba is painted the same shade of white and every roof the same shade of red and all have delightful gingerbread woodwork, which makes me think that shared taste can keep people confined for centuries to the same, few square feet of planet from massacring each other. Joan Bourque, a New York artist who moved here and runs the Sea Saba dive shop with her husband Lou, and who dared to leave the cedar shingles on the roof on their home unpainted, says neighbors still stop by to ask when she's planning to paint it red.

I was picked up at the airport by Glen Holm, Saba's director of tourism, who put the car in second gear and headed up the mountain to The Captain's Quarters in Windwardside, the village above Hell's Gate. The Captain's Quarters is a turn-of-the-century sea captain's home that's been transformed into a small hotel. The unobstructed view from your bed is of the cloud flecked Caribbean 1,500 feet below. Jackie O slept here when she brought Caroline and John, Jr. to Saba to scuba dive. I'm also told by knowledgeable Sabans that Queen Beatrix, then but a princess and on her honeymoon with Prince Claus, conceived Crown Prince Willem Alexander in Room #7.

Over drinks, Glen introduced me to a young man who gave his name as Hassell, the same as the road builder and also as Steve Hassell, the hotel's manager. I asked if Steve and he were related. He said they were first cousins. He also told me Glen was his first cousin as well. As it turns out, virtually everybody is related on Saba, and three names—Hassell, Peterson, and Johnson—fill almost every page of the local phone book.

Sabans understandably look alike. Most are pale with small, curved noses, sparrowlike cheekbones, and delicate lips. Visitors will also notice that they behave a little strange as well. Pop a simple question and a Saban will hesitate several beats before coming up with an answer. Cold sober, they act as if they've already had a few Heinekens. Inbreeding is one explanation for their behavior. Another is that Sabans may be having trouble understanding us and even each other. Educated in Dutch yet speaking English at home, they become eloquent in neither. A third possibility is that they just seem slow to high-powered Americans hot off the airplane.

If the Sabans project an out-of-whack quality, the island's climate only completes the effect. At a couple of thousand feet above sea level it feels more like the Rockies than the Caribbean. The temperature rises into the 80s during the day but plunges back into the 50s at night. The wind off Mt. Scenery, Saba's highest peak, gusts with Gothic Force, and when it rains, it rains as hard as it does during typhoon season in the South Pacific. The visitor whose goal is to get a suntan must make peace with the fact that even when there isn't a cloud anywhere else in the sky, the summit of Mt. Scenery can be hidden in them.

I was nervous about my inaugural deepwater dive. The first time I went diving, in the Red Sea, I panicked even thought I wasn't more than five feet under water. I couldn't get enough air into my lungs and I started to feel like I was suffocating. I gave the signal that I wanted to surface, and when I did, I ripped the mask from my face and gasped for air. My reaction had been completely emotional. There was enough air in the tank to fill my lungs to capacity for a half hour. But something had happened underwater, I was seized by terror unlike anything I'd experienced since childhood.

My reaction, while not entirely rational, had some basis. Diving isn't tennis, where the worst thing that can happen to you is that you'll lob a ball over the fence and embarrass yourself. If your equipment malfunctions, you're in trouble. If you panic underwater and streak to the surface—a completely natural reaction to my mind—the too-rapid change in pressure can cause agonizing pain, paralysis, and even death. Knowing the poten-

tial for disaster one demands more from a dive master than a deep tan and good teeth. You want somebody who shares your reverence for life, particularly your own, and who also has the nerves of a test pilot.

Lou Bourque, the director of the Sea Saba dive operation and my guide, seemed to possess these qualifications. He was visibly upset when one diver lost a five-pound weight, saying that on Saba, at least to a diver, lead is more valuable than gold; everything from T-shirts to diving equipment must be flown in and often takes months to arrive.

Lou said he'd wait for me in the water and plunged overboard. Greg Johnson, his first mate, showed me how to hold one hand over my mask and regulator and the other against the back of my head so I wouldn't lose all my equipment when I tried the same maneuver. The Florida couple who were also diving with us smiled encouragingly. I was suddenly struck by the preposterousness of believing I could fling myself into the ocean with a sixty-pound tank attached to my back and fifteen pounds of lead weights on my belt and not sink indefinitely. However, getting to this moment had been the goal of my trip, and if I chickened out now, this essay would be all travel and no adventure.

I took a deep breath and tumbled backwards into the water—I think I did a complete somersault. When my body eventually righted itself, Lou was motioning me to follow him away from the boat. We descended slowly through the clear water, stopping every few feet to pop our ears against the mounting pressure, and reached the sandy bottom in a couple of minutes where we waited for Deana and Cliff. They came soon, and as they did I felt an attachment to them of the sort I assume Neil Armstrong felt for Buzz Aldrin as he skipped toward him across the lunar landscape.

The three of us followed Lou into Tent Bar Reef, a coral garden filled with waving sea fans, brain coral the size of boulders, frilly purple leaf coral, and things I was later told were sponges but looked nothing like any I'd ever seen. One variety, the barrel sponge, was as hard as armor and shaped like a silo. Elkhorn coral, treelike and growing to ten feet in height, would have looked more at home in the sagebrush deserts of the Southwest. Sergeant major and brown chromis fish swam along beside us.

In the boat on the way back to shore, the can of pear nectar I was sipping may as well have been champagne considering my triumphant mood. I felt as though I had been initiated into a secret society whose exalted rulers were sea fans and fish, had been recognized as a kindred spirit and whispered secret knowledge.

They'd stopped serving lunch at the Captain's Quarters by the time we got back, but fortunately, the Chinese restaurant in Windwardside was still open. When I'd suggested to Glen that we have dinner there some night, his response had been less than enthusiastic. One visit made it apparent why. The restaurant seems to have eluded Saba's white paint, red roof standards of propriety. Several unshaven gentlemen, whose slackened expressions suggested they were here for the afternoon, stood at the bar guzzling Heinekens. A radio blared a blend of static

and reggae as young children chased each other around the table at which teenage couples played footsy between bites of eggroll. At some point the distinctive sound of breaking glass could be heard and all the children slinked out sheepishly. The Chinese couple who ran the restaurant continued to serve and clear throughout it all, unfazed. I liked the Chinese restaurant. It proved that Saba had a subversive streak. The pork sate wasn't bad either.

That evening I climbed the hill into Windwardside to visit Guido's, the island's Italian restaurant and discotheque. It had the requisite rotating mirrored ball, parquet dance floor, and concert-size speakers. The place was packed by eleven, with all the tourists and most of the native population in attendance when the Dutch navy marched in—thirty or forty young men in single file, all with closely cropped hair, most of it blond. The bartender told me their military service included clearing nature trails on the island.

The next day I went diving with Joan, Lou's wife, at an underwater pinnacle called Man O'War Shoals which rises seventy feet from the ocean floor to within fifteen feet of the surface. I plunged in without much of the previous day's apprehension and followed Joan down. At the

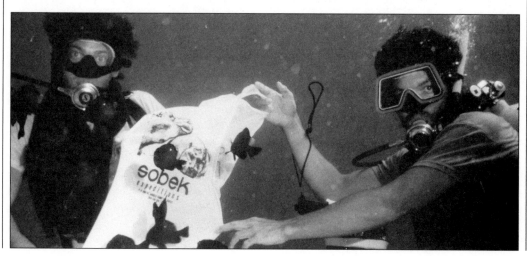

bottom a welcoming party of coneys, red fish with blue spots, hovered inches from our masks and even allowed us to touch them.

The pinnacle looked like the spire of a medieval cathedral but encrusted with coral and surrounded by thousands of fish that floated between us and the water's sparkling surface. We slowly made our way along its sides, stopping every few feet as Joan pointed out an arrow crab, its limbs as delicate as a daddy longlegs, a moray eel hiding in a crevice, and the fish—angel fish, black and yellow rock beauties, silver amberjack, French grunts, goat fish, and Spanish hogfish.

I tucked my hands behind by back and drifted with the current, feeling like I was flying. I was living my childhood fantasy of being able to soar over the landscape, swoop down for a closer look, graze the rooftops, and wave to the awestruck citizens. Only the citizens were fish and lobsters and their houses came in colors and shapes that even the most outrageous postmodern architect wouldn't attempt.

When I looked for Joan she was kneeling on the bottom, one hand prayerfully folded over the other. Diving is considered a sport, but it isn't really. It's more like a meditative retreat, sightseeing at its most sublime.

After a short break on the boat, we dove Ladder Labyrinth, so named because it's near the steep, handcarved thousand-step staircase that was the only access to Saba for earlier generations of visitors. As we descended I spotted a barracuda. I'm told that even though they look ferocious and are up to six feet long, they are generally harmless unless eaten; they cause more cases of fish poisoning than any other fish. Happily, this one was going in the opposite direction. With an escort of rose-colored blackbar soldier fish, and silver and yellow butterfly fish, we swam through a canyon of fissures, rock ledges, and overhangs from which tube sponges, looking like elephant trunks, dangled. A

stingray, half buried in the sand, fled with a single undulation of its winglike fins as we approached.

Lying in bed later that afternoon, I felt vaguely heroic but also sad that I had to go home the next day. There were twenty-two other dive sites on Saba I hadn't visited yet—underwater caves, tunnels, elkhorn forests. But I certainly didn't feel deprived. Diving was such a vivid, visceral experience I felt I could replay each dive in my head as easily as if I'd stuck a videocassette into a VCR. I was surprised that the aspect of diving that affected me most wasn't seeing the fish but rather having shared their territory. My favorite image isn't even of marine life but of the other divers, moving through the miraculous blue water exploring.

The sound of Christmas carols, accompanied by a guitar, came through the window. I'd almost forgotten about Christmas; sidewalk Santas and harried last-minute shoppers seemed like another world. Since it was Sunday, I assumed that a church service, Caribbean style, was in progress and decided to investigate. But as I climbed the hill into Windwardside and neared the source of the music, it took a decidedly secular turn with such old standards as "My Darling Clemantine" and "Red River Valley."

The singing wasn't coming from the church but from Scout's Place, an inn with a large terrace overlooking the sea. Several dozen people including almost everybody I'd met on Saba were there. Glen handed me a Heineken, Joan gave me a mimeographed copy of the music, and Lou served me a plate of hors d'oeuvres. As we launched into "Home on the Range," I asked Glen what the occasion was. He pointed to an elderly gentleman in a jacket and a tie seated at the center of the excitement and said it was his surprise ninetieth birthday party. It was hard to hear Glen over the music, but I think he said the fellow was a Hassell.

Environment

The Amazon Basin (EC 1)

ENVIRONMENTAL ADVENTURE—CLASS II

➤ *World's largest rain forest*

➤ *Model farms and alternatives*

➤ *Photographic safaris of jungle wilderness*

The focus of the planet's concern for saving the rain forests is, and must be, the rain forests of the Amazon Basin. The single largest ecozone in the world, source for a significant percentage of the atmosphere's oxygen, reservoir of a fifth of all the world's fresh water and home to one-third of all the plant and animals species on earth—the value of the Amazon is incalculable. Here, too, the battle for control of the Earth is most pitched: logging and agricultural projects denude vast tracts of land daily, and population pressures invade every narrow road to the heart of previously untracked wilderness, where durable native tribes confront fickle modern man. It is a complex world of its own, with complicated problems and no easy solutions, but we try to make sense of it on this special two-week sightseeing and fact-finding mission.

Randy Hayes, founder and president of Rain Forest Action Network, has taken special interest in the Amazon and will escort this journey to the Brazilian states of Mato Grosso, Pará, and Amazonas. Several quality lodges will host us, such as the Floresta Amazonica Hotel at Alta Floresta, a new city of 180,000 founded in 1976 in the midst of the Amazon. Here a model farm showcases the production of agricultural products suited to rain forest ecology, a nearby mine harvests gold from mineral-rich deposits, and an overnight journey up the Rio Cristalino shows us the rich flora of Amazonia.

Other stops include an overnight stay in the remote Xingu Reserve and a visit to the World Wildlife Fund reserve near Manaus. We go to the raw jungle at the center of the continent for two days, where we'll stay at the Ariau Jungle Tower, a lodge on the margins of the Rio Negro in Amazonas accessible only by riverboat. Here as almost everywhere throughout the trip, we'll meet the local experts and advocates of rain forest preservation, concluding with a panel discussion with grass roots organizations in Sao Paulo, the world's third largest city, on the Pacific coast at the Tropic of Capricorn. This is a journey of discovery, a holiday of education, and a call to save the rain forests of the Amazon.

ITINERARY:

Day 1: Miami to Rio de Janeiro.

Day 2: Alta Floresta.

Day 3: Cristalino River, camp overnight.

Day 4: Jungle trek and return to Alta Floresta.

Day 5: To Altamira.

Day 6: Xingu Reserve

Day 7: Return to Altamira.

Day 8: To Manaus; city tour and overnight.

Day 9: World Wildlife Fund reserve and overnight.

Day 10: Boat trip to Rio Negro lodge.

Day 11: Jungle lodge.

Day 12: Return to Manaus.

Day 13: To São Paulo.

Day 14: São Paulo rain forest conference.

Day 15: Departure for U.S.

PREMIUM

July

SOBEK Expeditions

Rain Forests of Indonesia (EC 2)

WILDLIFE AND ENVIRONMENTAL ADVENTURE — CLASS III

- ➤ *See the orangutans of Sumatra and Borneo*
- ➤ *Raft the Alas, river of the red ape*
- ➤ *Trek in the rain forest of Kalimantan*

Few regions of the world can boast the diversity found in Indonesia, the huge Southeast Asian country draped over the equator from the Bay of Bengal to the Pacific Ocean. Fifth in both population and area, Indonesia has long been regarded a sleeping giant in world politics, as shown by its membership in OPEC and status as the largest Moslem nation in the world. With the resurgence of concern over environmental degradation, Indonesia has again captured the public eye due to the rapid rate of destruction of rain forest areas on Sumatra, Borneo, and other islands. We will visit two of these controversial regions, combining adventure with environmentalism for a modern odyssey in an endangered world.

After sleeping and swimming away our jet lag in Bali, we fly to the northeast end of Sumatra, long regarded as a model of rain forest ecology and species but where increased logging and the policy of "transmigration" is threatening its most famous denizen, the orangutan. This large primate, at 250 pounds second only to the mountain gorilla in size, earns its name from the Malay orang utan, "man of the forest," and is today rarely seen in its deep forest habitat. We visit the Bohorok

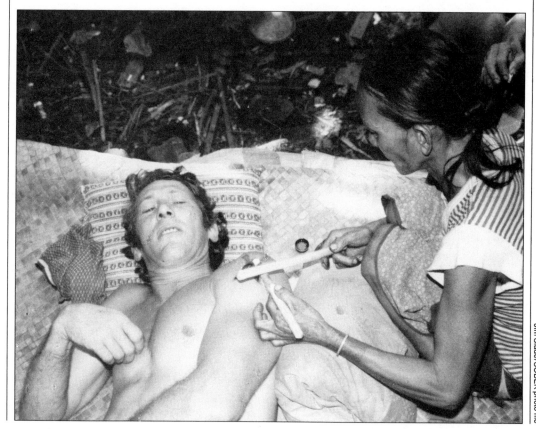

Jim Slade/SOBEK photo file

Orangutan Rehabilitation Centre where young apes captured in infancy to be raised as pets are reintroduced to the natural environment and eventually released. Then we journey across the Karo Batak Highlands to the Alas River, a mild whitewater run through Gunung Leuser National Park. Here gibbons, macaques, leaf monkeys, and even occasional orangutans continue to be sighted, making this four-day float a unique wildlife experience.

We fly on to Borneo, the world's third largest island, where the Indonesian state of Kalimantan once offered huge tracts of primary rain forest bursting with unusual life-forms. Here, too, the "reclaiming" of jungle by slash-and-burn agriculture threatens the sanctity of forests tens of millions years old. After traveling by canoe up the Mahakam River to the confluence of the Melkoet, we continue on foot to our first camp. Over the next two and a half days, our trek takes us through primary and secondary forest, slash-and-burn areas, and overgrown fields slowly returning to nature. Guides will be local Penihing Dyaks, as well as representatives of Indonesia's forestry department and rain forest action advocates. This expedition will be an informative and eye-opening one.

ITINERARY:

Day 1: Depart U.S.

Day 2: Lost to International Date Line.

Day 3: Arrive Bali.

Day 4: Bali.

Day 5: Fly to Jakarta and Medan.

Day 6: Bohorok.

Day 7: Karo Batak Highlands.

Days 8-11: Alas River.

Day 12: Fly Medan to Balikpapan.

Day 13: Up Mahakam River and begin trek.

Days 14-15: On trek.

Day 16: Down Mahakam, fly to Balik-papan, on to Jakarta.

Day 17: Return.

PREMIUM

August

SOBEK Expeditions

Threatened Primates of Africa (EC 3) ▲▲▲▲

WILDLIFE SAFARI— CLASS III

➤ *The chimpanzees of Gombe*

➤ *The gorillas of Rwanda*

➤ *Red colobus, baboons, and more*

While the arguments over humanity's ancestry continue, the very real threat of extinction still faces our primate relations. Whether we are more closely related to chimpanzees or gorillas, or spring from a still more ancient ancestor lost deep in the Oligocene Era, the fact remains that today, in the decreasing forest areas of central Africa, these proto-hominids are losing habitat and numbers in alarming proportions. Perhaps we can find somewhere within our larger brain size the wisdom to preserve these endangered species, for in their populations we may find our own secrets lurking—social or biological resources encoded in their behavior and physiology that we can draw on in our own continuing struggle for survival. In any case, merely to witness the interactions within chimp and gorilla family groups can be an education for each of us, and the Threatened Primates of Africa program gives us several such opportunities.

Leading the program is Dr. Michael

Mahale is a wilderness park at the base of a cloud forest-shrouded massif, and Gombe is perhaps the most famous of all primate study areas, for it was here that Jane Goodall made her breakthrough contacts with its wild chimpanzees. We will travel on foot through this roadless national park, amidst black and white colobus monkeys, baboons, bush bucks, crested guinea fowl, and hawk eagles, as well as the intelligent and graceful creatures that may well be our closest living relatives, the chimpanzees.

ITINERARY:

Day 1: Depart U.S.; overnight Brussels.

Day 2: Flight to Kigali, Rwanda.

Day 3: Kigali.

Days 4-5: Lake Kivu.

Day 6: Return to Kigali.

Day 7: To Bujumbura, Burundi.

Day 8: Steamship to Kigoma, Tanzania.

Days 9-13: Mahale and Gombe national parks.

Day 14: Fly to Dar-es-Salaam.

Day 15: Fly to Brussels.

Day 16: Return to U.S.

PREMIUM

October

SOBEK Expeditions

Ghiglieri, who has long combined twin careers as a primate biologist and river guide. His recent book, *East of the Mountains of the Moon*, is a popular account of his year of research in the mountains of Rwanda and of his insights into the several chimpanzee communities. He has also rafted with SOBEK on rivers in North America and Asia as well as in Africa, which makes him the ideal guide for this environmental adventure.

The program starts with five days in Rwanda, where we will explore on foot the forests of Lake Kivu, with their native populations of mountain gorillas. This largest of primate species is also one of the gentlest, living quietly within a limited range on a vegetarian diet of roots and leaves, as shown in the film *Gorillas in the Mist*. Then we travel by steamship from Burundi across Lake Tanganyika to Tanzania to begin the second leg of our journey, which takes us through Mahale and Gombe national parks, where chimpanzees have been extensively studied.

Wildlife of India and Nepal (EC 4)

ECOLOGICAL
ADVENTURE—CLASS II

➤ *In the sanctuary of the one-horned rhino*

➤ *Riverside rain forests of Bhutan*

➤ *Seek the tigers of Nepal*

A more diverse country is hard to imagine. Divided by religion and language, by class and climate, by economy and environment, India is not only one of the world's most populous countries but also one of the most complex. Part of this complexity is found in its remaining natural areas, where rare species survive from the ages before humanity overran the subcontinent. For nearly three weeks we explore these remnants of paradise and the creatures that inhabit them, ranging from the golden langurs of the Bhutan border to the tigers that skulk the deciduous forests of Uttar Pradesh. But be forewarned: game viewing in Asia is not like an African wildlife safari. In India and its neighbors, the animals are truly endangered, their numbers limited by the pressures of a hundred million people. Still, experienced game guides and well-located accommodations near proven viewing areas should enable us to sight some of the most exotic of Asia's wildlife.

Inevitably, our exploration of India begins in Delhi, where seven million people surround the remnants of Britain's Indian Empire. Soon we fly on to Assam, India's easternmost state, nearly isolated from the rest of the country by the pincer of Bangladesh and Bhutan. Here we reach Kaziranga National Park, habitat of a relatively large population of the one-horned rhino as well as wild buffalo, elephant, and countless waterfowl in the park's marshlands. Next, we explore the shores of the Brahmaputra River and the Manas Sanctuary on the Assam/Bhutan border, where troops of golden langur monkeys can be found.

Then it's on to the mountain kingdom of Nepal, where a two-day river run down the Trisuli and Narayani rivers takes us to an island wildlife camp on the Narayani. Here we can see the freshwater gangetic dolphin, the narrow-nosed crocodile known as the gharial, and other exotic wildlife including peacock, rhesus monkey, rhino, sambar, chital, and sloth bear. There are tigers in this region, but an even better opportunity for viewing them awaits us at "Tiger Haven" adjoining Dudhwa National Park in the state of Uttar Pradesh, just across the western border of Nepal. Two days here lets us seek wild tiger, leopard, and other game while camped near a pristine lake that seems a thousand miles from the congestion of Asia's cities and a million years from the modern world.

ITINERARY:

Day 1: Depart U.S.

Day 2: Arrive Delhi.

Days 3-5: Dudhwa National Park.

Day 6: To Patna.

Day 7: To Kathmandu.

Days 8-9: River run.

Day 10: Tiger Tops.

Day 11: Fly to Calcutta.

Days 12-14: Manas Sanctuary.

Day 15: To Gauhati.

Days 16-17: Kaziranga National Park.

Day 18: To Delhi.

Day 19: Return.

PREMIUM

January

SOBEK Expeditions

Rain Forest of Costa Rica (EC 5)

ENVIRONMENTAL SURVEY—CLASS I

➤ *Unusual Central American ecozones*

➤ *Cloud forest of Monteverde*

➤ *Tortoise nursery of the Caribbean*

I n a world that seems to have gone mad, Costa Rica shines like a light of sanity. It has been chosen by the United Nations as the site of the University of Peace because it alone among nations has no army. Its president won a Nobel Prize for his efforts to bring peace to Central America. And almost a tenth of all its land has been protected in national parks or wildlife sanctuaries, an enviable percentage indeed.

Because of its enlightened attitudes,

high altitudes, and fertile valleys, some people have called Costa Rica the Switzerland of the Americas—but here edelweiss, dairy farms, and snowy Alps are replaced by jungle orchids, banana groves, and active volcanoes. Costa Rica has an incredible diversity of habitats—high mountains, cloud forests, coastal swampland, low-lying brush and savannah, the Atlantic and Pacific coasts and volcanic pockets—all of which allow an amazing variety of flora and fauna to thrive.

We plunge right into this wonderland after an overnight stay in the capital city, San José, where an opera house modeled on the one in Paris might make us think we are in Europe after all. First stop is the famous cloud forest of Monteverde National Park. First protected by Quaker settlers in the 1950s, Monteverde offers miles of forest trails winding between ferns and mosses, beneath a dark canopy filled with colorful birds—including the rare resplendent quetzal, the most beautiful bird in the Americas. Next stop is Santa Rosa, site of Costa Rica's historical museum and an extensive acacia forest with howlers, white-faced and spider monkeys, deer, coyotes, and armadillos among many other native species.

Returning to San José via the Carara Biological Reserve—a transition zone between the high dry climate and the humid southern coast—we ready ourselves for a cross-country flight to La Selva, near the Nicaraguan border, a region difficult for tourists to reach in recent years. Here Costa Rica offers its richest coastal parks, including Braulio Carrillo with its jaguars, pumas, and 400 bird species, and nearby Tortuguero.

Tortuguero is perhaps the most famous beach in the world of natural history, for here four species of turtles lay their eggs each year, between the months of August and November. Over 100 eggs in two or three clutches are laid by a single female of the yard-long green turtle, a phenomenal number necessitated by the high predation rate on eggs, hatchlings, and young turtles. Other turtle species nesting at Tortuguero include the hawksbill, leatherback, and loggerhead turtles, all of which are endangered because of unprotected beaches in neighboring countries with Caribbean coasts. A visit to Costa Rica shows what a concerned government can do.

ITINERARY:

Day 1: Fly to San José, Costa Rica.

Day 2: To Monteverde via Poas Volcano.

Days 3-4: Monteverde.

Day 5: To Canas.

Day 6: Santa Rosa.

Day 7: Carara to San José.

Day 8: Fly to La Selva.

Days 9-10: La Selva.

Day 11: To Tortuguero.

Day 12: Tortuguero.

Day 13: To San José.

Day 13: Return.

PREMIUM

November-December

SOBEK Expeditions

Nepal Tree Planting Trek (EC 8)

ECOLOGICAL ADVENTURE—CLASS III

➤ *Community forestry work*

➤ *Stunning views of the Annapurna Range*

➤ *Festive celebrations with local villagers*

Our tree planting treks in the Nepal Himalayas not only bring you into cross-cultural contact with local people, they give you the opportunity to work with them in implementing ecological conservation. Over the twelve years that JOURNEYS has been offering Nepal trips we have been involved in environmental projects ranging from solar heating and biogas projects to trail clean-up treks to vegetable seed and warm clothing distribution. We also offer other conservation-oriented trips to Nepal and other areas of the Himalayas every year, including a Buddha's Birthday Tree Planting Trek.

After arrival in Kathmandu, you will join your Nepalese staff for a brief workshop in tree planting techniques. You will then trek with your staff and seedlings acquired from regional nurseries to an area of Nepal in the Gorkha region where we are assisting local communities in reforestation projects. The trekking will involve walking through mountainous terrain ranging in elevation from 3,000 to 9,000 feet. Trekkers walk four to seven miles per day with numerous nature- and culture-oriented stops en route. The types of trees and the locations of the planting vary with the season. All planting equipment is provided. Approximately six days are spent actually engaged in community forestry work. Your trip will offer excellent views of the Annapurna Range in central Nepal. Nine days are spent on the trail trekking to and from the planting areas and about four nights are spent in Kathmandu. Groups are accompanied by experienced, English-speaking Nepalese Sherpas. Group size is limited to twelve people.

Local villagers, the nearby Buddhist monastery, and the JOURNEYS staff create a festival atmosphere around the planting project, and you can expect a convivial, jubilant, and upbeat experience that makes for an adventure travel experience that is ecologically beneficial, challenging, intellectually satisfying and cross-culturally incomparable.

The trip may be extended with a whitewater rafting trip, a Chitwan elephant safari, or additional trekking with your Nepalese staff in another part of Nepal. Participants should be in good physical condition with some previous hiking and camping experience. JOURNEYS offers other nature-, culture-, and conservation-oriented trips to other areas of Nepal year-round. Participants are always welcome to stay on in Nepal for further group or independent exploration at very reasonable costs.

ITINERARY:

Days 1-2: En route.

Day 3: Arrive Kathmandu.

Day 4: Orientation to Kathmandu.

Day 5: Vehicle travel to Gorkha region.

Days 6-16: Trekking and tree planting.

Day 17: Return to Kathmandu.

Day 18: Kathmandu.

Day 19: Depart Kathmandu.

Day 20: Return.

MODERATE

March-October

JOURNEYS International, Inc.

Africa

Zambezi River (AF 1, AF 2)

ADVANCED WHITEWATER— CLASS IV

➤ *Ride the big waves of the Z*

➤ *Descend where Livingstone dared not*

➤ *One-, two-, or seven-day adventures*

Z ambia is the real Africa—still a true wilderness in many places, and a treasure trove of wildlife. And the highlight of any visit to this part of the country is Victoria Falls, or *Musi-O-Tunya* (the Smoke That Thunders). The falls are a mile-wide curtain of water falling over 350 feet (twice as high as Niagara) into a narrow chasm of rushing and boiling whitewater—one of the Seven Natural Wonders of the World that, even for the most jaded travelers, is never disappointing.

Michael K. Nichols/SOBEK photo file

In 1981 SOBEK, with sponsorship from The National Geographic Magazine and ABC Sports, made the first navigation of the Zambezi from the base of the falls to Lake Kariba, completing an exploration of the river left unfinished by Dr. David Livingstone when he canoed to the lip of the falls in 1855. It was the most magnificent river corridor SOBEK had ever explored, with rapids better than those of the famed Bío-Bío, and has since become our most popular international whitewater destination.

After the falls, the Zambezi plunges through an isolated African canyon, down through over 100 rapids to the calm waters of Lake Kariba. On our seven-day river trip, we run the entire section, an epic navigation of seventy remote miles. The first day alone boasts ten of the world's biggest rapids including the notorious boat-launcher, Number Five. After that, we encounter continuously thrilling whitewater and two spectacular waterfalls, where the river drops twenty feet over basalt cliffs. The falls are beautiful to behold, but they also mean portages. Fortunately, the portages are relatively short and the views of the falls and the rapids are breathtaking.

Besides the rousing rapids, the Zambezi offers wildlife, from crocodiles to hippos to shoreline antelope, and the chance to interact with subsistence fishermen who live along its banks. The fishing, by the way, is superb—the river brims with bream and tiger fish.

The seven-day trip begins at a hotel in Victoria Falls and includes six nights of camping under the clear African skies and good, fresh, river meals. SOBEK also offers a one-day trip (AF 2) which gives adventurers a chance to spend a single thrilling day negotiating the tumultuous ten rapids, and a two-day adventure that offers. . .well, two thrilling days. There's still plenty of time to take a side hike to a waterfall or visit a set of limestone caverns, or relax in preparation for the difficult climb out of the canyon. The drive back from the two-day trip passes through some fascinating African villages.

And finally, for those who are not interested in whitewater thrills, we offer a wildlife-viewing trip led by Makora Quest boatmen, who take you on a gentle section of the river in two-person canoes or rafts.

The Mighty Z is at the top of any river runner's list, but it's also a trip that is easily combined with the finest in African game viewing. Victoria Falls, Zimbabwe, is a center of operations for top quality outfitters specializing in Chobe National Park and the Okavango Delta—recognized by all the major wildlife foundations as the greatest place left on earth for game viewing.

ITINERARY (AF 1):

Day 1: Meet at hotel in Victoria Falls.

Day 2: To Livingstone, Zambia. Walk to Victoria Falls put-in; begin river trip.

Days 3-5 or 3-6: On the river.

Day 6 or 7: End river trip; return drive to Livingstone or Victoria Falls; hotel.

Day 7 or 8: Return.

ITINERARY (AF 2):

One-Day Trip:
Morning meet at Victoria Falls and river trip; evening take-out.

Two-Day Trip:

Day 1: Morning meet, run river to camp.

Day 2: Continue river trip to take-out; return to Victoria Falls.

PREMIUM

June-December

SOBEK Expeditions Zambia

Omo River (AF 9)

ULTIMATE RIVER
SAFARI—CLASS IV

➤ *The real wildlife of Africa*
➤ *Remote riverside cultures*
➤ *300 miles of adventure*

Ethiopia, the fabled Hidden Empire, famous for its rock-hewn churches, chanting priests, and spectacular mountain scenery, has entered the consciousness of the 1990s with massive media attention to its economic problems and social policies. But in spite of this, the traditional hospitality of this unique culture lives on. Tourism is officially encouraged and Westerners are greeted with a warm welcome. Moreover, the Omo watershed lies in the southwest, the most peaceful and prosperous part of the country. The Omo is a special place, especially for SOBEK. We started on the Omo in 1973; it was our first trip and is still one of our finest.

We call it "The African Queen," and that may be an understatement. For one thing, its scenery is spectacular: sheer inner gorges, columnar basalt amphitheaters, distant peaks, and innumerable side creeks and waterfalls. For another, it is a great place to spot wildlife. Hippos surface near the boats for a suspicious inspection, crocodiles bask in the sun, bushbuck silently take an afternoon drink, colobus monkeys fly through the trees—sometimes we even see lions, leopards, and wild dogs. And the birds are everywhere: fish eagles, Goliath herons, kingfishers, bee-eaters, storks, kites, and vultures.

The first SOBEK explorers to go down the Omo met tribesmen who had never seen a white man, and the people who live along the river are still among the remotest and least-visited people anywhere on earth. Our interaction with these friendly and beautifully decorated groups is something very special.

If all this seems like more than any one trip could possibly contain, you can choose between the Upper Half or the Lower Half—or go for the gusto and take on the full month-long Omo Experience. The Upper Half accents whitewater and wildlife, with day-hikes, hot springs, and a two night layover at one site from which we climb up the canyon to visit picturesque Wolayta villages. The drive back to Addis Ababa includes a night at beautiful Lake Langano.

The Lower Half starts out with the river in its deep canyon, but the river begins to mellow, and we see distant peaks, patchworked fields, and more and more remote groups of people. Birdlife density increases, and hippo counts per day reach their maximum. Here we encounter our first group of lower Omo peoples right on the river, and for the last seven days or so we encounter Bodi, Mursi, Kwegu (Bacha), Nyangatom, and Karo tribes. Each group has its distinctive dress and decoration: fantastic hairdos, enormous clay lip plates, ear plugs, bark cloth and beaded leather skirts. The trip ends near the Omo National Park, a magical place of dry plains ringed by the distant mountains of the Sudan.

Both portions of the river include a little of everything the Omo offers but with a different balance. Taken together, the Omo rises from the remarkable to the magnificent, a wild and beautiful immersion in an almost prehistoric world.

ITINERARY:

Day 1: Addis Ababa.

Day 2: Drive to river and begin descent.

Days 3-11: Upper Half trip.

Day 12: Soddo Bridge; Upper Half group returns to Addis; Lower Half group joins river from Addis.

Days 13-26: Lower Half on the Omo.

Day 27: End river trip; flight to Addis Ababa.

Day 28: Return.

MEDIUM

October-November

SOBEK

Rufiji River Safari (AF 13)

WILDLIFE FLOAT— CLASS III

➤ *Drift through the Selous Reserve*

➤ *Tanzania's largest wildlife park*

➤ *Daily guided foot safaris*

This float down the Rufiji River is a superb introduction to Tanzania's legendary Selous Game Reserve, subject of Peter Matthiessen's *Sand Rivers* and the largest and wildest reserve in Africa. With an area of over 18,000 square miles, the Selous is home for vast numbers of wildlife, including the continent's largest elephant and rhino populations. But this is no place of zebra-striped minibuses and lodges with gaudy gift shops. The Selous has only a sparse and virtually unused network of tracks, and tourism development is confined to its margins. This is Africa as Livingstone saw it. As you follow the game trails in the bush, you can be sure that, apart from a rare Game Department foot patrol, no one has passed this way in years.

The trip begins with a ride from Dar-es-Salaam on a railway that cuts through Tanzania and offers the world's best wildlife viewing from a train (outside, perhaps, of a theme park). We end up at the comfortable cabins of Stiegler's Gorge Safari

Camp, where we spend one or two days resting and taking game walks and drives. Then we begin our ride on the river near the upper end of Stiegler's Gorge. In the gorge we ride the rapids and do some exciting river rafting, and when we emerge into calmer waters we begin our serious wildlife viewing. Hippo-grazed swards of grass shaded by acacias and baobabs provide idyllic campsites, with convenient bathing on nearby rock ledges. The landscape is open here, and experienced scouts lead us through the gently miombo woodland for morning and afternoon game walks, looking for impalas, waterbucks, buffalo, elephants, giraffes, lions, hyenas, and wild dogs.

Next we enter the labyrinth of channels, swamps, and lakes that the Rufiji created when it left its original bed in 1973. This area is especially rich in birdlife: fish eagles, herons, Egyptian geese, myriad storks, bee-eaters, and African hoopoes. We also frequently surprise buffalo and elephants on the banks, and there are so many hippos we vie with them for right-of-way.

At Lake Tagalala, we add a touch of class to our trip at a magnificent campsite with deep shade, smooth lawns, and nearby hot springs. We spend two nights here and then push off for the last leg of the trip—a fantastic area of tall doum palms rising out of the water, some drowned, some still flourishing. After ten days on the river we finally reach take-out at the tented Rufiji River Camp where a friendly staff greets us with cold Safari Lager.

The physically fit can combine this river trip with the Mt. Kilimanjaro Trek (AF 14); and those who wish to see the famous game-viewing areas of northern Tanzania can combine it with a Tanzania safari (AF 56).

ITINERARY:

Days 1-2: En route.

Day 3: Dar-es-Salaam.

Days 4-5: Train to put-in.

Days 6-14: Rufiji River safari.

Day 15: End river trip at tented camp.

Day 16: Return to Dar-es-Salaam.

Day 17: Free day in Dar; evening return.

PREMIUM

December-January, June-July, November-December

SOBEK

Kilimanjaro Climb (AF 14)

STRENUOUS TREK— CLASS IV

➤ *Hike to 19,340-foot Uhuru Peak*

➤ *Dramatic ascent of Africa's pinnacle*

Kilimanjaro, an extinct volcano, is the highest solitary peak in the world, the superb remnant of a gargantuan lava flow that pushed itself through the ancient rock of Africa fifteen or twenty million years ago. It towers 19,340 feet above sea level, dominating its surroundings as no other mountain does, looming in regal majesty over the East African plains. Our ascent of the mountain takes us through an unbelievable range of climatic zones, from equatorial rain forests to arctic snows.

There is a relatively easy ascent to the top along the Marangu route, but this trail is followed by large numbers of climbers. Seeking, as always, the less trammeled ways, we have chosen another route, rarely traversed but safe and not too difficult.

The Machame trail, winding underneath the spectacular glaciers of the southern face of Kilimanjaro, requires two extra days of climbing, but this allows us some extra time to acclimate before attempting the summit.

The trip begins in Arusha, Tanzania, where we spend a day to recover from jet lag. Then we drive to Machame Town and begin the climb. All days involve 4 to 7 hours of hiking, with the exception of the summit push, which is long and tiring (up to 16 of hours trekking). Symptoms of altitude sickness are possible, even likely, but our guide will have tips on how to keep them to a minimum.

The first two days we hike to 12,600 feet—through the rain forest, into open stands of heather, and then onto the gentle slopes of the Shira Plateau. The next day we acclimate and explore the area. After that we climb to up to 15,000 feet and then descend to a beautiful campsite 2,000 feet below. The next day we make a dramatic climb right up the Breach Wall and trek into the Karanga Valley, with great views down to the Masai steppe and up to the spectacular glaciers and icefalls of Kili's south side.

On our sixth day on the mountain, we make the summit push, beginning at about one o'clock in the morning. Daybreak finds us near the crater rim, looking down on a magnificent sunrise, and then it's another hour to Uhuru Peak at 19,340 feet.

We descend the mountain via the tourist route to Kibo Hut, and then go another easy eight miles to Horombo Hut where we sleep in comfortable bunks.

Our final day on the mountain is a strenuous thirteen-mile descent, but we are rewarded at our hotel by infinite supplies of hot water and a farewell dinner. The climb can be combined with a float down the Rufiji River (AF 13) or an extension to the famous parklands of Tanzania (AF 56) to further explore the land of mankind's origins.

ITINERARY:

Day 1: Arrive Arusha, transfer to Kibo Hotel.

Day 2: Orientation at Kilimanjaro.

Days 3-7: Hike Machame trailhead (10,000 ft.) to Barafu Hut (15,500 ft.)

Day 8: Climb summit and begin descent.

Day 9: Descent to Kibo.

Day 10: Kibo Hotel.

Day 11: Return or join AF 13 in Dar-es-Salaam.

PREMIUM

January, June-July, November-December

SOBEK

Sinai Adventure (AF 22)

OVERLANDING TOUR—CLASS II

➤ *St. Catherine's Monastery*

➤ *Camel trekking*

➤ *The reefs of the Red Sea*

Lift the veil from the land of mystery; draw on the wisdom of the ancients from the wellspring of time. This trip has been designed to give the adventurous time traveler a look into the ancient world as it survives today. Using buses outfitted for desert camping, we head out from modern Cairo into the past, crossing a World War II battle zone and heading into the Tih Desert where we find historic forts and monasteries including the mountain retreat of St. Catherine.

Here we hike up Mt. Sinai in search of Moses' burning bush. Next, a camel trek in the company of Bedouin guides takes us through the canyons of northeast Sinai,

and we end our trip at the Red Sea, with snorkeling and seafood feasts. The world's great religions come from the desert, and for the adventure traveler as well, these arid lands are a font of mystery and inspiration.

ITINERARY:

Day 1: Cairo.

Days 2-3: Na'ama Bay.

Day 4: Nuweiba.

Day 5: Camel trek.

Day 6: St. Catherine.

Day 7: Mt. Sinai; return to Cairo.

Day 8: Return.

MODERATE

Year-round

Transglobal B.V.

River of the Pharaohs (AF 23)

ARCHAEOLOGICAL TOUR—CLASS II

➤ *Felucca Sailing the Nile*

➤ *The Valley of Kings*

➤ *Relax on the Red Sea*

Land of pyramids and temples, foundation of modern civilization, and source of centuries of speculation and mystery, Egypt has refused to relinquish its grip on mankind's soul. Even today it seems balanced at the center of conflict and contradiction: not quite part of Africa and not wholly Middle Eastern. Just as Egypt cuts its own course in history, so, too, does the Nile cut its unique course through time: it's the longest river in the world, and it's history is equally long. For over two weeks, we explore this Mother of Rivers and the civilizations that have flourished along its banks, including three full days aboard a felucca, the traditional sailing vessel of the Nile. This unusual combination tour lets us explore Egypt in a timeless fashion, sailing by day through the valley where agriculture was born, camping by night beneath the stars of the earliest astronomy. Our sail ends at Edfu, a temple site downstream of the huge Aswan Dam and gateway to the famous Luxor region. Here we visit the temples and tombs that have made Egypt synonymous with antiquity: Karnak, ancient Thebes, the Tomb of Tutankhamen and Kom Ombo, even the temple of the crocodile god Sobek, the inspiration for the world's toothiest adventure company. We round out our expedition with trips to the Great Pyramids of Giza, the Nubian villages and coral gardens of the Red Sea, and Cairo—truly a journey of discovery in one of the world's most remarkable countries.

ITINERARY:

Days 1-2: Cairo.

Day 3: Giza; board train to Aswan.

Days 4-5: Aswan.

Days 6-8: Felucca cruise.

Day 9: End cruise; drive to Luxor.

Day 10: Valley of the Kings.

Day 11: Drive to Hurghada on Red Sea.

Days 12-13: Red Sea.

Day 14: Bus to Cairo.

Day 15: Return.

MODERATE

Year-round

Transglobal B.V.

Sahara Overland (AF 26) ▬▬▬▬▬

TREK/OVERLAND— CLASS III

➤ *Walk or drive through the best of the Sahara*

➤ *Summit Algeria's highest mountain*

➤ *Camp as T. E. Lawrence did*

The Sahara is the most extraordinary desert in the world. Its heart is the Hoggar in Algeria. Discover this enchanting world of natural beauty on an extended trek, or on day walks from a four-wheel-drive truck.

To walk in the silence of the desert, to sleep under a starry canopy, to live peacefully where time has been frozen tens of thousands of years, is to experience the real desert. When the sun meets the rocky horizon at the end of a day of walking, it is easy to understand why this silent land hypnotizes all who wander through it. The Hoggar Step-by-Step makes use of vehicles only to get to the trailhead and from trail's end. Otherwise, we are alone on foot in the vastness of the Sahara, in the hourglass of the sands of time.

Each day is different: forests of rock, citadels of stone spires, hidden gueltas, lunar landscapes, are just some of the landscape components. On foot the most striking scenes are reached: Mt. Tahat, Algeria's highest point, Illaman, the Hermitage of de Foucault, Tezoulaigs, Saarinan, and more. In the encampments, by the light of the embers, the Tuareg guides tell their tales, tea is sipped by all, and the impossibly grand sky wraps the horizons.

The Citadels of the Tassilis Du Hoggar reveals the impressive variety of country offered by this region of the Algerian Sahara. The 4WD vehicle brings together fantastic sites too far to walk between in this time frame. A few hours in the vehicle and the magic corners of Youf Hehaket, Tahaggart, and Tagrera are reached.

In the course of the days, seeking out the prehistoric paintings and petroglyphs, the desert teaches, reveals its secrets. Life persists everywhere in this barren land, and the Tuareg guides turn the correct stones, and showcase the hidden treasures of the Sahara.

ITINERARY, Walking Trip:

Day 1: To Lyon, France.

Day 2: To Algiers.

Day 3: Fly to Tamanrasset; drive to desert.

Days 4-5: Mt. Tahat.

Day 6: Assekrem.

Day 7: Spires of Tezoulaigs; Aguergas.

Day 8: Tamanrasset.

Day 9: Algiers.

Day 10: Paris.

Day 11: Return.

ITINERARY, 4WD Trip:

Day 1: To Lyon, France.

Day 2: Algiers.

Day 3: Tamanrasset; the Hoggar.

Day 4: Youf Haharlal.

Day 5: Prehistoric art of Youf Hehaket.

Day 6: Walking in the Tassilis of the Hoggar.

Day 7: Tagrera.

Days 8-9: Walks amid rock formations and desert.

Day 10: Algiers.

Day 11: Paris.

Day 12: Return.

MEDIUM

October-April

SOBEK

Grand Safari (AF 28) ▰▰▰▰▰▰▰

RUGGED 4WD
SAFARI—CLASS III

➤ *Fish River Canyon*
➤ *Kalahari Desert*
➤ *Okavango Delta*

The magic of Africa is captured in its many moods: the starkness of sun-baked plains, the tranquillity of hidden streams, the furtive, tentative lift of an impala's head. We experience these moods for over three weeks as we safari through Namibia, Botswana, Zimbabwe, and South Africa on a grand tour of not only animal life but native traditions and colonial history as well. Here are all the sights that we imagine when we whisper "Africa" —elephants lumbering through the acacias, giraffes running at full gallop, a lion motionlessly eyeing an oryx calf.

But the real discoveries lie in the sights that seem to arise almost dreamlike out of the landscape: the rough tumble of the Orange River over Augrabies Falls; the arid beauty of the Kalahari, home to the slight Bushmen and to a handful of strange but hearty animals; the magic of Fish River Canyon, a seventy-mile gash in the arid Namibian landscape. There's the inland delta of the Okavango where dugout canoes take us to tranquil islands in a natural paradise, and there's The Smoke That Thunders, the enormous tumult of Victoria Falls, where we have a chance to challenge the huge rapids of the Zambezi. All this, and more, awaits us on this four-wheel-drive safari out of Johannesburg, where words like "spectacular" are as commonplace as they are true.

ITINERARY:

Day 1: Leave Johannesburg and begin safari.

Day 2: Augrabies National Park.

Days 3-4: Fish River Canyon.

Days 5-6: Namib Desert.

Days 7-8: Walvis Bay, coastal Namibia.

Day 9: Windhoek.

Days 10-11: Kalahari.

Days 12-13: Okavango.

Days 14-15: Moremi Wildlife Reserve, Botswana.

Days 16-17: Savuti Channel.

Days 18-19: Chobe.

Days 20-21: Victoria Falls.

Days 22-23: Return south via Makgadik-gadi Salt Pans, Botswana.

Day 24: Johannesburg and return.

MODERATE

March-July, September-January

Afro Ventures

Botswana Safari (AF 30) ~~~~

OVERLAND/SAFARI—
CLASS III

➤ *Camping in wildlife reserves*
➤ *Inland delta of Okavango*
➤ *Spectacular Victoria Falls*

The real Africa is more incredible than any dime novel or summer cinema entertainment. It's a land where huge rivers turn desolation into a wildlife heaven, where a milewide waterfall plummets hundreds of feet into narrow gorges,

where flocks of flamingos flood the skies.

Our Botswana Safari is an ideal way to strike out into the heart of Africa, with extended stays at the Moremi Wildlife Reserve in the Okavango Delta, in the elephant country of Chobe National Park, and at Victoria Falls where we bask in the cool spray and test the turbulent white-water of the Zambezi River. Botswana is a country the size of France, with almost a quarter of its area devoted to wildlife conservation, some of it administered by the native Botswana tribes. Firsthand encounters with crocodiles, hippos, buffalo, and lions make this camping safari one for the young and strong of heart.

ITINERARY:

Day 1: Johannesburg to Botswana.

Days 2-4: Maun, Okavango Delta.

Days 5-6: Moremi Wildlife Reserve.

Days 7-10: Chobe National Park.

Day 11: Victoria Falls.

Day 12: Zambezi River run.

Day 13: En route.

Day 14: Ben Lavin Nature Reserve.

Day 15: *Johannesburg.*

MEDIUM

Year-round

SOBEK

Namibian Ventures (AF 35) ▲▲▲▲▲▲

OVERLAND/NATURAL
HISTORY—CLASS II

➤ *Mountainous desert sand dunes*
➤ *German colonial heritage*
➤ *Bushmen of the Kalahari*

Towering sand dunes, vast plateaus of aridity, flocks of flamingos pink against the cerulean sun, and a paradoxical heritage makes Namibia unique in all Africa. We explore all the known attractions of this vivid and constantly changing landscape, from its world-record dunes to its German colonial character, as well as pay our dues in the game parks of this southwestern African nation. Towns like Swakopmund, Luderitz, and the capital of Windhoek boast an anachronistic German heritage, while ornately dressed Hetero women, wizened tribesmen, and descendants of the Bushmen bespeak a different background. We travel by minibus or four-wheel-drive to several game-viewing areas, including the famous Ethosha Pan, spend two full days in the celebrated Namib Desert, and visit the stark Grand Canyon-like terrain of Fish River. A close look at a country often overlooked but never equaled.

ITINERARY:

Day 0: Arrive Johannesburg.

Day 1: To Kuruman.

Day 2: Kalahari.

Day 3: Hardap Dam.

Day 4: Windhoek.

Days 5-8: Ethosha Pan.

Day 9: Brandberg Mountains.

Days 10-11: Swakopmund and Moon Valley.

Days 12-13: Sossusvelei Canyon.

Days 14-16: Fish River Canyon.

Day 17: Augrabies Park.

Day 18: Kimberly.

Day 19: Johannesburg.

Day 20: Return.

Note: Shorter 15-day itinerary also available.

MODERATE

Twenty-day Itinerary: April-October
Fifteen-day Itinerary: January-February/November-December

SOBEK

Serengeti Tented Safari (AF 36)

OVERLAND CAMPING SAFARI—CLASS III

➤ *The great Rift Valley*
➤ *Wildlife of Serengeti and Ngorongoro*
➤ *Olduvai Gorge*

The superior variety of natural wonders in Tanzania makes this overland safari a classic in the world of adventure, a nonstop barrage of wildlife and scenery that thrills the soul. There is simply no match for the sheer number, variation, and accessibility of wildlife to be found here, from the plains of Serengeti to the surface of Lake Manyara. Traveling in comfortable and practical safari vehicles, we survey the world's largest permanent population of big game at Ngorongoro, mingle with the Masai in their homeland, touch the original hearths of humanity in Olduvai Gorge, and traverse the centuries of evolution in between.

Our route begins at Arusha in the shadow of Kilimanjaro, then crosses the foothills to the Great Rift Valley and Masai-land. Four days of traditional overland travel take us to Serengeti National Park, where our sightseeing includes a visit to the museum of the celebrated Leakey digs at Olduvai Gorge. Finally we return to Arusha via Ngorongoro and Lake Manyara National Park, washing off the sands of time in a comfortable hotel. Whether we are cruising along the soda-crust shores of Lake Natron or contemplating the long rocky road of human evolution in the Olduvai Gorge, Tanzania will keep us on our toes with amazement and surprise.

ITINERARY:

Day 1: Arusha.

Day 2: Begin safari, drive to Rift Valley.

Days 3-5: Great Rift Valley.

Days 6-9: Serengeti.

Day 10: Olduvai Gorge.

Day 11: Ngorongoro.

Days 12-13: Lake Manyara.

Day 14: Arusha.

Day 15: Return.

PREMIUM

January-March, May-October, December

Overseas Adventure Travel

The High Atlas (AF 43)

TREK/CULTURE—
CLASS III

➤ *Trek the Sahara mountains*

➤ *Climb North Africa's peak*

➤ *Sip tea with the Berbers*

Sprawling across the southern horizon, the snowcapped peaks of the Atlas Range create an imposing background for the magical city of Marrakech. Here in the former Imperial capital we get acquainted with the North African cultures while exploring the palaces, souks, and marketplaces, then travel on to road's end in the remote Moroccan backcountry. Our two-week trek is based in the tiny Berber village of Arroumd, where we take time to get acquainted with the Berber culture while adjusting to the altitude. We share the houses and food of the mountain people and participate in their mint tea ceremonies. With local guides and pack mules we trek among the terraced valleys and high passes, visiting remote mud and wood hut villages, enjoying the Berber hospitality, crafts, and folklore. Some nights are spent in village homes, some in alpine huts, and some under the stars. We also have the opportunity to climb Mt. Toubkal (13,665 ft.), the highest peak in North Africa. The climb is strenuous but not technically difficult, and we are rewarded by breathtaking views of the Atlas Mountains stretching off to the Sahara. Our itinerary combines an intriguing blend of the color and culture of North Africa's highest mountains and their hardy inhabitants.

Two different treks are offered: the more strenuous is a circuit of Mt. Toubkal over several passes and also takes u to the fringes of the Sahara, culminating in a climb of Mt. Toubkal. The more moderate trek is a loop of the most interesting areas, again finishing with an ascent of Mt. Toubkal.

There are other alternatives as well, and the first couple of days of both treks are used to limber up on day walks, to familiarize ourselves with the area, and to discuss the possibilities with the trek leader. The walking will take us up through forested foothills and into deep valleys. Most of the walking is on mule trails, though sometimes the going can be rough. On the trek, mules carry personal gear, so it is necessary to carry only a light day pack.

ITINERARY:

Day 1: Arrive Marrakech.

Day 2: Marrakech.

Days 3-11: To the High Atlas; trekking.

Days 12-14: Marrakech.

Day 15: Return.

MODERATE

April-October

SOBEK

Zambezi Wildlife Safari (AF 45) 〰

WILDLIFE SAFARI —
CLASS I

➤ *Boating safari and game drives*

➤ *Exclusive lodges and tree huts*

➤ *Whitewater on the Zambezi*

This classic African adventure follows trails blazed by Livingstone and Stanley, Sir Richard Burton, and Teddy Roosevelt. Picture yourself on safari amidst herds of elephant, zebra and giraffe while lions circle prey. Picture yourself relaxing on a colonial veranda as the sun kindles a flame of colors on the horizon. Picture yourself on a raft, adrenalin rushing as the oarsmen negotiate one of the world's best white-water river runs. This is the Technicolor Africa of your dreams, a safari into the heartland of the continent, comfortably packaged to maximize wildlife and adventure and minimize hardship.

While many of the open spaces in the great stretch of African savannah that spans the distance from Kenya to South Africa are crowded with villages and civilization, we visit two of the less-visited game parks where the uncrowded expanses still exist. They are enough off the beaten track to make them SOBEK-style adventure destinations, yet they offer first-class accommodations that will make your safari more enjoyable. We start at an

Brian Clark/SOBEK photo file

exclusive resort on Fothergill Island in Lake Kariba, where fish eagles, velvet monkeys, and hippos serenade us with African songs and prepare us for the bush. The food is excellent here, our hosts are friendly, and we have a chance to look for game by vehicle, by boat, or on foot.

Then we venture out for three days at Hwange National Park to enjoy Africa at its highest—in individual tree huts ten feet off the ground, each with first-class facilities. Here, also, are vast herds of Cape buffalo, often numbering over 1,000, elephant, zebra, giraffe, wildebeest, eland, and antelope. It is also one of the last strongholds where the white Rhino can regularly be seen.

As a finale, we go to the pride of Africa, Victoria Falls, staying in the Victoria Falls Hotel, which was built in the early part of the century and retains a wonderful aura of faded romanticism, including acres of gardens and a casino. The next day we walk to the foot of the falls to take a thrilling one-day river trip on the Zambezi River, which is actually one of the world's finest whitewater runs, a day of action that includes ten rapids as challenging and as big as anything on the Grand Canyon stretch of the Colorado River.

This is a classic, safari trip, combining luxury accommodations, countless close encounters with the ancient magic of Africa, and a day of rushing adrenalin.

ITINERARY:

Days 1-2: En route.

Day 3: Arrive Harare; transfer to Kariba and Fothergill.

Days 4-5: Fothergill Island.

Day 6: Flight to Hwange, drive to Sikumi.

Days 7-8: Sikumi Tree Lodge.

Day 9: Victoria Falls.

Day 10: Zambezi River (seasonal) or Victoria Falls.

Day 11: To Harare and return.

MEDIUM

January, April, June-December

SOBEK

Parks of Botswana (AF 46)

CAMPING SAFARI—
CLASS II

➤ *Inland delta of the Okavango*
➤ *Camp in Chobe National Park*
➤ *Wonder of Victoria Falls*

The remarkable inland delta where the waters of the great Okavango River come to their quiescence in the vast Kalahari Desert is the setting for natural life marvels beyond imagining. The delta is a zoological wonderland of wildebeest, antelope, lion, rhino, elephant, and resplendent oryx, to mention just a few of the many creatures that inhabit the inland marshes and isolated isles of this unique ecosystem. Using Land Rovers, bush planes and dugout canoes, we survey the crystal clear channels of the delta and then head for other lesser-known national parks in Botswana.

Our second stop is the wildlife reserve at Moremi, one of Africa's best and least-visited sanctuaries. After that we go to Chobe in the heart of elephant country, and from Chobe it's only a short ride over to Victoria Falls, where free time allows for options such as a visit to the botanical gardens and a crocodile farm or a flight over the enormous spectacle of The Smoke That Thunders, Victoria Falls. If the trip coincides with rafting season, you'll even join a one-day descent of the Zambezi through ten of the world's biggest rapids. Botswana is unique among African nations: less frequented by tourists than Kenya or Tanzania and equally full of wildlife. For a quick glimpse of a natural wildlife paradise, this trip is ideal.

ITINERARY:

Day 1: Meet in Maun, Botswana; fly to Okavango Delta camp.

Day 2: Okavango.

Days 3-4: Moremi Wildlife Reserve.

Days 5-7: Chobe National Park.

Days 8-9: Victoria Falls.

Day 10: Return or join other packages.

Note: Reverse itineraries on some dates

MODERATE

Departs year-round

Afro Ventures

Kenya Wildlife Safari (AF 48)

TENTED CAMP AND LODGE SAFARI—CLASS II

➤ *Samburu National Reserve*

➤ *Mt. Kenya and Aberdare Mountains*

➤ *Masai Mara National Park*

Kenya is synonymous with big game, and what better way to see the animals and scenery that come from *Out of Africa* than to rove through its celebrated parks? This overland safari is a journey through the history of African exploration, a chance to witness the wealth of plains game that have given Kenya its fame. The complete package tour, featuring comfortable accommodations in a variety of tented camps and game lodges, begins with a free day in Nairobi, where we begin to sense the pulse of African life.

Then it's off to the equatorial mountains, Mt. Kenya and the Aberdares, for some game viewing. From there we head north to Samburu, a region of vast semi-desert that harbors unusual wildlife and proud nomadic tribes. And for a contrast we go to the Great Rift Valley, where Lake Baringo offers water-skiing and rowing as well as bird-watching and game viewing. Our survey of Kenya ends with two full days in Masai Mara, homeland of the colorful and proud Masai nomads.

ITINERARY:

Day 1: Arrive Nairobi.

Day 2: To Mt. Kenya.

Day 3: Aberdares.

Days 4-5: Samburu; Larsen's Camp.

Days 6-7: Lake Baringo.

Days 8-9: Masai Mara; Mara River Camp.

Day 10: Nairobi.

Day 11: Return.

MEDIUM

January-April, June-October, December

SOBEK

Trans-Africa (AF 50)

OVERLAND—CLASS III

➤ *Truckin' across the Dark Continent*

➤ *Adventure from Abyssinia to Zimbabwe*

➤ *Segments from 4 to 21 weeks*

Kebos/SOBEK photo file

The essence of Africa is distilled on a transcontinental truck expedition, a modern motorized homage to the great safaris of the past. We travel through landscapes little-altered by the march of progress, peopled by tribes whose way of life has remained unchanged for thousands of years. This rugged trip requires the ability to cope with the delays and hardships made inevitable by primitive conditions, harsh weather, and long distances. Yet our journey is a celebration of extraordinary scenery, people and wildlife.

In northern Africa, Arab, Berber and Moor rub shoulders in the crowded bazaars; across the High Atlas, Berbers give way to Tuareg nomads as we enter the fringes of the immense Sahara, a varied landscape of 100-meter-high dunes, ancient volcanic ranges, and gravel plateaus. South of the Sahara the black tribes take over, first Hausa and Fulani in the Sahel, then numerous small groups,

each with distinct beliefs and traditions as we enter the Cameroons.

Continuing through the rain forest of Zaire we emerge into the vast plains of East Africa, with its fantastic diversity of large tribal groupings. This is still an explorer's continent, much as it was in the Nineteenth century. If you want it to yield you some of its secrets, join us on one or all of the legs of a Trans-Africa safari between London, Kano (Nigeria), Nairobi (Kenya), and Johannesburg (South Africa) or the reverse. Segments last from four to nineteen weeks, and each one is a special adventure unto itself.

ITINERARY:

Day 1: Begin London, Nairobi, or Johannesburg.

Note: Complete trip lasts nineteen weeks; Nairobi to London portion lasts fifteen weeks. Various segments of the trip may be booked separately upon arrangement. Alternate departures follow reserve route.

MODERATE

Year-round

SOBEK

Serengeti and Gorilla Safari (AF 55)

CAMPING AND LODGE SAFARI — CLASS III

➤ *Mountain gorillas of Rwanda*

➤ *Lions of the Serengeti*

➤ *Masai tribespeople*

The sunlit plains and misty forests of Tanzania and Rwanda are home to the grandest wildlife parade on earth. Among the many famous creatures here are two of the planet's most distinguished species—the great predator cats studied by George Schaller and the mountain gorillas befriended by Diane Fossey, the "Woman in the Mists."

But aside from the famous observers these creatures have drawn, the region is also a land of great beauty, a dazzling display of creation worthy of the most jaded photographers. From the black chests of the gorillas to the crimson markings of the carmine bee-eater, every shade of color is here: the delicate pink of flamingo flight-feathers, the subtle earth tones of a gazelle, the menacing green of a crocodile, the camouflage hues of the cheetah—all test Kodachrome and Fujicolor to their limit.

In the background are the plains of the Serengeti, the volcanoes of Rwanda, and lakes Manyara and Victoria. This trip, which combines sightseeing with a gorilla trek, is an intense, cross-country exposure to the living miracle of African wildlife.

ITINERARY:

Day 1: Arrive Arusha.

Day 2: Overland safari begins with drive to Lake Manyara.

Days 3-4: Ngorongoro Crater.

Days 5-8: Serengeti.

Days 9-11: Lake Victoria.

Day 12: Kigali, Rwanda.

Days 13-16: Parc National des Volcans and Gorilla trek.

Day 17: Kigali and return.

Note: Reverse itineraries on some dates.

PREMIUM

January-March, May-October, December

Overseas Adventure Travel

Treasures of Tanzania (AF 56)

SAFARI—CLASS I

➤ *Views of Kilimanjaro*
➤ *Wildlife of the Serengeti*
➤ *Scenery of Ngorongoro*

Of all Africa's nations, Tanzania has made the most of its wildlife and scenic resources, perhaps because it's got the most to make: from the ragged badlands of Ngorongoro Crater to the top of Kilimanjaro, Tanzania is a land blessed with diversity, opportunity, and the big game that has come to symbolize a continent. This relatively quick tour of Tanzania allows us to see the highlights of this vast country in just over a week's time, without sacrificing either the comforts of home or the marvels of the land. From our welcome at the popular colonial-style Norfolk Hotel in downtown Nairobi, capital of Kenya, we head out to neighboring Tanzania for our first stop: Lake Manyara Lodge overlooking the Great Rift Valley. Two days of game drives in the famous Serengeti National Park bring us close to gazelle and giraffe, water buffalo and wildebeest, impala and lion. Then we head to Olduvai Gorge, with its "history of prehistoric man" museum, and on to the great caldera of Ngorongoro, where many wild species of the great plains roam. It may seem like a short trip, but it just might encompass more than a million years of human life.

ITINERARY:

Day 1: Arrive Nairobi.

Day 2: Drive to Arusha and Manyara.

Days 3-4: Serengeti.

Day 5: To Ngorongoro via Olduvai.

Day 6: Ngorongoro.

Day 7: Nairobi via Arusha.

Day 8: Return.

PREMIUM

January-April, June-October, December

United Touring International

Madagascar Discovery (AF 57) ▲▲▲▲▲▲▲

WILDLIFE AND CULTURE—CLASS I

➤ *Perinet Lemur Reserve*

➤ *Flora of the Spiny Forest*

➤ *Markets of Antananarivo*

The island that time forgot is Madagascar, a thousand-mile-long piece of the Eocene floating in the Indian Ocean off the African coast. Here evolution conducted its experiments in isolation from the rest of creation, allowing the early primate genus of lemurs to flourish as nowhere else in the world. The bold shifak lemur is found in Madagascar's unique Spiny Forest, a sharp-edged world of unusual vegetation; the indri and the ring-tailed lemur are found in the forest at Perinet; and over twenty species of lemurs are present all throughout the island, promising the traveler fascinating close encounters with these strange and lovable animals.

But a journey to Madagascar is a unique destination in other respects as well. For some the highlight of the trip will be the bizarre rituals of ancestor worship practiced by the native Malagasy— vibrant ceremonies and funeral rites that take place in the villages. Others will remember the Zoma, the crowded market at the foot of Antananarivo's royal palace in the historic capital. Still others will want to head underwater to see the bursts of submarine color found among the off-shore islands of the Indian Ocean. Once a French colony, Madagascar has managed to retain the customs of its traditional people and its ecological mysteries as well. It combines the beauty of a tropical island paradise with some of the most fascinating forms of flora and fauna on earth. And no one will be able to forget the eerie calls of the lemurs, which seem to be the very voice of the ancestor spirits themselves.

ITINERARY:

Day 1: Arrive Antananarivo ("Tana").

Day 2: Flight to Ft. Dauphin.

Days 3-4: Spiny Forest and Berenty Reserve.

Day 5: Fly to Tana; drive to Antsirabe.

Day 6: Perinet Lemur Reserve; return to Tana.

Day 7: Return via Nairobi.

PREMIUM

Year-round

Liounis and Cortez Expeditions

Mahajamba River (AF 60)

RAFT / NATURAL HISTORY — CLASS III

➤ *Madagascar's secrets*

➤ *Lemurs and virgin forests*

➤ *Rafting on the Queen River*

Breck O'Neil/SOBEK photo file

Madagascar. The name evokes images of a remote and exotic land, far away from everyday life. The Red Island lives up to its full billing. It is as distant from the United States as it can be and as different as you would expect.

Although it's the world's fourth-largest island and boasts countless miles of mountains, rivers and rain forests to beckon the curious, Madagascar has barely been discovered by travelers. It is the island that time forgot. And what an island! The 250 miles that separate it from the southeast African coast make it a world apart, with a unique Afro-Polynesian culture, a fantastic variety of endemic plants and animals, and a rich history interrupted only by occasional invasions of seafaring foreigners.

Join us on a gentle rafting trip through the hills and villages of Madagascar, then extend your stay if you wish to spend time in the Perinet Reserve, a rain forest station that's known for its flora and lemur population and is located in a beautiful coastal town and on the broad beaches of the lush island of Sainte Marie.

ITINERARY:

Day 1: En route.

Day 2: Paris.

Day 3: Antananarivo.

Day 4: To the river.

Days 5-12: On the river.

Day 13: Tsaratanana; derig.

Day 14: Antananarivo.

Day 15: Return.

EXTENSION:

Day 15: Antananarivo.

Days 16-17: Train to Tomasina.

Day 18: Fly to Ste. Marie Island.

Days 19-21: On Ste. Marie.

Day 22: Antananarivo.

Day 23: Return.

MODERATE

April

SOBEK

Raft Morocco (AF 65)

WHITEWATER — CLASS III

➤ *The middle Atlas Mountains*

➤ *Wildflowers and wild water*

➤ *A Marrakech express*

Through the mountains of Marrakech and Fez run many rivers waiting to be discovered by whitewater enthusiasts. Three of them, the Oued Sebou, Oum Er Rbia, and the Assif Ahanesal, offer an exciting introduction to the diversity of the Land of the Berbers.

This unique outdoor tour, offered by the pioneering French whitewater company, Atalante, affords us an opportunity to visit two bustling Moroccan cities, Marrakech and the ancient capital Fez, and explore the remote countryside via raft.

The most challenging of the three rivers we'll visit is the Assif Ahanesal which plummets through narrow gorges lined with weird rock formations. Inaccessible by land, the riverside is home to hordes of curious monkeys who peek out at us from behind the rocks.

We'll camp in the cedar forest beside Aguelmane Azigza Lake before descending Oum Er Rbia where the wildflowers that line the shore give the river its nickname, "The Pink River." This too is an exciting river, dropping steeply at first into rapids, waterfalls, and waves. In the calmer lower sections, you'll have the chance to see Berber villages where the people observe their timeless traditions.

The Oued Sebou is a technically difficult river, impressive for its thundering volume. If we tear our eyes away from the whitewater that surrounds us, we'll see villages perched atop the steep canyon walls.

If you're up for a sample of the exotic world of international whitewater, there's no better trip! Play it again, Sam!

ITINERARY:

Day 1: To Paris.

Day 2: Marrakech.

Days 3-7: On the rivers.

Day 8: Marrakech.

Day 9: Return.

PREMIUM

March-April

SOBEK

Luangwa Walking Safari (AF 67) ◣◣◣◣◣◣◣

WILDLIFE WALK— CLASS III

➤ *Africa's best-kept secret*
➤ *Comfortable lodges and safari camps*
➤ *Close encounters with big game*

Africa's best-kept secret is Zambia's spectacular Luangwa Valley National Park, a 3,500-square-mile paradise that comes pretty close to being Eden. Here can be found one of the greatest concentrations of game animals anywhere in Africa today—including lion, the rare rhino, giraffe, nearly every kind of antelope you've ever heard of, over 350 species of birds, and some 50,000 elephants.

And best of all, you can see this explosion of wildlife not from a safari bus or the hotel lounge but from a bush camp on the banks of the Luangwa River. From a fully appointed game lodge, groups of up to seven people slowly cross the Luangwa parklands in the company of a trail leader and an armed game guard, and make camp at a site chosen for its proximity to game and scenery. Thatch huts with comfortable facilities (hot showers, laundry service and good food!) serve as a wilderness base for daily morning and evening hikes, a place to share tales of close yet safe encounters.

Along the trail, surprises are the order of the day: leaping impala herds and screeching baboon troops, loping giraffes and skulking hyenas—all part of this real-life glimpse of the landscape where man was born a million years ago.

ITINERARY:

Day 1: Lusaka, Zambia, to Chibembe Lodge.

Day 2: Walk to trail camp.

Days 3-4: Walking safari.

Day 5: Return to lodge.

Day 6: Fly to Lusaka; return.

MEDIUM

June-October

Wilderness Trails

Kenya Coast/Tanzania Wildlife ‿‿∿∿∿‿ (AF 200)

VARIETY PACKAGE—
CLASS III

➤ *Mosques and minarets of old Lam*

➤ *Serengeti splendor*

➤ *Ngorongoro Crater*

This trip offers the unique combination of the magnificent Swahili culture of old Lam, mixed with what can only be described as the greatest animal show on earth, the wildlife parks of Tanzania. What a variety for those seeking an introduction to Africa!

We catch one of the most famous trains in Africa down to Mombasa where we spend time on the old colonial south coast with three relaxing days at "Nomads," a neat collection of local bungalows on the white sands of beautiful Diani Beach. Next it's off to the airport for our short flight to the charm of old Lam, a unique Swahili island and one of the first Arab settlements on the African coast. The town's labyrinthine streets and black-veiled women evoke the atmosphere of

the slave trade of days gone by—an island without vehicle transport, where traditional Arab dhows still ply back and forth. We stay at "Peponis," right on the beach at Shella, a fishing village with mosques and minarets overlooking the mouth of Lam Harbor. Here you can explore the narrow back streets and barter with the locals for a wide variety of African artifacts, or just sit and watch skilled artisans carve beautiful designs on the massive Arab-style doors, a craft which has made this island famous. No trip to Kenya would be complete without a visit to this romantic island hideaway.

For the second part of our trip, we return to Nairobi before heading down to Tanzania. What trip to this amazing country would be complete without a journey through the Serengeti game reserve? Sometimes a vista of seemingly endless and almost treeless plains, sometimes dotted with the flat-topped acacia trees that so many of us associate with our image of the real Africa. Thirty-five species of game and over three hundred and fifty species of birds abound in this incredible "zoo without fences." Bring plenty of film!

Olduvai Gorge is next, the site where Dr. Leakey and his wife worked for so many years before discovering the earliest remains of modern man. Makes you really feel at home!

In Ngorongoro Crater, 2,000 feet deep and ten miles wide, we find a virtual paradise of flora and fauna. Ngorongoro is the world's largest intact volcanic crater and is believed by many to be the original "Garden of Eden." This animal haven surely must be one of the original wonders of Africa.

On the return journey to Arusha, we discover the incredible Lake Manyara with its vast population of flamingos, ducks, waders, and egrets and the tree-climbing lions, famous for their habit of lazing around in the low branches of trees, as though time has just stood still.

ITINERARY:

Day 1: (Sunday) Meet in Nairobi, take overnight train to Mombasa.

Day 2: Arrive at Mombasa, transfer to "Nomads."

Days 3-4: In Mombasa.

Day 5: Fly to Lam.

Days 6-7: In Lam.

Day 8: Fly to Nairobi.

Day 9: Drive to Arusha.

Day 10: Drive Serengeti.

Day 11: In Serengeti.

Day 12: Drive to Ngorongoro Crater.

Day 13: Drive to Lake Manyara.

Day 14: Return to Arusha.

Day 15: (Sunday) Return to Nairobi

MEDIUM

January-October

World Expeditions

Gorillas and Wildlife (AF 201)

CULTURAL
OVERLANDING—CLASS II

➤ *Vast game reserves*

➤ *Mountain gorillas of Rwanda*

Many of the traditional cultures of Africa are being replaced by the Twentieth-century "progress," and our generation may be the last to experience them before they are changed forever. This safari combines Kenya, with its breathtaking scenery and vast game reserves, with a visit to the endangered mountain gorillas of Rwanda which must be a highlight for anyone visiting Africa.

We start in Nairobi and head off down the escarpment, into the famous Rift Valley, for the beginning of a week that will eventually take us to Lake Nakuru, Masai Mara, and Samburu game reserves. These carefully selected parks will satiate even the most avid animal lover. But this is only a warm-up before we return to Nairobi and fly to Kigali to commence a two-week safari that many would believe could only happen in Hollywood.

The second part of this trip has been designed especially for those with some true expedition blood in them. This safari is, and will remain for the next year, an exploratory trip into the Kivu region in search of colorful tribes and the magnificent fauna for which this area is famous.

We will not take group after group on the same route. Each successive trip will vary as much as the prevailing conditions will allow. This will reduce the impact tourism may inflict on a fragile environment and enable us to enjoy many first encounters. We still plan to ascend the active volcano of Nyiragongo and trek to the misty domain of the incredible mountain gorilla. We may spend two or three days trekking through a remote part of the Rwandan hills, or go off in canoes to explore the islands on Lake Kivu itself, or search for pygmies that are rumored to exist on the western side of the lake. No two trips will be exactly the same. On this safari we are certain you will enjoy an exciting, intimate experience that will guarantee memorable and enduring moments for you and for the people you visit.

ITINERARY:

Day 1: (Sunday) Meet in Nairobi.

Day 2: Morning drive to Masai Mara.

Day 3: In Masai Mara.

Day 4: Morning drive to Lake Nakuru.

Day 5: Morning drive to Samburu.

Day 6: In Samburu.

Day 7: Return to Nairobi.

Day 8: Fly to Kigali.

Day 9: Drive to reserve.

Days 10-13: Climb to gorillas, bush treks, climb Nyiragongo, exploratory excursions.

Day 14: Return to Reserve.

Days 15-19: Explore Lake Kivu area.

Day 20: Fly Kigali/Nairobi.

Day 21: In Nairobi.

Day 22: (Sunday) Trip finishes Nairobi.

MEDIUM

February-December

World Expeditions

Madagascar Exploratory Expedition (AF 202) ▲▲▲

WILDLIFE WALK— CLASS II

➤ *Exotic island flora and fauna*

➤ *Socialize with friendly lemurs*

➤ *Turquoise lagoons of Nosy Be*

No place is as different from the rest of the world as Madagascar. And this is a fittingly different and remarkable trip. Remote, unique, exotic, and richer in an indigenous flora and fauna than any country in the world, Madagascar has the world's largest and smallest chameleons, rare palms, black parrots and a variety of exceptionally pleasing, and often tame, easy to observe animals called lemurs. Many unique species of birds, insects, animals, and plants here are threatened with destruction. Most species occur nowhere else in the world.

This is a trip that really focuses on tak-ing you to the richest and most spectacular ecosystems of Madagascar. Led by English/French/Malagasy-speaking guides Serge Harizo and Sylvie Rabesahala, we travel by air, rail, boat, foot, and jeep to some of the most remarkable and remote areas of the island. We vary the itinerary by season and in accordance with our discoveries of what fits in a JOURNEYS-style trip. The extensive exploration includes renowned natural areas Montagne D'Amber National Park, Perinet Special Reserve, Berenty Reserve, Isalo National Park, Bezaha Mahataly Research Area, Ranoma-fana Proposed National Park, and the zoma (weekly market).

Areas of greatest concentrations of lemurs and other wildlife will receive primary attention, but we will also introduce you to the remarkable cultures of Madagascar and their practices of ancestor worship. We will relax on tropical beaches, socialize and interact with the very friendly lemurs, partake of night jungle hikes in search of nocturnal fauna, and luxuriate in the solid tropical hardwood decor of colonial-style hotels.

This is the most extensive, thorough, guided, nature-oriented small group trip to Madagascar. We encourage itinerary, leadership, and cost comparisons. Groups limited to ten participants.

We can offer individualized, custom itineraries to any areas of Madagascar at any time of the year. Madagascar works well as an extension to an East Africa Safari Itinerary.

ITINERARY:

Days 1-2: USA/Nairobi.

Day 3: Arrival in Antananarivo.

Days 4-6: Tana/Diego-Suarez/Montagne D'Amber National Park.

Day 7: Diego-Suarez/Tana/Perinet.

Days 8-9: Perinet Reserve.

Day 9: Perinet/Tana.

Day 10: Tana/Antsirabe.

Days 11-12: Antsirabe/Ranomafana.

Days 13-14: Ranomanfana/Isalo National Park.

Day 15-16: Isalo/Tollara/Betloky.

Days 17-20: Betloky/ Bezaha Mahataly.

Day 21: Bezaha/Tollara/Taolanaro.

Days 22-23: Taolanaro/Berenty.

Day 24: Berenty/Taolanaro.

Day 25: Taolanaro/Tana.

Day 26: Tana.

Day 27: Return to USA.

MEDIUM

April-October

JOURNEYS International, Inc.

South America

Bío-Bío River (SA 1)

CHALLENGING
WHITEWATER—CLASS IV

> *A full deck of rapids*
> *Hike to active volcano*
> *Personalized video*

For whitewater river runners, the Bío-Bío needs no introduction. Since the first descent of the river by SOBEK in 1977, the Bío-Bío's reputation for non-pareil action has reached every corner of the boating world. It is Chile's largest river, cascading almost continuously in its course from the Andes to the South Pacific, and it is the wildest river SOBEK runs commercially, with rapids that sur-pass the finest in the United States. Such a river dictates caution, and the river guides have worked hard to develop routes in the rapids and a variety of safety techniques that guarantee the safest possible ride.

Since the Bío-Bío is a first-class river, this is a first-class trip to back it up. In Santiago, we stay at the Carrera Hotel, the city's finest, and in Victoria, near put-in, we overnight at the Manzanar Hot Springs Hotel—a rustic resort whose fine hot baths should clear up the final stages of jet lag.

Our eight days on the Bío-Bío are ones of seemingly choreographed pyrotechnics. Gentle at first, flowing through the soft, rolling countryside of the *Uhuasco*, Chile's cowboy, the Bío-Bío allows us to get a feel for it before it abruptly changes. Soon metamorphic and granitic gorges suddenly squeeze in, pinching the channel and creating Class IV and V whitewater sections. During the full eight-day run we ride almost one hundred rapids. But even the longest rapid takes but a half-minute, and we have plenty of time to soak in the scenery and

hot springs along the way. We fish for trout, hike to an alpine lake rivaling Yosemite in beauty, stretch back on soft beaches and marvel at the night sky and the stars of the Southern Hemisphere. On a layover day we can hike towards the snowy summit of Volcan Callaqui, a smoking 10,000-foot volcano that looms directly over the river for most of its run. Interaction with the people who live along the Bío-Bío—farmers, cowboys, and Indians—is another highlight of the trip, including an *asado*, a Chilean feast of roasted, freshly slaughtered sheep or goat.

After take-out, we bus to the town of Chillan where we browse its gigantic, sprawling market, one of the largest and most colorful in Chile, and then it's all aboard a train for a five-hour ride back to the Carrera Hotel.

Because everyone who takes this trip wants to savor it for a lifetime, a professional videographer kayaks along on every Bío-Bío run and puts together a personalized video for each participant. This is a trip you'll be showing to your grand-children.

ITINERARY:

Day 1: Santiago; begin train journey.

Day 2: Arrive Victoria; drive to Manzanar Hot Springs.

Day 3: Begin river trip.

Days 4-11: On the river.

Day 12: Santa Barbara to Chillan.

Day 13: Train to Santiago.

Day 14: Return.

MEDIUM

December-March

SOBEK Expeditions

Torres del Paine (SA 3)

HIKING/SCENIC— CLASS III

➤ *Chile's endless charm*

➤ *Torres del Paine National Park*

Punta Arenas, the former whaling station, lies at the uttermost ends of the earth, in the southern extremes of Chile on the Straits of Magellan. It is our gateway to Torres del Paine National Park, a captivating assemblage of reeling mountains and brooding glaciers, of rampaging rivers and quiet fjords. The famous Towers of Paine, skyline-scratching extrusions of granite, dominate the parklands.

Here, for four days, we have many features to explore, including the park's mini icebergs, rock escarpments, guanacos (similar to llamas), avestruz (ostrichlike birds), pink flamingos, and mammoth Gray Glacier. We can take gentle strolls mixed with fishing and guanaco viewing, or we can take challenging treks into the wilds behind the Paine massif.

This is territory for the stalwart adventurer, although it is also home to many fascinating peoples. Some of its original inhabitants, the Tehuelches Indians, first seen by Darwin, wore virtually nothing in this harsh climate except guanaco capes over their shoulders! We at least have long summer days during North America's coldest and shortest months to bask in this exotic landscape, starting in Punta Arenas, a port town of 80,000 people, and one of the jumping off points for Antarctic tours.

ITINERARY:

Day 1: Puerto Montt.

Day 2: Punta Arenas.

Days 3-6: Torres del Paine.

Day 7: Punta Arenas.

Days 8-9: To Santiago and return.

MEDIUM

December-February

SOBEK Expeditions

Inca Ways (SA 5)

MODERATE TREKKING— CLASS III

➤ *Trek the Inca's domain*

➤ *Raft the Sacred Valley*

➤ *Explore Machu Picchu and Cuzco*

There is no better way to immerse yourself in the cultures of Peru, past and present, than on this hiking and rafting adventure through the heart of the ancient Incan Empire. We begin with back street walks in exotic Cuzco, the 11,000-foot pre-Pizarro capital of the continent. Here the crisp, clear mountain light intensifies the Indian marketplaces and illuminates the faded colonial splendor of the seventeenth-century churches and town squares. We spend a day walking and acclimating and then drive to the Sacred Valley of the Incas for two days of rafting the mild whitewater of the Urubamba River, a far tributary of the Amazon.

This river route gives us a backdoor look at life in a timeless agricultural valley as we float past ancient farms, villages, and markets, and explore some massive ruins, including the ancient fortress of Pisac. We spend the night in a charming country

Leatha Aicano/SOBEK photo file

inn, and the next morning we float beneath terraced hillsides and glacial peaks until the river narrows and we race by a series of watchtowers and fortresses that once guarded this important valley. We end up in the Indian town of Chillca where we leave the Urubamba and begin hiking the Inca Trail.

On the trail, a beautifully intact granite path built over 600 years ago, we trek with porters in classic Himalayan style. We walk from six to nine miles a day, carrying only a day pack, and enjoy the magnificent scenery, which ranges from alpine grassland to tropical cloud forest. The trail itself is an impressive feat of Incan architecture and engineering. We start out at about 10,000 feet, among cacti and scrubby, red-flowered ''tara'' trees, and by the second day we are in a world of glacier-fed cascades bordered by elderberries and wild cherries. Our camp, above timberline, is in a mossy, evergreen cloud forest with a view of jagged, snow-covered peaks. On the third day we reach the highest point of the trek, Warmiwanuska Pass, at 14,200 feet.

Here, surrounded by white-crowned peaks, we begin the awesome descent to Machu Picchu—through tropical cloud forest, over a second pass at 12,900 feet, and down a dramatic stairway to camp at Chakicocha, facing the ruins of Sayac-marca. Our final day on the trail is perhaps the most dramatic of all as we follow a ridge, walk down another beautiful winding staircase, and finally enter Machu Picchu via the ''Gateway of the Sun.''

We have until dusk to explore this ancient citadel, inhabited by priests and chosen princesses over half a millennium ago, or to walk in the surrounding natural preserve—a landscape full of trailside orchids and butterflies, strange native animals, even a bird (a barred fruiteater) that looks like a volleyball. We spend the night at Hotel Machu Picchu and the next morning either continue our exploration of the ruins or hike up Wayna Picchu for a condor's view of the entire complex and the canyon surrounding it. In the late afternoon we board a train that carries us back to Cuzco.

In Cuzco, we explore the city with new eyes, sensing something of how this Incan capital must have felt to the Indians who regarded it as a holy Andean Mecca. We too, after all, have followed the footsteps of the Incas to the heart of their domain.

ITINERARY:

Day 1: Arrive Lima.

Day 2: Lima.

Day 3: Fly to Cuzco.

Day 4: Rafting the Urubamba.

Day 5: End rafting, begin trek.

Days 6-7: On trek.

Day 8: Arrive Machu Picchu.

Day 9: Machu Picchu; train to Cuzco.

Day 10: Cuzco.

Day 11: Lima.

Day 12: Return.

MEDIUM

May-August, October

Explorandes

Source of the Amazon (SA 8)

WHITEWATER RAFTING
AND TREK — CLASS IV

➤ *Canyons of the high Andes*

➤ *Class V-plus action*

➤ *Trek to Machu Picchu*

The Apurimac is blessed from birth, where it emerges as an elegant snow stream spilling from the high peaks of the Peruvian Andes to the humid Amazon Basin far below. Thus the world's largest river begins its 4,000-mile run to the sea with a tributary worthy of its rank, a challenging whitewater run bursting with high-class rapids and overflowing with sky-high scenery. Our run on the uppermost section of the river navigable by rafts takes five days and is not a trip for the faint of heart. Its two-mile-high elevation makes every day a rarefied challenge, and its whitewater is definitely worth all our attention.

Following the river trip, we have another challenge to face: a six-day trek along ancient stone paths to the spectacular ruins of Machu Picchu, most famous of the Incan ruins. From isolated Quechua villages, over 15,700-foot passes, to camps in the stony shadows of forgotten Incan outposts, we explore the backcountry of Peru in a way few travelers ever can.

Extra time at Machu Picchu and in Cuzco completes this adventure the way it begins: with a full draught of the wonder of Peru.

John Tichener/SOBEK photo file

ITINERARY:

Day 1: Lima.

Day 2: Fly to Cuzco.

Day 3: Drive to river; begin descent.

Days 4-6: On the Apurimac.

Day 7: End river trip, begin trek.

Days 8-12: On trek.

Day 13: End trek at Machu Picchu.

Day 14: Machu Picchu to Cuzco.

Day 15: Cuzco.

Day 16: Fly to Lima.

Day 17: Return. (Note: River trip only)

Note: Days 1-7 are available separately.

MODERATE-MEDIUM

June-July

Rioandes

The Galápagos Islands (SA 13) ▰▰▰▰▰▰▰

NATURAL HISTORY
CRUISE—CLASS I

➤ *The enchanted isles of Melville*

➤ *The birthplace of Darwinism*

➤ *Wildlands and wildlife galore*

The dramatic novelty of the Galápagos has given rise to both wild speculation and hard science. Early whalers thought there was magic in these scattered isles off the coast of Ecuador long before Darwin gave them notoriety in the academic world. And by the time Herman Melville wrote of ''The Encantadas,'' many thought that all life on Earth originated on them. They are nothing if not odd: ugly clusters of volcanic rock covered with algae slime from the ocean and coarse yel-

low grass inland, with a tropical rain forest adding lushness to the landscape here and there. And they are populated by animals that date back more than three million years—tortoises and iguanas that may be the descendants of prehistoric animals.

The Galápagos beg for an explanation. There is a seething sense of creation in progress, with beaches stained red and black and green, iguanas that look like minature dinosaurs, and birds that look and sound like no others in the world. It's easy to see why Darwin's trip here helped him formulate his theory about natural selection and the process of evolution— that animals, plants, and birds adapt to an environment for survival. About 50 percent of the animals here were original residents of the islands and other bird and marine species were eventually carried here by wind or water currents.

We take a look at this unnatural, natural paradise in the best way possible— cruising from island to island on small boats captained by expert naturalists. From the moment we set foot on our first island, we realize that wildlife watching here is like nowhere else in the world. Fear of man is missing. With palpable innocence, sea lions jump in to play alongside skin divers; iguanas sit patiently for portraits; boobies and frigate birds pursue their mates with lusty abandon. We'll see the unique, flightless cormorant, swim and play with Galápagos fur seals, snorkel at the mysterious Devil's Crown (an eroded, submerged volcanic cone), and visit Puerto Ayora, the world-famous Charles Darwin Research Station.

The list of natural wonders endemic to the Galápagos goes on and on: it may be the only place in the world, for instance, where snorkelers can sight, in a single afternoon, sea turtles, blue-footed boobies, iguanas, rays, and small sharks. What makes this particular trip to the Galápagos special is the boat, which is specifically designed for comfort and wildlife viewing, and the quality of the naturalists on board, who can point out the details that so intrigued Darwin—details like variations in beak shapes and behavior that can only be seen with a biologist's practiced eye.

These islands, comprising a 3,029-square-mile natural preserve, may be the only remaining habitat of substantial size where man has conserved huge quantities of wildlife before capsizing the natural balance of nature. As we visit them and learn how to see, we'll discover miracles and mysteries that may make lifelong naturalists of all of us.

ITINERARY:

Day 1: Arrive Quito, Ecuador.

Day 2: Fly to Baltra, Galápagos; board yacht.

Day 3: Tower Island.

Day 4: Isabela, James, and Rabida islands.

Day 5: Santa Cruz Island.

Day 6: Floreana Island.

Day 7: Hood Island.

Day 8: Barrington and South Plaza islands.

Day 9: Baltra Island; return flight to Quito.

Day 10: Cotopaxi National Park; evening return to Quito.

Day 11: Return.

MEDIUM

Year-round

SOBEK Expeditions

Easter Island (SA 14)

HORSEBACK RIDING— CLASS I

➤ *Massive, mysterious stone sentinels*

➤ *Five days of horseback riding and hiking*

➤ *South Pacific solitide*

The mysteries of Rapa-Nui have stimulated the imagination of visitors ever since a Dutch explorer first anchored his three ships on this South Pacific island on Easter Sunday, 1722. The consummate artistry of the looming heads or *Moai*, the massive size of the pedestals (some as high as 160 feet), and the enigmatic disappearance of the carvers themselves are sources of wonder and conjecture. Although legend suggests that the Moai walked to their destination from the stone quarry at Rano Raraku Volcano where they were sculpted, archaeologists believe they were carried on wooden boards pulled like a sled by ropes made of tree fibers. Cooked potatoes were rubbed along the bottom of the boards to make them more slippery.

This island, 2,300 miles west of the Chilean coastline, was completely isolated as recently as the 1960s, when its only contact with the outside world was a Chilean warship that visited once a year with provisions. And although tourists have now discovered it in small numbers, there is definitely a spooky remoteness to the place, and we sense the isolation and mystery as we spend five days riding horses and hiking over the countryside of this volcanic moat and camping on beaches and at the base of the inscrutable stone sentinels.

ITINERARY:

Day 1: Santiago.

Day 2: Fly to Easter Island.

Days 3-6: Visit island by horse.

Day 7: Fly to Santiago and return.

MEDIUM

December-February

SOBEK Expeditions

Rivers of Costa Rica (SA 27)

RIVER RAFTING—
CLASS III

➤ *Class IV Río Chirripo*

➤ *Class IV-plus Río Pacuare*

➤ *Class V Reventazon*

Geography begets sport in Costa Rica, the cornerstone of any adventure tour in Central America. With its spine of mountains splitting the country into numerous drainage basins, the terrain of this beautiful country is ideal for short but demanding river runs from cloud forest to coast.

There's the Chirripo, with fifty miles of abundant rapids, waterfalls, side hikes, birdlife, otters and iguanas, all amidst the lush foliage of the tropical jungle. And there's the Pacuare, which races through a narrow forested gorge and drops sixty feet per mile—a true jungle river where our paddle-play may be watched by tapir and jaguar, ocelot and deer. Last, there's the Bursting River, the Reventazon, with a world-class gradient of 125 feet per mile and Class V rapids such as Land of a Hundred Holes, Burning Rocks, the Sieve, and El Horrendo.

Two separate itineraries, determined by the time of year and recent rainfall, offer runs of two of these rivers plus time to explore the other natural wonders of Costa Rica and the capital city of San José. From the top of steaming Poas Volcano to the 300-foot plunge of Veragua Falls to the depths of the Hundred Holes, Costa Rica has more than enough excitement to carry even the most jaded traveler through nine days of natural wonderland.

ITINERARY, Dry Season (January-June):

Day 1: San José.

Days 2-4: Río Pacuare.

Days 5-6: Reventazon.

Day 7: Poas Volcano.

Day 8: San José.

Day 9: Return.

ITINERARY, Wet Season (July-December):

Day 1: San José.

Days 2-4: Río Chirripo.

Day 5: Veragua Falls.

Day 6: San José.

Days 7-8: Río Pacuare.

Day 9: Return.

MEDIUM

Year-round

Costa Rica Expeditions

Agua Azul Kayaking (SA 28)

RAFTING / KAYAKING—
CLASS V

➤ *Challenging rapids*

➤ *Amazonian rain forests*

The fabled forests, mountains, ruins, and blue rivers of Chiapas provide the perfect scene for kayak exploration. The carpet-thick jungles of this Mexico-Guatemala border region, once the center of highland Maya culture, are deeply carved throughout by warm turquoise waters and filled with a wide variety of exotic hardwoods, vines and epiphytes, palms and a thick tangle of undergrowth. (The film, *Romancing the Stone*, was shot in Chiapas.)

We explore and run various tributaries in the headwater region of the Rio Usumacinta, including the Jatate and the Santo Domingo. In startling contrast to the serene valleys and remote mahogany villages, there are narrow gorges filled with waterfalls, rapids, and subterranean passages that make every day a new discovery. Along the way, we pass through Indian villages populated by descendants of the Mayans who live on subsistence agriculture. Our guide will help us establish a rapport with the Indians and understand some of their customs.

This is a kayaker's fantasy trip: easy to reach yet extraordinarily isolated, more in the nature of an expedition than a regular commercial run; truly a challenging way to see a forgotten corner of the Americas.

ITINERARY:

Days 1-2: To Tuxtla.

Day 3: San Cristobal.

Days 4-19: Jatate, Usumacinta, and Santo Domingo rivers.

Day 20: Head home.

MODERATE

February-March

SOBEK Expeditions

Barranca del Cobre (SA 36)

TREK / NATURAL
HISTORY — CLASS IV

➤ *Descend steep canyon walls*

➤ *Investigate ancient cave dwellings*

The Copper Canyon in northern Mexico is one of the Western Hemisphere's unknown wonders: a vertical world of rock and mystery almost as deep and much more inaccessible than the Grand Canyon. From our rendezvous in the west Texas town of El Paso, we travel to the colonial-style town of Chihuahua, Mexico. From there, the fabled Ferrocarril Barranca del Cobre takes us deep into the Sierra Madre Occidental, along the rim of this fabulous and fabled gorge cut by the Río Urique. Then it's down, down, and down some more, with pack animals and native guides, into a world of tropical canyons, hot springs, centuries-old cliff dwellings and the villages of our hosts, the indigenous farmers and goat herders of the canyon. These people, the Tarahumara, are the world's most remarkable runners, comfortable racing distances that would make a marathon seem a stroll—50, 100, even 150 miles without a stop.

Our own hikes are more modest at 6 to 12 miles a day with plenty of time to explore life along the river, swim, hike, and photograph the eroded rock formations, or simply bask in the warm springs. On our final hike out of the canyon, we climb 3,000 feet in one day. In the reeling world of the Barranca del Cobre, every step takes us closer to the extraordinary.

ITINERARY:

Day 1: El Paso to Chihuahua.

Day 2: Train to Barranca.

Day 3: Hotel Cabanas.

Days 4-7: Trekking.

Day 8: Hotel Cabanas.

Day 9: Train to Chihuahua.

Day 10: Chihuahua.

Day 11: El Paso and return.

MODERATE

March-May, September-December

SOBEK Expeditions

Andean Odyssey (SA 37)

VARIETY PACKAGE—
CLASS II

➤ *Raft the Urubamba*

➤ *Ruins of Machu Picchu*

➤ *Includes international airfare*

Journey to the Empire of Gold in comfort on this hotel-based tour of the fabulous realm of the Incas. This trip covers much of the same territory as trip #SA 5 (Inca Ways) but with no overnight trekking or camping out. The full package includes a flight from Miami to Lima, Peru's capital, where we'll have a day to explore the city's cosmopolitan charms, and a spectacular plane ride up and over the Andes to Cuzco. Here we spend a full day in this timeless town, drinking in the sparkling mountain air and exploring the fine stonework of plazas and palaces, all created centuries ago by Incan and colonial craftsmen. Then we begin a two-day rafting trip down the Rio Urubamba, which races through the agricultural oasis of the Sacred Valley of the Incas. Amidst fig trees and terraced fields we challenge the spritely rapids by day, and relax over-

night in the comfort of a colonial riverside inn.

Finally, we begin the ride to Machu Picchu on a narrow gauge alpine train and chug deep into the granite gorge of the Urubamba, following the route that was just being surveyed when young Hiram Bingham walked the roadbed asking if there were ruins in the area. We go from dry highlands down to the tropical jungle and then back up until we reach the base of the majestic citadel of Machu Picchu. Here we have plenty of time to explore the vast network of terraces, temples, and tombs, that were probably once inhabited by the final Incan ruler and his nobles as they escaped from the Spaniards into what appeared to be the security of the jungle. We spend the night next to the ruins at Hotel Machu Picchu.

Back in Lima we have another day to visit the wicker market, or walk to the Pacific Coast, or just relax after this stimulating journey—not only to a beautiful place and an exotic culture but through time and into the heart of a world whose hallmark, for us, is mystery.

John Tichener/SOBEK photo file

Cordillera Blanca (SA 39)

CHALLENGING TREK—CLASS IV

➤ *Hike the high Andes*

➤ *Panoramas of light and stone*

➤ *Full pack support*

Leatha Alcano/SOBEK photo file

South America's most perfect trek is found in the Cordillera Blanca, an Andean range in northern Peru. Towering mountain walls, arid glacial basins, and flowered meadows offer a memorable arena for this five-day trek between a dozen peaks that surmount the barrier, each reaching 15,000 feet into the cerulean sky. Our trek is fully supported by pack animals to carry our gear, and guides to set up camp, so we are able to hike comfortably one spectacular day after the next.

Beginning in Huaraz, in an immense glacial valley fronting the Cordillera, we begin our northward trek with a warm-up hike near the blue Llanganuco Lake at the base of Peru's highest peak, Huascaran. The next day we continue trekking as we cross the continental divide, passing through rangeland into deeply glaciated terrain, ascending steeply to Punta Union, our high point at 15,584 feet. Distant river canyons, towering snowcapped pinnacles, lone Alpine lakes, and one of the world's most beautiful mountains, Alpamayo (19,700 ft.), all combine on this short, awesome trek to inflame our senses and consume our souls.

ITINERARY:

Day 1: Arrive Lima.

Day 2: To Huaraz.

Day 3: Llanganuco Lake hike; begin trek.

Day 4: Trek Huaripampa Valley.

Day 5: Punta Union to Quiswarpampa camp.

Day 6: Lake Jatuncocha, to Llamcorral camp.

Day 7: End trek at Cashapampa; drive to Huaraz.

Day 8: Lima.

Day 9: Return.

MODERATE

April-October

Explorandes

Patagonia Panorama (SA 45)

NATURAL HISTORY—
CLASS III

➤ *Animal sanctuaries of Argentina*

➤ *Penguin colonies of the Atlantic*

➤ *Trekking in Tierra del Fuego*

Reaching from the Tropic of Capricorn south toward the Antarctic Circle, Argentina embraces an enviable array of environments, from the wine tasting rooms in Buenos Aires to the thundering glaciers of Perito Moreno; from the broad pampas of the Patagonian plains to the wilds of Tierra del Fuego. Clearly, variety is the hallmark of this million-square-mile land, and variety is what you get on this eighteen-day panorama of its natural wonders.

At the foot of the Andes we see the caves, waterfalls, and fossil deposits of Witches Cavern and savor a barbecue lunch with gauchos and thousands of red-pelted guanacos in La Payunia Reserve. On the coast we navigate the Valdes Peninsula and watch for elephant seals, sea lions, Magellanic penguins, and even whales. A flight over the troubled waters of the Strait of Magellan takes us to the Land of Fires, where a dozen different ecosystems cluster on the island at the end of the continent and creatures such as pink flamingos, the world's largest woodpecker, and three kinds of wild geese make their appearance.

We hike for two days in this magical land and then head for our last major destination, the spectacular glacier Perito Moreno that bisects Lago Argentino with a wall of blue ice. Travel has seldom provided as many rewards in so short a time, and the New World has never seemed newer and more eye-opening than it does in Argentina.

ITINERARY:

Day 1: Morning arrival in Buenos Aires; city tour.

Day 2: Fly to Llancanelo Lake; overnight Malargue, Mendoza.

Days 3-4: La Payunia Reserve.

Days 5-6: Los Alerces National Park.

Day 7: Fly to Trelew.

Days 8-10: Sea mammals of Valdes Peninsula.

Day 11: Fly to Ushuaia, Tierra del Fuego.

Days 12-13: Hike in national park.

Day 14: Fly to Rio Gallegos, Patagonia; overnight Lago Argentino.

Days 15-16: Los Glaciares National Park.

Day 17: Lago Argentino.

Day 18: Fly to Buenos Aires and return.

PREMIUM

November

Lihue Expeditions

Amazon Adventure (SA 46) ▲▲▲▲▲

NATURAL HISTORY
PACKAGE—CLASS I

➤ *Canoe the Rio Napo*

➤ *Daily wildlife hikes*

➤ *Colorful riverside lodge*

The Amazon is a place of grand dimensions indeed, but it is also a world of lush and quiet detail where many a lifetime has been spent documenting the plant and insect species of a single square mile. Even the shortest visit is a revelation, and we attain ours by basing our adventure out of a research station-turned-jungle lodge at the spectacular confluence of the Amazon with the Rio Napo.

From Lima, we catch a dawn flight to Peru's Amazon port, Iquitos, where we board a launch for a fifty-mile cruise to Explorama Lodge and Research Station, a place to explore further the intricacies of this ecozone or to chase butterflies and lounge beside enormous ferns and yard-wide Victoria Regia water lilies.

From Explorama, we take a two-day journey deep into the forest, cruising through wide, braided, river channels on a palm-thatched local riverboat made from one large tree trunk. After establishing a base camp, we navigate as far into the jungle as water levels permit. Our goal is to take a close look at the rain forest and its inhabitants with the help of people who devote their lives to understanding them.

We visit the villages of the Yagua Indians, hunt caiman from canoes, and trek into the jungle, accompanied by the howls of howler monkeys and the caws of macaws. The birdlife alone is enough to fill a notebook with pages of discovery—blue and yellow macaws, toucans, hoatzin, giant kingfisher, and more, each as colorful as the eye can imagine. More than just a vacation, this trip is a chance to understand the world's richest ecosystem and perhaps, to make a difference in its future and in ours, as fates here are inexorably intertwined.

ITINERARY:

Day 1: Arrive Lima.

Day 2: Fly to Iquitos; cruise to lodge.

Days 3-5: Jungle Lodge.

Day 6: Iquitos to Lima.

Day 7: Return.

MEDIUM

February, April-September, November-December

SOBEK Expeditions

Cordillera Huayhuash Trek (SA 50) ⚡⚡⚡

TREKKING—CLASS V

➤ *Hidden Andean valleys and lakes*

➤ *Seven Andean passes over 15,000 feet*

➤ *Three weeks of high adventure*

Cloud-scraping Andean passes are the portals to the wonders of the high cordillera of Peru, where we spend two weeks on one of the great trekking routes of the world—the Huayhuash circuit. Seven tendon-stretching passes ranging from 15,400 to 16,400 feet guard the hidden valleys and lakes of the Huayhuash, and test the mettle of the fittest of trekkers. The passes offer a commensurate reward for the challenging trek, an Alpine splendor that has few equals anywhere.

Careful acclimation and a moderate pace make this high altitude circuit feasible, and a well-planned series of layover days allows both recovery and exploration of lakes Carhuacocha and Jahuacocha—two bright-blue glacial lakes from which hanging glaciers stretch thousands of feet like ladders up to a snowy heaven. The Indian population from whom our regular trekking staff is drawn is both friendly and knowledgeable, sharing traditional perspectives on life in the inhospitable heights of the Andes.

Far-reaching vistas of peaks, broad glaciers, and cascading mountain creeks, and a variety of landscapes—barren, lush, icy, and rocky—entertain the eye at every bend. Rise to the challenge of an Andean high!

ITINERARY:

Days 1-2: To Lima.

Days 3-5: Huaraz.

Day 6: Chiquian.

Days 7-19: On trek.

Day 20: Chiquian.

Days 21-22: Lima.

Day 23: Home.

MODERATE

July

SOBEK Expeditions

The Lost World (SA 57)

WILDERNESS
EXPLORATION—CLASS III

➤ *Tabletop mountain sanctuary*

➤ *Rugged hikes and cave camps*

➤ *Twin plunge of Angel Falls*

It was after attending a lecture on Mt. Roraima, a tabletop mountain in Venezuela's steamy jungles, that Sir Arthur Conan Doyle plunged into writing ''The Lost World,'' his fable about prehistoric creatures surviving in present day South America. While we find no pterodactyls on this *tepui*—a local name for the mountains—we do find the fabulous: an oasis of plant and animal life elevated above the misty jungle including unique species that live only on this isolated summit.

Our two-day trek takes us up a natural ramp to the 9,094-foot summit of the Roraima where we find an alternate universe of sculpted rock formations, odd-shaped crystals, bizarre carnivorous plants, and clear pools ringed with strangely beautiful flowers. It's like exploring a Japanese garden whose Zen architect, going for mystery and meditation, has pulled out all the stops. After two days on the summit, where we camp like Doyle's explorers in a huge cave, we continue our Venezuelan voyage with a view of Angel Falls, discovered by tropical bush pilot Jimmy Angel in 1935. With 3,212 feet of spill, it is the highest waterfall in the world. At the end of this trip, we'll feel like little Alice did in Wonderland, having taken a journey that tested all logic and found it wanting.

ITINERARY:

Day 1: Arrive Caracas; continue to Puerto Ordaz.

Day 2: Drive across Gran Sabana to San Francisco de Yuruani.

Days 3-4: Trek to Mt. Roraima.

Days 5-6: Explore Roraima.

Days 7-8: Descent trek to Kavanayen Mission.

Day 9: Puerto Ordaz.

Day 10: Ciudad Bolivar to Canaima.

Day 11: Orchid Island and Angel Falls.

Day 12: Caracas and return.

MEDIUM

March, October-November

Tropical

Baja Cycle (SA 61)

BICYCLING—CLASS III

➤ *See Baja from a wheelside seat*

➤ *Snorkel and swim in turquoise seas*

➤ *Cycle through plum-colored canyons*

Pedal the beautiful badlands of Mexico's Baja California in a leisurely clockwise loop. Drink in the unique contour and coloration as the pastel desert shimmers in the heat and the plum-colored canyons and rumpled mountains glisten like hammered gold. Luxuriate on unmarked white sand beaches, your own piece of paradise that stretches to the horizon.

From La Paz to Buena Vista we pedal through cactus country, the foothills of the Sierra de la Laguna where we are treated to awe-inspiring views of the Sea of Cortez. On our way down to the hillside city of San José del Cabo, we cross the Tropic of Cancer and stop at sleepy villages for cold drinks and fresh seafood. Then it's on to the confluence of the Pacific and the Gulf of California where Mexican Highway 1 abruptly ends and the scrub-dotted desert meets the turquoise seas. Here we break to swim, snorkel, dive, fish, shop and sail. Then it's back north along the Pacific shoreline and up a rarely traveled but incredibly scenic road to La Paz, the end of our idyllic seven-day odyssey.

The expertise, experience, and enthusiasm of the guides ensure an unforgettable adventure. It is the perfect one-week, two-wheeled tour.

ITINERARY:

Day 1: Loreto, Baja California.

Days 2-6: Sea of Cortez.

Day 7: Return.

MEDIUM

December-January

SOBEK Expeditions

Rivers of Ecuador (SA 62)

RAFTING AND CULTURE— CLASS III

➤ *Two days of paddle rafting*

➤ *The emerald waters of the Pacific*

➤ *River safari into the Cayapas jungle*

Many of the world's great discoveries have been made along the equator. Humankind's earliest ancestors lived along the cross hairs of Africa; rice and corn first became domesticated in the equatorial climes of Southeast Asia and

Peru; and Darwin's insights into evolution followed his visit to the Galápagos Islands that straggle the planet's midsection. In Ecuador we discover our own equatorial wonders, including the lively rapids of the Río Toachi and the isolated Cayapas Indians of the Pacific coast.

We start with a city tour of Quito, a Spanish colonial city built on the ruins of the Incan empire. Called the Florence of the Americas for its colonial treasures of art and architecture, Quito is a city worth returning to, and so we will. First we drive to Cotopaxi, Equador's largest volcano and a spectacular national park. Then we descend through a landscape of active volcanoes and earthquake faults to the Toachi River. Our two-day paddle of the Toachi takes us through moderate rapids and by the isolated villages of the Colorado Indians—a total of fifteen miles through the aptly named Valle Hermoso.

Finally we head for the warm waters of the Pacific at Esmeraldas where, after a day of relaxing, we set out to explore the Cayapas River. Two days of jungle explora-tion by riverboat take us deep into the homeland of the Cayapas Indians, one of the many indigenous tribes still surviving along the equator in modern Ecuador. Upon returning to Quito, we find that even our brief encounter with the mysteries of the equator is enough to focus a new perspective on our world.

ITINERARY:

Day 1: Arrive Quito.

Day 2: To Cotopaxi.

Day 3: To Alluriquin and begin rafting.

Day 4: Down the Toachi to Valle Hermoso.

Day 5: To Esmeraldas.

Day 6: Begin river safari.

Day 7: Cayapas River.

Day 8: Return to Esmeraldas; fly to Quito.

Day 9: Otavalo Indian market; afternoon free.

Day 10: Return.

MEDIUM

May-November

Rioandes

Patagonia Explorer (SA 64) ‸‸‸‸‸

OVERLANDING—CLASS II

➤ *Canoeing through multicolored forests*
➤ *Trekking in Tierra del Fuego*
➤ *Patagonian splendor*

Pampas, peaks, and fjords are just a few of the components of the wild land at the end of the earth, Patagonia. Its history and reputation are intimidating—images of hardship and discomfort, of vast distances and great expanse, are closely associated with it. The extremes of Patagonia's weather and topography justify some of this, but the natural wonders of the area are surprisingly accessible.

In just two weeks SOBEK covers the best of Patagonia—Punta Arenas, Torres del Paine National Park, Lago Argentino, Moreno Glacier, Cerro Torre and Cerro Fitz Roy, the pampas, Tierra del Fuego, Ushuaia, and the Strait of Magellan. In our own heavy-duty van our small group meanders at a relaxed pace through the marvels of southern Chile and Argentina, enjoying the wilds in comfort. Don't hesitate to discover for yourself the farthest reach of the earth.

ITINERARY:

Days 1-2: Santiago.

Day 3: Punta Arenas.

Days 4-5: Torres del Paine.

Days 6-8: Lago Argentino.

Days 9-10: Glaciares National Park.

Day 11: Crossing the pampas.

Days 12-13: Tierra del Fuego.

Day 14: Punta Arenas.

Day 15: Santiago.

Day 16: Return.

PREMIUM

December-January

SOBEK Expeditions

Belize Barrier Reef (SA 65) ‸‸‸‸‸‸

SEA KAYAKING— CLASS III

➤ *Paddle offshore the Maya Mountains*
➤ *Camp on Caribbean cays*
➤ *Two weeks of tropical adventure*

The fastest-growing sport in adventure travel is sea kayaking—the self-propelled investigation of the interface between land and ocean. And in Belize, the model of stability in Central America, the environment is ripe and ready for a sea kayak exploration extraordinaire of the world's second longest barrier reef.

Stretching over 175 miles in a nearly unbroken wall, the Belize Barrier Reef protects the coastal Maya Mountains from the currents of the Caribbean and creates a sheltered lagoon twenty miles wide. It is in this lagoon, full of coral gardens and marine life, that we paddle our kayaks— surrounded by aqua blue waters that beg for diving, photography, fishing, and play. A local fisherman accompanies our small group to the offshore islands and reefs, harvesting a fresh feast nightly and sharing his knowledge of the sea and local culture.

Soon we'll be climbing coco palms and diving for shellfish with the best of them, going native with surpising ease.

At the end of our trip we head inland for a special tour of a manatee lagoon and a jaguar preserve, then hike into the jungle to visit an unrestored Mayan ruin. Finally, we paddle down a flat water stream out to the sea. There's more to Belize than readily meets the eye, and this trip by sea kayak is the way to discover it.

ITINERARY:

Day 1: Arrive Belize City, travel to Placencia on coast.

Day 2: Rig for trip and begin sea kayak tour.

Days 3-7: Sea kayaking Barrier Reef; island camping.

Day 8: Placencia.

Day 9: Manatee lagoon.

Day 10: Mayan hike.

Day 11: Jaguar preserve.

Day 12: Flat water river paddle.

Day 13: Drive to Belize City.

Day 14: Return.

MEDIUM

February-April

Slickrock Kayak Adventures

Costa Rica Explorer (SA 66)

NATURAL HISTORY
PACKAGE–CLASS I

➤ *Raft the Reventazon*

➤ *Air inclusive package*

➤ *Cloud forests and coasts*

Robert Harrison/SOBEK photo file

For those who have "discovered" Costa Rica, it is a country worth exploring in depth and detail time and again. Here, we delve into its amazing variety of flora and fauna with naturalists accompanying us most of the way.

Soon after our arrival in San José, the colonial capital city, we head out for a day of Class III whitewater rafting on the Reventazon River. This is a classy river, suitable for first-timers, yet rollicking enough for veterans. It is also a back door through some lush and wild country. Then we drive with a naturalist to Poas Volcano National Park and go to the 8,800-foot summit of what has been called the most beautiful active volcano in the hemisphere. Here the fantastic fauna of a high-altitude cloud forest grows right near the volcano's steaming crater, last afire only a decade ago.

Continuing through the misty cloud forests of the country's central cordillera, we arrive in Monteverde, a cloud forest reserve that is home to six different ecological communities and one of the world's most beautiful birds, the resplendent quetzal. We explore this area with a naturalist guide, and then fly by charter plane to Tortuguero National Park and the fabulous Tortuguero Lodge, a world-famous fishing resort known for its beautiful grounds, its tarpon and snook angling, and the thousands of green sea turtles that come up on the deserted beaches in front of the lodge from June to September to nest.

After two days in Tortuguero, we board the boat for a voyage to Limon through a canal system that connects the city with some isolated settlements in the rain forest, and in Limon we board a special narrow gauge train to San José. By trip's end we should have a new respect for this tiny, peaceful country that seems to have taken pains to protect rather than to exploit its natural blessings.

ITINERARY:

Day 1: Fly Miami to San José.

Day 2: Rafting.

Day 3: To Poas and Monteverde.

Day 4: Monteverde.

Day 5: San José.

Days 6-7: Tortuguero.

Day 8: Limon.

Day 9: Jungle train to San José.

Day 10: Return.

PREMIUM

Year-round

SOBEK Expeditions

Mayan Adventure (SA 68)

CULTURAL INTRODUCTION — CLASS I

➤ *Clear waters of Atitlán*
➤ *Jungle ruins of Tikal*
➤ *Colonial capital of Antigua*

Guatemala was the center of the ancient Mayan culture and it is still one of the richest cultural areas in Central America: Mayan life is alive in the highland villages and in the overgrown temples of the rain forest. For the amateur anthropologist or for the traveler eager to learn more about the prehistory of the New World, this trip is an ideal introduction to Guatemala's illustrious past. From the moment your eyes behold the crystal-clear waters of Lake Atitlán a separate reality takes over. Here lakeside markets are among the most colorful on earth, specializing in world-famous traditional weaving styles that are modern expressions of ancient Mayan art. Even the faces of the Indians look like New World gods.

Another kind of antiquity is found in Antigua, the peaceful old colonial capital leveled by earthquakes and volcanic eruption time and again since its founding in 1543. Then it's off to the Peten, the rain forest of lowland Central America where the Mayan culture reached its greatest heights. We visit several of the best-known sites, including Ceibal with its evidence of peaceful coexistence between Mayan and Toltec cultures, and Tikal with its elaborate buildings and game courts revealed through decades of excavation. At the end of our trip we will have discovered that antiquity truly lives in Guatemala and not just in the imagination.

ITINERARY:

Day 1: Guatemala City.

Day 2: Chichicastenango and Lake Atitlán.

Day 3: Antigua.

Day 4: Guatemala City.

Day 5: Petexbatun Lagoon.

Day 6: Aguateca ruins; Flores overnight.

Day 7: Tikal; return to Guatemala City.

Day 8: Departure.

MEDIUM

Year-round

SOBEK Expeditions

Manu National Park (SA 69)

NATURAL HISTORY / CANOE—CLASS III

➤ *Cloud forests*

➤ *Venture via canoes*

The National Park of Manu is the largest tropical park in South America, covering 1,800,000 hectares of pristine environments. Designated by the United Nations as a Biosphere Reserve, it is an area virtually untouched by the hand of Western Man—a unique ecozone of serene beauty encompassing highland savannahs, cloud forests, and lowland jungles, a land of clear oxbow lakes, birds, primates, and other small mammals. On our journey we'll explore a wide variety of tropical habitats and look for special species of plants and animals such as jaguar, tapir, capybaras, and river otters.

The trip begins in the fabulous, high Andean market city of Cuzco. From here we drive into the Paucartambo Valley, through the cloud forest and lowland jungles, and then over the pass at Acyanaco and along the fringes of the park. Then, with dugout canoes powered by outboard motors, we float down the Alto Madre de Dios River to its confluence with the rapids-filled, chocolate waters of the Manu River. After camping here on a riverine beach, we'll venture into the heart of Manu, passing tropical birds and riots of tropical vegetation. For the next several days we'll meander through the waterways and lakes, discovering the wildlife and primitive resplendence of a pure jungle wilderness. This is an intimate encounter with a small patch of the primeval.

ITINERARY:

Day 1: To Lima.

Day 2: To Cuzco.

Day 3: Drive to Salvación in the lowland jungle.

Day 4: To Boca Manu by canoe.

Days 5-8: Exploring Manu by canoe and trail.

Day 9: Salvación.

Day 10: Cuzco.

Day 11: Lima and return.

MODERATE

May-November

SOBEK Expeditions

Flight of the Condor (SA 70)

FLYING/NATURAL HISTORY—CLASS II

➤ *Beach clambakes and a gaucho barbecue*

➤ *Robinson Crusoe Island*

A grand voyage of contrasts in environment and color, from the subtropical South Pacific paradise of Robinson Crusoe Island to the blinding-white frozen continent of Antarctica—such is our trip on the *Condor Darwin*. In a specially modified DC-3, with increased window space for unparalled aerial viewing, we wing over 2,000 miles of some of the earth's most spectacular and seldom seen landscapes. The plush interior of the *Condor Darwin* is in the executive configuration with a capacity of just sixteen, so we have ample room and comfort as we pass above the coldest, most hostile seas in the Southern Hemisphere.

Starting from Santiago, Chile, we fly across the Pacific to Robinson Crusoe Island, where Alexander Selkirk spent three years as a castaway and became the inspiration for Daniel Defoe's classic novel. The island is now a World Biosphere Reserve, and we explore it by foot and by mule. Then we fly over the snowcapped volcanoes and deep-blue lagoons of Chile's Lake District to Puerto Montt, gateway to Patagonia. Then it's farther south to explore glaciers, lakes, and rivers brimming with trout. At Torres del Paine National Park we encounter guanacos, black-necked swans, and, if we're lucky, condors. Finally, a flight over Tierra del Fuego, Cape Horn, and the Drake Passage takes us to a Chilean Air Force strip on the Seventh Continent, Antarctica! Soar to the ultimate adventure.

SAMPLE ITINERARY: *Condor Darwin* Southbound

Day 1: Santiago.

Days 2-4: Robinson Crusoe Island.

Day 5: Puerto Montt.

Day 6: Roselot.

Day 7: Lago San Rafael.

Day 8: Lago O'Higgins.

Days 9-10: Torres del Paine.

Day 11: Puerto Williams.

Days 12-13: Antarctica.

Day 14: Punta Arenas.

Day 15: Return.

PREMIUM

October-February

SOBEK Expeditions

The Jivaro Indians (SA 71)

CULTURE – CLASS III

➤ *Walk among Incan ruins*
➤ *Experience cultural Immersion*

Journey to the tangled depths of the isolated Ecuadorian jungle in search of the Jivaro Indians, the world-famous headhunters of the Amazon. The Jivaros (or "Shuar," as they call themselves) are the only Indians in South America who still practice the ancient art of headshrinking, and until about twenty-five years ago the only heads they shrank were human ones!

This exciting sixteen-day expedition begins in Quito, a city that is the center of aristocratic Hispanic culture in Ecuador and is built on the ruins of a conquered Incan city. Here we'll visit ethnographic museums and meet our English-speaking guide. Then we fly over the southern Andes to the colonial city of Cuenca, the original home of the Panama hat, where we'll explore the archaeological site of Ingapirca, the northernmost ruins of the Incan Empire. Next we drive to Cajas National Park (at 13,000 ft., one of the highest in the world), where we mount horses and head into the Mazan Woods, a 600-year-old virgin forest. Then it's downhill, through the clouds, into the Amazon Basin. By small plane we'll head to Miazal in the foothills of the Cutucu Mountain Ridge and from there travel by canoe into Shuar country.

The next week is spent plying the serpentine rivers of the Amazon, stopping and staying at Shuar villages, learning and living the rain forest life. We'll meet their shamans, participate in their ceremonies, absorb their customs and unique culture, join in blowgun hunts, bathe in their hidden thermal springs, and eat their exotic foods. This is an extraordinary encounter with rites and passages and people on the living edge.

ITINERARY:

Day 1: Quito.

Days 2-5: Highlands excursion; parks, markets, and the Andes on horseback.

Days 6-10: Jivaro expedition; in the village experiencing everyday life.

Day 11: Macas.

Day 12: Quito.

Day 13: Saquisili Indian market.

Day 14: Quito.

Day 15: Otavalo.

Day 16: Return.

MEDIUM

November-February; July-August

SOBEK Expeditions

Antarctic Scientific Expedition (SA 72)

RESEARCH ADVENTURE – CLASS III

➤ *Adventure at the bottom of the earth*
➤ *Really cool scientific research*

Antarctica is a world treasure, an entire continent that knew not the footsteps of humankind until this century. As such, it is a test case for our resolve to save the Earth, and by joining the Antarctic Scientific Expedition you can do your part, while enjoying a fascinating look at this unique and isolated world. After arrival in Punta Arenas, Chile, a flight to King George Island and the Antarctic

Peninsula allows a first glimpse of the forgotten continent, in preparation for nearly a week of interactive research with scientists from around the world.

Locations and projects for each departure will vary, but some of the research to be undertaken includes studying penguin and seal colonies, reading magnetometers and doing other geological research, and making human impact studies. No formal experience is necessary, and guides and liaisons with the scientific community will ensure that the trip is safe and comfortable. Let Antarctica be more than a white expanse on your globe. Let it be an inspiration for the rest of your life, a place where you made a difference.

ITINERARY:

Day 1: Arrive Punta Arenas.

Day 2: Fly to King George Island.

Days 3-12: Tour Antarctic Peninsula and participate in research.

Days 13: Return to Punta Arenas.

Day 14: Fly homeward.

PREMIUM

November-December

SOBEK Expeditions

La Manzanilla Kayak/Camping Tour (SA 200)

KAYAKING/CAMPING— CLASS II

➤ *Kayak the Manzanilla Lagoon*

➤ *Visit the village of Barra de Navidad*

➤ *Body surfing and bird-watching*

Meet your group on a secluded beach in the jungles of southwestern Mexico, just three hours south of Puerto Vallarta. The exact location is Tenacatita Bay outside the forgotten fishing village of La Manzanilla. Palapa huts surrounded by swaying palm trees serve as our base camp for this eight-day kayaking and camping adventure. From here we hike in the jungle to the deserted beach of Tomarinda, paddle to the "aquarium" for some snorkeling, deep sea fishing "Mexican style," and then paddle south for two days along the coast to the village of Barra de Navidad, one of the largest winter nesting grounds for the double-crested cormorant. In the intricate, uncharted waterways of Manzanilla Lagoon we look for great herons, snowy egrets, king fishers, and alligatorlike caimans. And in the village of La Manzanilla we can practice our Spanish and bargain with the locals, or just hang out and observe everyday life. Expect the unexpected on this trip, as well as great body surfing, hiking, fishing, kayaking, and bird-watching.

ITINERARY:

Day 1: Arrive Puerto Vallerta.

Day 2: Jungle hike, snorkeling.

Day 3: Tenacatita Bay.

Days 4-5: Paddling.

Day 6: Leisure.

Day 7: Manzanilla Lagoon.

Day 8: Puerto Vallarta.

Cost includes: boats, camping and cooking gear, food, and all ground transportation.

MODERATE

December-January

Outback Expeditions, Inc.

Europe

Haute Route Ski (EU 10)

SKIING—CLASS III

➤ *Ski the top of Europe*

➤ *Traverse glaciers*

➤ *Cozy Alpine huts*

The high-level route traverses glacier passes among the great Alpine peaks, from Chamonix in the west to Saas Fee in the east. This is the most famous and highly prized ski tour in the Alps, holding a unique attraction for ski mountaineers, tourers, and a large number of fit cross-country skiers who yearn and yodel for the high country.

The classic high level route covers a distance of eighty miles and can be divided into two stages, with alternative side routes offering equally powerful powder prospects. Chamonix, the capital of Alpine activities on rock and ice, hosts us for four days as we ski among the most majestic and dramatic mountains in Europe—Tiolet, Dolent, Droit and Charbon among others. Then we move up to other haute route huts—Trient, Chaanrion, and Vignettes—including a fantastic run down to Zermatt, Switzerland, beneath the classic form of the Matterhorn.

ITINERARY:

Day 1: En route.

Day 2: Arrive Geneva, depart for Chamonix.

Days 3-5: Chamonix.

Days 6-10: Haute Route.

Day 11: Zermatt.

Days 12-14: Monta Rosa Hut.

Day 15: Saas Fee.

Day 16: Saas.

Day 17: Chamonix.

Day 18: Return.

MEDIUM

April

Alpine Adventures

Sierra Nevada (EU 13)

MODERATE BACKPACKING— CLASS III

➤ *Backpacking through Andalusia*

➤ *Delicious food of southern Spain*

➤ *Historic inns*

The southern slopes of the Sierra Nevadas are known as Las Alpujarras, and a distinctive Moorish influence pervades the customs, food, and architecture in this region. On this trek through the area's wooded valleys and open highlands, we witness a timeless way of life, and share a culture rooted deep in history.

We will visit remote Andalusian hill villages, white-walled and decorated with hanging flowers, as well as tour the most romantic and enchanting of Spanish cities, Granada. We'll stay at Lanjaron, a Moorish spa town, and Canar, a tiny mountain village perched like an aerie on the rocks above the valley of the Guadalfeo. We'll hike through forests of pine and eucalyptus to the snow line, and cool off in the Río Chico. In the National Park of Sierra Nevada we will find mountain buck, chamois, and partridges, and perhaps the royal eagle. And all along our route we'll sample the delicious Alpujarran cuisine, including *gazpacho andaluz* (cold, tomato-based soup), *choto al ajillo* (lamb and garlic), and *truchas con jamón* (trout with ham).

We end the hike where the land meets the sea, at the little town of Salobrena, at a castle looking out over the bay. This is a civilized backpacking tour, and we end it happy and well-fed.

ITINERARY:

Day 1: Fly London to Málaga.

Day 2: Lanjaron.

Days 3-12: On trek.

Days 13-14: Granada.

Day 15: Return to London.

MEDIUM

May, July-August

Exodus Expeditions

Classic British Walks (EU 14) ◣▬▬▬▬▬▬

HISTORIC WALKING TOURS— CLASS II/III

➤ *Rolling hills and misty moors*
➤ *Smuggler's caves and medieval castles*
➤ *Time travel through literary history*

To walk in Britain is to chase the great voices of literature—the Scotland of Burns, the Lake District of Wordsworth, the Irish moors of Yeats, the wild coast of du Maurier, the Cotswolds of Shakespeare. Each of these eight-day walking tours is based on day hikes that challenge one's literary and historical imagination more than muscular endurance, although this is not a trip for couch potatoes. We do explore the British Isles on foot, walking from six to twelve miles a day. The point is to focus our attention not on conquering mountains but on the landscape and its wealth of romantic tales and historical richness. And we're helped in this task by experienced local guides, three square meals a day, and a van to transport our luggage. At night we almost always stay in historic inns or public houses.

In the Scottish Highlands we hike up craggy peaks and across vast, empty moors, looking for red deer, mountain goats, golden eagles, and wildflowers. The mountain scenery is superb, the paths are rugged, and the names of the places we go as enigmatic as the people: Stob Dearg; Sgorr Dhonuill; Ven Nevis (Britain's highest mountain); and Loch Eilde Mor.

In the Lake District, long a favorite of English trekkers, we hike along rolling fells, babbling brooks, and serene lakes. Here, as Wordsworth said, "All that is needed is an eye to perceive and a heart to enjoy." We start in Keswick, where we climb Blencathra and Shiddaw via Sharp

Edge, and the next day hike to Buttermere. From there it's on to Wasdale,
Seathwaite, Patterdale, and finally to the
"poet's village" of Grassmere.

In the Irish Moors and Mountains
Walking Tour, we hike through lush green
hill country dotted with rock walls, Gaelic
graveyards, and medieval castles. In addition to Mother Nature, we encounter
endless historical and natural surprises,
not to mention Irish folk music in the
pubs and a touch of the blarney. Starting
in An Laithreach in the Wicklow Mountains, we travel to Galway, and then to the
town of Doolin, the center of folk music
in western Ireland.

In the Southwest Coast of England,
we capture the atmosphere of Daphne du
Maurier's *Jamaica Inn*, visit the Poldark
mines of Zennor, pass through Lamorna
Cover, home of spy novelist John Le
Carré, and stand at the westernmost tip of
England. The walk begins in the Roman
city of Bath and from there we head out
the coastal path, where the wild Atlantic
swell crashes into the cliffs. Along the way
we attend, if possible, an open-air play at
the Mynack Theatre and visit the monastery at St. Michael's Mount.

In the Cotswolds, we start at Stratford
upon Avon and from there walk from garden, to church, to museum, to showpiece
village to manor house, to more gardens,
to sights so picturesque they sometimes
seem unreal. This is a world of gentle hills,
beautiful plantings, and fine old houses,
and our walk through it gives us time to
explore some of its civilized pleasures.

SAMPLE ITINERARY,
Lake District:

Day 1: London to Carlisle; overnight
Keswick.

Day 2: Ascend Blencathra via Sharp Edge.

Day 3: Hike Derwent Fells to Buttermere.

Day 4: Hike Black Sail Pass to Wasdale.

Day 5: Wasdale to Seathwaite via Scafel
Pike.

Day 6: Drive to Patterdale; hike Helvelyn
Cirque back to Seathwaite.

Day 7: Hike to Grassmere; drive to
Ambleside.

Day 8: Return to London.

MEDIUM

Lake District: *May, July-August*

Southwest Coastal Path: *April-May,
July, September*

Scotland: *June, August*

Ireland: *June*

Costwolds Way: *July*

SOBEK Expeditions

Tour du Mont Blanc (EU 15) ▲▲▲▲▲▲

ALPINE HIKING —
CLASS III

➤ *Switzerland, Italy, and France*

➤ *Hike through the great Alps*

➤ *Family hotels and mountain huts*

A classic Alpine hiking tour takes us
among the highest mountains in
Europe, crossing the snow-braced passes
of the three countries that converge in the
Alps. Here, we are in the birthplace of
modern mountaineering. The scenery
here is a photographer's dream: tumbling
glaciers and soaring peaks, idyllic valleys
and distant visions. And it's capped by
15,771-foot Mont Blanc, of such
monumental scale that it towers over
Western Europe like a cosmic law.

This thirteen-day package involves
moderate hiking to elevations no greater
than 9,045 feet, which we reach on our

fourth day of hiking at Tete du Nord des Fours. We walk for ten of the thirteen days, with several short bus shuttles to different trail systems. During our nights in mountain huts we will experience the international spirit of the Alps. These rustic chalets serve as remote yet lively centers for a colorful entourage of trekkers, and breathe a poetic Old World ambience. The trip originates and ends at the famous French mountain resort of Chamonix, and it is here that our fond farewell dinner leaves us longing still for the high country above all borders.

ITINERARY:

Day 1: Arrive Chamonix.

Day 2: Bus to Les Houches; begin hike.

Day 3: To Glacier de Bionnassay, Col de Tricot.

Day 4: Les Contamines to Chalet de la Balme.

Day 5: Tete du Nord des Fours; overnight Refuge des Mottets.

Day 6: Hike to Courmayeur, Italy.

Day 7: Courmayeur.

Day 8: Bus to Switzerland; hike over Grand Col Ferret.

Day 9: Bus to Champex; hiking to Trient.

Day 10: Trient to Tre la Champ, France.

Day 11: Hike to Chamonix.

Day 12: Depart.

MEDIUM

July-August

SOBEK Expeditions

Transylvanian Alps (EU 23)

MOUNTAIN TREK— CLASS III

➤ *Visit Count Dracula's castle*
➤ *Charming medieval cities*
➤ *Mysterious mountains and misty moors*

Of all the mountains in Europe, none are more shrouded in mystery than the Transylvanian Alps. The Bran Castle, home of Dracula, drapes an unearthly aura over the rugged Romanian terrain of misted lakes and barely believable wildlife. We take two weeks to traverse the entire length of these Alps (traveling only by daylight), highlighted by an easy ascent of Mt. Moldoveanu (8,344 ft.), highest in Romania.

Accommodations will be in selected mountain chalets, where the cuisine reeks of the protective "stinking rose," garlic. The July departure features the annual folk festival at Durau, and two days of trekking in the Ceahlau Mountains, while on the September trip we spend the full moon at Dracula's castle. Anything can happen in Transylvania, so be prepared for the experience of this lifetime—or the one beyond.

ITINERARY:

Day 1: Bucharest.

Day 2: To Busteni; begin trek.

Days 3-14: On trek.

Days 15-16: Sibiu.

Days 17-19: Curau folk festival (July); or Bran Castle (September).

Days 20-21: Bucharest.

Day 22: Return.

(**Note:** Shorter seventeen-day itinerary also available.)

MODERATE

July-September

Above The Clouds

The Mountains of Greece (EU 25) ∿∿∿

MOUNTAIN TREK—
CLASS III

➤ *Traditional hillside villages*

➤ *Ancient, snowcapped peaks*

➤ *A Mediterranean beach awaits*

The great limestone crags and the chasms of the Pindos Mountains march to the sea from the northwest corner of Greece, creating a buffer that has isolated this region from time. Little has changed here since King Phillip of Macedonia, and even the tourist industry has ignored the area and left it peacefully alone. The landscape is awe-inspiring; peaks cluster here, Smolkas and Gamila and Vasslitsa reach the 7,500-foot range; sheer cliffs stretch thousands of feet to the bottom of massive gorges; beech and fir blanket the hills.

Although we stay in inns and huts, we carry our own gear into the wild heights, visiting neat villages surrounded by terraced hillsides, glimpsing the graceful Grecian goats, and ascending to the summits if our enthusiasms so carry us. Then take it easy—the soft coast at Parga waits to soothe your weary legs, the Mediterranean sun to warm your tired bones.

ITINERARY:

Day 1: Arrive in Corfu, ferry and bus to Ioannina.

Day 2: Ioannina.

Days 3-11: Mountain hiking.

Day 12: Ioannina.

Days 13-14: Parga.

Day 15: Return.

MODERATE

June-September

Exodus Expeditions

Aegean Odyssey (EU 42) ⚡⚡⚡

SAILING
ADVENTURE—CLASS I

➤ *Cool breezes and Aegean sun*

➤ *Skippered 30- and 50-foot yachts*

➤ *Retrace Odysseus' route*

Island-hopping his way through the Mediterranean, Odysseus left his mark not only on literature, but on the world's conception of adventure travel. At the heart of his journey was the sailing ship, and our "Aegean Odysseys" make full use of its charms. Packages of one to four weeks permit passengers to sail the seas between Greece and Turkey, visiting a handful or a harvest of Grecian isles in the Cyclades and Dodecanese island groups. Highlights might include the Temple of Poseidon at the edge of the Attic Peninsula; the beautiful piney isle of Kea and the mineral springs of nearby Kithnos; the historical landscape of Thira, that some believe is the volcanic ruin of Atlantis; the island of Delos, the divine birthplace of Apollo and Artemis; or perhaps Patmos, where St. John experienced the Revelation in the Cave of the Apocalypse.

Each island is different, with its own individual history and mythology to link time and imagination; each island is caressed by the rosy fingers of dawn. Kakavia, baklava, and retsina enliven our cuisine in local taverns, and capable skippers illuminate our sea trek with the lusty, bloody, powerful, and hilarious legends of ancient times.

ITINERARY:

Day 1: Departure from Athens, Paros, Patmos, or Rhodes.

Days 2-6: On cruise.

Day 7: Services end midday, or can be extended for additional weeks by previous arrangement.

MEDIUM

April-October

Eurotrek

Tour de France (EU 45)

MODERATE BICYCLING — CLASS II

➤ *Wheel through the wine country*

➤ *Pedal by prehistoric cave paintings*

➤ *Bike from Burgundy to the Bay of Biscay*

France is a cyclist's dream. Magnificent scenery, historic monuments, the wine regions and famous castles, fortifications, and medieval towns can all be experienced from a dense network of well-kept, small back roads, used infrequently by motorists. For fourteen days we are free to choose from a wide variety of routes as we

cross through the very heart of the country, connecting the historic grape-growing centers of Beaune, Pommard, Volney, and Mersault.

Beginning in Zurich, our route includes such well-known regions as Burgandy, the Dordogne, the fabulous castles of the Loire Valley, the Garden of France, and for a grand finale, the Cevennes Mountains from north to south, through the famous Tarn Gorge.

You can take your own bike, which can easily be transported by the support coach that accompanies the tour throughout the ride, and you can choose to cycle stages of ten, twenty-five, or even fifty miles. The coach carries all our camping, cooking, and personal gear—an arrangement that is easy on your back and allows you more time for enjoying the sights and savory flavors of France.

ITINERARY:

Day 1: Basel, Switzerland; begin cycle.

Day 2: Burgundy.

Days 3-5: Auvergne.

Days 6-9: Dordogne Valley.

Days 10-11: Hourtin Plage.

Days 12-13: Loire Valley.

Day 14: Basel, trip ends.

MEDIUM

June-September

Eurotrek

Western Ireland (EU 48) ▲▲▲▲▲▲

CULTURAL — CLASS II

➤ *Hike back in time to Ole Ireland*

➤ *Stay in historic B&Bs*

➤ *Bend elbows in the finest pubs*

While most of Ireland has left behind its native tongue and much of its past, one section of the country carries on many of its cultural traditions as in days of old. Throughout Connemara and the Aran Islands, the traveler has the distinct feeling of having stepped into the pages of historical Ireland. Age-old rhythms persist here, embodied by the traditions of the local musicians and instrument makers, the shepherds and weavers of woolen goods, the world-famous local pubs and the raising and racing of the legendary Connemara horses.

We will drive along the fabulous coast road to Clifden, climb the magnificent hills of the Benna Beola, the Mweelrea, and the Maumturk mountains, and ride boats to some of the offshore emerald isles and bird sanctuaries. We'll explore Raigh,

in the heart of James Joyce country, and the Clonmacnoise Heritage Site on the River Shannon. We will dip deeply into the local culture, staying at homey Bed and Breakfasts, and walking through some of the most picturesque countryside Europe has to offer.

ITINERARY:

Days 1-2: Galway.

Days 3-8: Connemara district.

Days 9-10: Aran Islands.

Day 11: Ferry to Galway.

Day 12: Train to Dublin.

Day 13: Dublin.

Day 14: Return.

MEDIUM

August

Above The Clouds

Chatkal River (EU 53) 〰

RIVER RAFTING — CLASS IV / V

➤ *Challenging whitewater rafting*

➤ *Indigenous culture of Kazakhstan*

➤ *Central Asia's unknown Tien Shan Range*

The mystery mountains of Asia are the Tien Shan, a tough cluster of 14,000-foot peaks so isolated that legends of their grandeur led early explorers to guess they were twice as high.

Slicing through them is the Chatkal River, SOBEK's newest whitewater discovery—a bouncing beauty of a river with Class IV-plus rapids and exploratory side hikes. Through an action extravaganza

like this doesn't need the contrast of cultural interest, this one has it. We explore the highlights of Moscow, visiting the Kremlin, the famous cathedral of St. Basil's, the Rembrandts at the Pushkin Museum, Lenin's Tomb, and even GUM, Russia's largest department store. From Moscow we fly to Kazakhstan, just north of Afghanistan, for an altogether different look at Soviet culture. Here we find ethnic Turkmen, Kirghiz, Uzbek, and other seminal peoples of Central Asia.

Our 160-mile race down the Chatkal lasts eight days, during which the rapids become increasingly challenging, including at least one possible portage over a Class V drop. Fishing, stunning scenery, isolated Moslem villages, and the exotic nature of Central Asia combine with world-class whitewater to create a magical adventure. If you've run the best rivers of the West, now's your chance to challenge the best of the rest—the Chatkal of the Soviet Union.

ITINERARY:

Day 1: Moscow.

Day 2: City tour.

Day 3: Fly to Kazakhstan; drive to Chatkal.

Day 4: Rigging and begin river trip.

Days 5-12: On the Chatkal.

Day 13: End river trip, drive to Khira.

Day 14: Aral Sea.

Day 15: Fly to Moscow.

Day 16: Return to U.S.

PREMIUM

September-October

SOBEK Expeditions

Whitewater France (EU 54)

MODERATE RAFTING— CLASS III

- ➤ *Ride wild rivers*
- ➤ *Sample civilized Paris*
- ➤ *The Grand Canyon of France*

Not far from the fashionable beaches of St. Tropez are the southern Alps, which boast beautiful and impressive river valleys. Here, untamed rivers are watered by snow-covered mountains and the glaciers of Haute Savoie flow under warm Mediterranean skies. For nine days we navigate the waters of four of these rivers—short and sweet trips to little-known valleys.

We begin with the Argens, a new dis-covery that snakes through forested wilderness with surprises at every bend. The Durance is next, with powerful branching waters, eroded precipices, poplar-punctuated river meadows, and large shady campsites. Then the Grand Canyon of the Verdon, with challenging whitewater and natural wonders reminis-cent of its American namesake. And finally the Var, where a wide, unspoiled mountain valley leads into the Gorges de Daluis, and deeply fissured red rock walls encase raging whitewater with brief inter-vals of lush greenery. This is a whitewater holiday where you might least expect it: the rivers of southern France.

ITINERARY:

Day 1: Zurich; by coast to France.

Day 2: The Argens.

Day 3: Hike the Grand Canyon of the Verdon.

Days 4-5: The Verdon.

Days 6-7: The Var.

Day 8: Côte d'Azur.

Day 9: To Zurich and return.

MEDIUM

April-July

Atalante

Rioni River (EU 56)

MODERATE WALKING AND RAFTING—CLASS III

- ➤ *Day hikes in the Caucasus Mountains*
- ➤ *A week of class III whitewater*
- ➤ *Moscow city tour*

The Caucasus Mountains separate the Black Sea from the Caspian Sea and, in a larger sense, Asia from Europe. They are, accordingly, a region of extreme sig-nificance, not only geographically and politically but historically as well. Here Hercules rescued the Greek god of fire, Prometheus, and Jason sought the Golden Fleece; here Christianity and Islam have fought a 1,400-year duel over the allegiance of the mountain inhabi-tants; and here we find snowcapped peaks more than three miles high, capped by 18,470-foot Mt. Elbrus, the crown of Europe.

Naturally this sturdy range is a birth-place to rivers as well, and we focus our attention on the Rioni, a swift-moving stream of Class III rapids passing through deep canyons and isolated villages. Nearby are ancient monasteries. We also hike the Caucasus to meet the people of this pivotal land, and they share with us the local wine and hospitality. On this trip as in all our excursions in Russia, we are hop-ing the ''trickle-down'' theory works in reverse, and our riverside friendships will enrich relations between the superpowers.

ITINERARY:

Day 1: Arrive Moscow.

Day 2: City tour.

Day 3: Fly to Kutaisi; bus to Utsera.

Days 4-7: Day hikes in the Caucasus.

Day 8: Begin rafting the Rioni.

Days 9-11: Rafting.

Day 12: End river trip; drive to Kutaisi.

Day 13: Fly to Moscow.

Day 14: Return.

PREMIUM

July

SOBEK Expeditions

Trek the Central Caucasus (EU 57)

MODERATE TREKKING— CLASS III

➤ *Pristine mountain heights*

➤ *Soviet Georgian hospitality*

➤ *Two 3-day treks*

The Andes, the Alps, the Himalayas, and now the Caucasus. This latter one is by all counts a major mountain range, blessed with a dozen 15,000-foot-plus peaks and capped by the highest mountain in Europe, Mt. Elbrus, over 3,000 feet higher than Mont Blanc and 4,000 feet higher than the Matterhorn. Here glacial systems have carved rugged couloirs, high waterfalls, and isolated tarns, and the scent of Alpine wildflowers wafts across the thin air of the little-visited trails. Now is the time to trek the Caucasus, when a rare window of opportunity has been opened by glasnost. For the first time in nearly a century, the people of East and West can share the glories of Russia's great mountain range.

The adventure begins on a chair lift to the foot of the Donguz-Orun Pass. The pass affords spectacular views of Elbrus and is our gateway to the Nakra River Valley, which we descend on a forested trail dotted with clusters of wild strawberries and raspberries. Between treks we stay at a mountaineer's camp in Mestia, the capital of Svanetia, a rarely visited district of Soviet Georgia known for its mountain people and good food. From Mestia we trek up the Yosemite-like Dolra Valley to a campsite beneath Bichow Pass (11,500 ft.). The pass, which crosses the Bichow Glacier, is one of the most dramatic in the Caucasus.

The trip can be combined with the Rioni River (EU 56) to give a fuller look at the wild wonders of this noble mountain range. And remember, no matter how tough the trail, every step you take will be a step toward peace.

ITINERARY:

Day 1: Arrive Moscow.

Day 2: City tour.

Day 3: Fly to Caucasus, drive to trail head and begin trek.

Days 4-5: On trek, Yusengi and Dolra river trails.

Day 6: Mestia.

Days 7-11: On trek, Nakra River trails.

Day 12: End trek, return to Mestia.

Day 13: Fly to Moscow.

Day 14: Return.

PREMIUM

June-July

SOBEK Expeditions

Journey to Kazakhstan (EU 58)

TREKKING AND CULTURE—CLASS IV

➤ *Trek the Tien Shan Mountains*

➤ *The watershed of East and West*

➤ *Nomadic cultures of Central Asia*

Buried in the heart of Asia are the Tien Shan Mountains, home to the legendary Kirghiz and Kazakh tribes. As empires rose and fell to the east and west of the Tien Shan, the nomadic people who inhabit these mountains continued the eternal cycle of grazing their flocks, casting a hardened eye at the dance of progress outside their domain. Now we have an opportunity to explore the dazzling landscapes of Kazakhstan even as this last unexplored boundary between Russia and China contemplates entrance to the twenty-first century.

Eleven days of trekking, sometimes in the company of horses, take us through a world where rock spires pierce the high skies, powerful glaciers move with invisible deliberation, and the ancient caravan routes still wind between the riches of the East and the marketplaces of the West. One of our destinations is Pobedy Base Camp beneath Victory Peak, at 24,406 feet a mountain of grand scale indeed. Our route is rendered accessible—and interesting—by truck rides, pack horses, fixed ropes, inflated rubber boats, and a helicopter flight. When we visit the squat yurts of the Kirgiz nomads, we glimpse a life-style that may pass within a generation, giving us the dubious privilege of being among the last to witness this ancient culture.

ITINERARY:

Day 1: Arrive Moscow.

Day 2: Moscow city tour.

Day 3: Fly to Alma-Ata.

Day 4: Karakala camp.

Day 5: Acclimatize to environment.

Day 6: Drive to trail head and begin trekking.

Days 7-16: On trek.

Day 17: Helicopter flight to Karakala.

Day 18: Visit yurt camp.

Day 19: Drive to Alma-Ata, return to Moscow.

Day 20: Moscow.

Day 21: Return.

MEDIUM

June-August

SOBEK Expeditions

Adventure USSR (EU 59)

CULTURE AND VARIETY—CLASS III

➤ *Trek and raft the Pamirs*

➤ *Explore Lake Baikal*

➤ *Ancient ruins of Samarkand*

The land of opportunity for adventure travel is unmistakably the Soviet Union, a sprawling land of natural wonders and human heritage. From the cornucopia of possibilities, SOBEK has selected two areas to focus on during this trip: the Uzbekistan in Soviet Central Asia, where ancient Islamic and tribal cultures still thrive, and the Lake Baikal region of Siberia, an area of great concern to Soviet environmentalists. On this trip we combine tours of the architectural delights of Imperial Moscow and ancient Samarkand, with trekking, rafting, and biking excursions in the Pamirs and around Baikal.

Moscow's grandeur starts it all, followed by a flight to Samarkand in Soviet Central Asia, a town where the emirates of the ancient Silk Road were defeated by the Czar's armies in the nineteenth century. Samarkand is an up-to-date Soviet city, but it is also an exciting mix of peoples, history, and architecture. It is one of the world's oldest cities—capital city for Tamerlane the Conqueror (1336-1405)—and it is full of masterpieces of Islamic architecture: Tamerlane's version of the Taj Mahal, the Gur Emir's infamous crypt, and Registan, which Lord Curzon called the "noblest public square in the world."

A two-hour drive brings us to Penjikent, site of archaeological excavations of an eighth century city and gateway to our Pamir trek. Here we are in the shadow of some of the world's highest mountains. The Pamirs are the central knot from which five of the planet's greatest mountain ranges flow, spreading out from it like spokes on a wheel: the Tien Shan, the Kun Lun, the Karakoram, the Hindu Kush, and the Great Himalaya itself. We trek through this area, passing by the Muzgor Lakes, and hiking along mountain ridges separated by the unusual phenomenon of earth walls deposited by a passing glacier. We cross two 11,000-foot passes and end the trek with a hike through a stunted forest in the shadow of snow-covered peaks. To cap it off, we drive to a nearby Class II river and spend an enjoyable day of rafting.

Then its on to Lake Baikal in Siberia, the world's deepest lake and one of its clearest too. The remoteness of the area and of the Siberian villages and people in them make this an enthralling region to explore, and we do it on foot, on horseback, and, if we choose, by raft. SOBEK is

working with a peace and environmental organization in the USSR which will be partly responsible for operating this trip. And they will help us to understand Soviet environmental issues—including the threat to over 1,100 species of marine life that inhabit Lake Baikal. The lake is threatened by industrial and agricultural development, and it is our hope that we can promote environmental concerns in the area by demonstrating the benefits of responsible tourism.

And if all this only whets your appetite for more, there is an optional one-week, lodge-based adventure in the Caucasus Mountains near Mt. Elbrus, Europe's highest peak. The superb culture and scenery of this Caucasian-influenced area adds a nice contrast to the Asian and Mongol feel of Uzbekistan and Siberia.

ITINERARY:

Day 1: Arrive Moscow.

Day 2: Moscow city tour.

Day 3: Samarkand.

Days 4-7: Pamirs trek.

Day 8: Rafting.

Day 9: To Lake Baikal.

Days 10-12: Hike, bike, cruise lake.

Day 13: Return to Moscow.

Day 14: Fly to U.S.

Caucasus Option:

Day 1: Moscow.

Days 2-6: Lodge near Elbrus; hike, ride horses, enjoy local culture.

Day 7: Fly to Moscow.

Day 8: Return to U.S.

PREMIUM

July-August

SOBEK Expeditions

Mountains of Tuscany (EU 60)

WALKING TOUR—
CLASS III

➤ *Villages and vineyards of northern Italy*

➤ *Hike the Apuan Alps*

➤ *From Genoa to Florence*

The backbone of Italy is the Apennines mountain range, which arches from Genoa down the seam of the boot to Mt. Etna at the toe. At the leading edge of this range are the Apuan Alps, which border the rich wine-growing region of Tuscany, a province of great historic as well as vinicultural importance. Here the Etruscan civilization arose, Galileo studied falling bodies, and the literary language of Italy was born.

We spend most of our two weeks in Tuscany exploring the rugged Apuan Alps on a long and sometimes difficult trek, rising early to hike through beech and chestnut woods en route to Alpine meadows. Along the way we stay in mountain huts or small hotels. Finally we reach the dazzling white peaks of Pania della Croce, Monte Sagro, and Monte Tambura, each shouldering its way over a mile into the blue skies of northern Italy.

On the last day, we go to Florence, one of the centers of European culture from Renaissance times. The Medici family ruled here during the fourteenth century and their sponsorship helped spark the creative fires of Dante, Boccaccio, da Vinci, and Michelangelo among others. Our aspirations are more modest: a loaf of panna, a jug of vino, and a thousand fond memories.

ITINERARY:

Day 1: Genoa to Campocecina.

Day 2: Minuciano.

Day 3: Campagrina.

Days 5-6: Strazzema.

Day 7: Isola Santa.

Day 8: Passo della Radici.

Day 9: Lagosanto.

Days 10-11: Boscolungo.

Day 12: Lago Scaffaiolo.

Day 13: Pracchia.

Day 14: Firenze (Florence).

MEDIUM

July-September

SOBEK Expeditions

Travels without a Donkey (EU 61)

WALKING IN FRANCE—
CLASS II

➤ *Hike the highlands of the Loire*

➤ *150 miles of timeless trail*

Over a century ago Robert Louis Stevenson set out to cross the Cevennes Range in southern France in the company of a single intractable ass. His resulting book, *Travels with a Donkey*, is a charming look at a country that seemed antiquarian even then. Now we can follow his route on this walking tour, which begins in Le Monastier, in the meadows and forests of the upper Loire River Valley, and takes us over the Cevennes, the range that protects central France from the Mediterranean breezes.

We hike some 150 miles over the downland range of Lozere to the great gorges of the Cevennes, and then descend, through the chestnut forests of the windward slopes, to the coastal plains of the Mediterranean. Here at trail's end in St. Jean du Gard, we reward our efforts with the ruby beverage of Carignan, the most productive red wine grape in the world.

Staying at family-run hotels or village inns and enjoying the good simple foods of southern France and ''vin de table'' throughout, this easy hike shows us that in some places in the world change is beside the point.

ITINERARY:

Day 1: Montpellier to Le Monastier sur Gazeille.

Day 2: Goudet.

Day 3: Costaros.

Day 4: Pradelles.

Day 5: Luc.

Day 6: La Bastide Puylaurent.

Day 7: Chasserades.

Day 8: Le Bleymard.

Days 9-11: Le Pont-de-Montvert to Florac.

Day 12: St. Privat de Vallongue.

Day 13: St. Germain-de-Calberte.

Day 14: St. Jean-du-Gard.

MEDIUM

May-June, August-September

SOBEK Expeditions

Arctic Safaris (EU 62)

AERIAL ADVENTURE—
CLASS I

> *The fumaroles of Iceland*
> *Greenland's Inuit villages*
> *Explore the lonely Faroe Islands*

The remote corners of northern Europe have been a footnote to history, bypassed by the rise and fall of civilizations. Yet this is just what the adventure traveler seeks—new perspectives on old lands. On this trip we look into the overlooked, with an itinerary tailor-made for the particular interests and priorities of a small group. The mode of transport is a nine-passenger propjet, the Mitsubishi MU-2.

After meeting in Reykjavik, Iceland, each six-person tour group will have its choice of three major destinations in Europe's Arctic reaches, each with hotel accommodations. The Faroe Islands are a lonely outpost in the North Atlantic Sea between Iceland, Norway, and Scotland. Here we can explore a magnificent landscape of rocky slopes, fresh green grasses, rugged coasts, and rare bird species. In the other direction, Greenland's Ammassalik region offers the traveler insight into the traditional life-style of the Inuit, the farthest east-ranging of the Eskimo people who crossed into the New World from Siberia. And, of course, there's Iceland itself, a geological museum adrift in the Atlantic, with hot springs, volcanoes, and fumaroles galore.

SAMPLE ITINERARY:

Day 1: Fly to Reykjavik.

Day 2: Visit Vestman Islands; fly to Kulusuk, East Greenland.

Day 3: Boat cruise.

Day 4: Fly to Faroe Islands.

Day 5: Faroes; return to Akuregri, North Iceland.

Day 6: Reykjavik.

Day 7: Return to U.S.

PREMIUM

July-August

Odin Air

Spitsbergen (EU 200) ∿∿∿

TREK/SAILING — CLASS III

➤ *Explore an Arctic desert by midnight sun*

➤ *Sail through a labyrinth of glaciers*

➤ *Observe abundant wildlife*

The largest island of the Svalbard Archipelago, Spitsbergen lies some 621 miles northwest of Norway, around the seventy-ninth parallel. It is one of the Arctic lands nearest to the North Pole; its latitude is about the same as Thule, Greenland. Nevertheless, this island is notably warmed by the Gulf Stream waters. Its climate is therefore milder than Greenland's or northern Canada's under the same latitudes. During the short Arctic summer, the scenery is lush and the days seem endless in the midnight sun. A fascinating world!

Spitsbergen is certainly among the most beautiful deserts in the world. One can hardly imagine its unbounded fullness, its icy chaos, its cold silence, and its sun's unalterable light. It is a labyrinth of huge glaciers strewn with eroded rocky crests. However, it is not a place reserved for great sportsmen only. Its relief offers mild difficulties and its slopes are perfect for cross-country skiing. Level differences are small and glaciers have few crevasses. Animal life is abundant and strictly preserved: Arctic reindeer, seals, and innumerable birds in summer; sometimes an Arctic fox, or even a polar bear in spring.

The tour is not strenuous, but it is adventurous and exciting, with four days in Longyearbyen and three days sailing. The hikes generally last three to four hours. The sailing tour heads north and we will visit the Ny Alesund Research Station and Smeerenburg, which is the last solid ground before the permanent Arctic ice. You cannot get closer to the North Pole by ship.

ITINERARY:

Days 1-2: Longyearbyen.

Days 3-9: On the trek.

Day 10: Longyearbyen.

Day 11: Return.

PREMIUM

July-August

Arctic Adventours

Oceania

Watut River (OC 1)

ADVANCED WHITEWATER—
CLASS IV

> *Savage rain forest rapids*
> *Papuan highlands tribes*
> *Join a sing-sing*

For visual images of a Stone Age culture coming smack up against the twentieth century, Papua New Guinea is unequaled. Many of the native men still wear nothing but grass and leaves, bark, bones, and shells. But you might see them in one of the new phone booths, installed recently by the Australians, direct-dialing Sidney or Rome. This immense island is also a land of natural contrasts: tropical forests, high mountains, coral reefs, and raging rivers. One of these rivers, the Watut, is perfect for a fantastic whitewater run.

On this trip, we take a week's ride down the Watut—the wildest river run in the Pacific Rim, as it channels through a gorge carved in the lowland forests of Papua New Guinea's north coast. Draining the razorback peaks of central New Guinea's Owen Stanley Range, the river begins with a deceptively hushed glide through mining country, site of an Australian gold rush half a century ago. But then it explodes as it enters the Kuper Mountains where 150 major rapids punctuate as many river miles. The Watut is comparable to California's Tuolumne, West Virginia's Gauley, or Idaho's Selway, but it offers more than exhilarating rapids and more exotic flora and fauna. Its 3,000-foot gorge is sheathed with tangled jungle and capped with clouds; its banks are lined with mango, papaya, and coconut trees; the air is full of the songs and cries of egrets, night herons, Papuan hornbills, and the colorful eclectus parrot and the riflebird. On our route down the river we pass under vine suspension bridges and visit a shimmering 100-meter waterfall.

The native people who live along the river are also an integral part of our rafting experience. The first Western explorers to reach the Watut came in 1913 in two whaling boats, looking for gold. When they came to the rapids they stashed the boats and went upriver on foot, only to be ambushed by the natives of the area, the Kukukukus. Most were killed; one managed to escape, wounded, to tell the tale. The Kukukuku have the reputation of being one of the fiercest of New Guinea's tribespeople as well as one of the oldest, coming from the Australian mainland 60,000 years ago. But times have changed, missionaries have come, and we find the local people to be extremely friendly and more than willing to trade with us for artifacts such as the traditional string bags, pigs-teeth necklaces, and Kundu drums. And if they happen to be having a feast, or a sing-sing, we'll be invited.

The wildest river run in the Pacific Rim is more than just a thrill, although it is that, too: it's a trip to a unique confluence of place and time.

ITINERARY:

Day 1: Fly Port Moresby to Lae.

Day 2: Drive to river; begin trip.

Days 3-5: On the Watut.

Day 6: End rafting; return to Lae.

Day 7: To Port Moresby and return.

MEDIUM

June-September

Niugini Adventures

Franklin River (OC 12) ━━━━

CHALLENGING
RAFTING—CLASS IV

➤ *The full spectrum of whitewater*

➤ *Untouched wooded wilderness*

➤ *The Great Ravine*

Australia's wildest whitewater is on the Franklin, a demonic and tantalizing run on the wooded isle of Tasmania. Our ten days on the river give us time to explore the eucalyptus groves lining the stream, find shelter in case of rain and make portages when necessary. This is not an easy river trip but a great one, demanding intense concentration, patience, and enthusiasm in the tricky rapids.

From its icy headwaters in the Cheyne Range through its narrow gorges, serene pools, boulder-strewn drops, and radical S-turns, the Franklin calls on the complete spectrum of whitewater skills even before it enters the Great Ravine. And

once in the Ravine, the Churn, Corruscades, Thunderrush, and Cauldron push boatmen to the limit for the three nail-biting days. Yet the small scale of the river demands the use of Avon Redshank rafts, which are less than 12 feet and roomy enough for only four.

Emerging from the Ravine, we look back in wonder at the limestone cliffs, glacial headwalls, wheeling and screeching cockatoos, rich rain forest, and especially at the remarkable rapids that have demanded the best that we have to offer for the last few days. Exactly when we return to Hobart depends to some extent on the river and the weather as well as on our determination.

ITINERARY:

Day 1: Meet in Hobart, drive to river.

Days 2-9: On the river.

Day 10: Return to Hobart.

Note: Duration from 8 to 12 days depending on weather.

MODERATE

December-March

World Expeditions

Whitsunday Dive (OC 15) ⚡⚡⚡

DIVING ADVENTURE—
CLASS III

➤ *Australia's sunshine state*

➤ *Kaleidoscope-colored aquatic life*

➤ *Coral-fringed islands*

Neptune's kingdom awaits the certified scuba diver. And what better place to earn certification than the Great Barrier Reef of Australia, one of the prime diving areas in the world. This easy week-long course almost guarantees success. Certification is internationally recognized, instructors are the best, and with this adventure comes a blessing that will last a lifetime: the whole world will become your diving platform.

The intensive instruction is centered around Whitsunday Island off the Queensland coast, with a teacher-to-student ratio of one-to-four for the best possible underwater education. A week of unparalleled diving for the advanced diver can also be arranged. Rainbow corals, undersea ravines, sunlight refracting through warm tropical waters, untold millions of fish—this is the dream-world you will be able to enter at will when you have completed this experience.

ITINERARY:

Day 1: Proserpine.

Days 2-5: Whitsunday Island.

Day 6: Great Barrier Reef.

Day 7: Return.

MEDIUM

Year-round

Barrier Reef Diving Services

Nymboida River (OC 16)

MODERATE RAFTING— CLASS III

➤ *Untouched rain forests*

➤ *Idyllic camping*

➤ *Fast and furious rapids*

When the water is up, in the Australian autumn, the Nymboida is the most reliable beginner's run in New South Wales, rushing through bushland and thick rain forest out to the sea. We begin our trip in Coff's Harbour, a popular Pacific coast resort accessible by train or plane, and then drive some rough roads through dense brush that bring us to Dorrigo, our put-in for the Nymboida.

Our first day on the river is filled with practice riffles that warm us up for the rousing best—a raft of wild rapids that power us through the ever-changing countryside for the next three days. Playful platypuses, wallowing wallabies, and leaping lizards carouse along the watercourse, while kingfishers dive and ducks dip. Let the nimble Nymboida turn you on to rafting Aussie-style.

ITINERARY:

Day 1: Coff's Harbour, NSW.

Days 2-5: On the river.

Day 6: Coff's Harbour and return.

MODERATE

November-April

World Expeditions

Rob Lesser/SOBEK photo file

Cape York Rock Art (OC 35)

CULTURAL QUEST—
CLASS II

> *Hike to the dawn of dreamtime*
> *Explore lost art of the Aborigines*
> *Encounter roos and dingoes*

The wilderness of Cape York in the far north of Australia is full of rock art galleries: etchings and still not fully explored carvings of the Gugu-Yelangi Aborigines. Our trek leaders, who in some cases were actually involved in the rediscovery and recording of these treasures, take us to some of the hundreds of caves hidden in the gorges of the Quinkan Reserve to see some of the finest specimens of petroglyphic art—pictographic descriptions of aboriginal culture and the dawn of the Dreaming. We get to the isolated reserve via four-wheel drive, traveling through a rugged sandstone country of open eucalyptus forest, pristine streams, and a wealth of natural history. Once there we find that time long ago slowed to a backcountry pace, and we camp in comfort near the headwaters of the Little Laura River. In the morning we wake to a riot of blue-winged kookaburras and flashing honey-eaters, and as the days progress we are likely to encounter kangaroos, dingoes, freshwater crocs and tortoises, eels, and brush turkeys. The chances of seeing anyone else once we leave our bush camp at Jowalbinna is minimal. This is an adventure full of magic, undertaken by guides who have a very special knowledge of this area; it is our privilege to accompany them.

ITINERARY:

Day 1: Cairns to Jowalbinna Bush Camp.

Days 2-3: Explore Quinkan Reserve.

Day 4: Afternoon return to Cairns.

MEDIUM

Year-round

Trezise Bush Guide Service

Sail the Tall Ships (OC 37)

SAILING ADVENTURE—
CLASS II

> *The Great Barrier Reef*
> *The romance of the sea*
> *Sailboarding and snorkeling*

Sailing a square-rigger is exhilarating and romantic, and sailing the *Coral Trekker* around Australia's Whitsunday Islands is a chance to catch the trade winds in some of the world's best sailing waters. A chain of ancient mountainous islands erupts from the Great Barrier Reef to create the Whitsundays and their relatively sheltered channels, and our journey takes us through this area from isle to isle, bay to bay. There is nothing quite like feeling the deck beneath your feet, the wind in your face, and watching the great square sails fill.

Our itinerary is flexible and unhurried. Basically, we spend long tropical days swimming and relaxing, with the option of joining the crew for some real hands-on experience in running a tall ship. There's also the opportunity to learn sailboarding or snorkeling and to scuba dive if you are certified. The Great Barrier Reef is one of the richest ecosystems in the world, and there's no end to what we can discover underwater, living in and around the coral, drifting in the current, and speed-swimming through the tropical waters.

Certainly it is a realm so alien to man that its creatures are finally unknowable. Schools of fish move by so fast they seem to be on some kind of laser track, and hundreds of tiny, iridescent fish just drift with the current. Stingrays float along the ocean floor, and clown fish hide in the arms of sea anemones, but fish are only half of the wonder. The coral gardens come in all colors, shapes and sizes—some hard, some leathery, some soft like sea-weed. There are canyons and gorges and forests of coral—purple-tipped coral, coral covered with sponges and tunicates, coral encrusted with tube worms.

Our nights are spent on gloriously deserted beaches, alive with birdlife and with the echoes of our aboriginal predecessors. There are barbecues and beach parties, with plenty of fresh, whole-some food, and either tents on land or bunks on the boat, to sleep in. There's opportunity for lots of activity on this trip, but if soaking up the sun among the tropical seas is all you're after, there's no more exotic way to do it—and you don't even need a license.

ITINERARY:

Day 1: Arrive Shute Harbor, Queensland; join cruise.

Days 2-6: Sailing the tall ships.

Day 7: Shute Harbor and return.

MEDIUM

Year-round

Coral Trekker Sailing Safari

Snowy River (OC 38)

WHITEWATER
RAFTING—CLASS III

➤ *The legendary Snowy River*

➤ *Wild rapids*

➤ *Leisurely beach camping*

Australian folklore springs from the Snowy River, and so do a multitude of rapids, a span of scenery, and a hoard of wildlife. Eight major adrenalin-pumping rapids and many smaller ones test the mettle of the novice or experienced rafter, while the serene Tullock Ard Gorge soothes the soul. With white sand beaches for camping, abundant wildlife, and good swimming throughout, we have all the ingredients for an estimable experience of exceptional excitement.

Our put-in is at McKillop Bridge, near Buchan, Victoria; from there to our take-out six days later, there is plenty of time for rest, relaxation, and a raft of thrills as we spin and torque through the Great Dividing Range, one of Down Under's best river runs.

ITINERARY:

Day 1: Meet near Canberra; begin river trip.

Days 2-5: On the Snowy.

Day 6: Take-out near Buchan.

MEDIUM

October-January

World Expeditions

New Zealand Mountaineering (OC 46)

MOUNTAINEERING INSTRUCTION—CLASS IV/V

> *Intermediate or advanced training*
> *Scenic Mount Cook on the South Island*

There's room at the top even for newcomers to the alpine sports; and this complete instruction program teaches you how to get there. New Zealand's finest mountaineering guides teach the basics and fine points of glacial travel, roped traverses, belaying, self-arrest, ice and rock holds, knots, and ice cave building. Perhaps best of all, the course takes place on the flanks of New Zealand's grandest peak: Mount Cook, peaking out at 12,349 feet above the South Pacific.

Two separate programs allow prospective climbers to develop at their own level. The week-long Mountain Experience Course is an introductory program, building skills and confidence toward ascents of moderate difficulty. The Technical Mountaineering Course is a longer, tougher, more advanced course for those with some previous mountain experience. It offers twelve days of detailed instruction in all aspects of mountaineering and culminates in extended high mountain travel and ascents. These are the same elevated classrooms where Sir Edmund Hillary learned the skills that took him to the world's highest peak. Why not you?

ITINERARY:

Day 1: Arrive Christchurch; begin course.

Days 2-6 or 2-11: Mountaineering course.

Day 7 or 12: Return.

MEDIUM

January–March, November–December

Alpine Guides

New Guinea Wanderer (OC 52)

CULTURAL TREKKING—CLASS III

> *Four days highland trek*
> *Three days coastal resort*

In the Tari Basin in the highlands of Papua New Guinea are the Huli, some 40,000 tribespeople who are noted for their flamboyant appearance, particularly when bedecked with flowers and elaborate wigs made of human hair—an intimidating sight when the Huli practiced regular

Richard Bangs/SOBEK photo file

warfare. We hike for four days through the homeland of the Huli, the high Tari Basin, which is crisscrossed with deep trenches once used for battle. Today the Huli are peaceful, although other aspects of their culture remain intact. The men still decorate themselves just to go to market; the woman still sleep with the pigs; and pigs and kina shells are still as valuable as gold. Most tribal disputes are settled by payment with one or the other. Our time among the Huli will be a return to a simpler, friendlier age, as we attempt to learn about Huli culture from a people who are more than willing to share it with us.

After trekking in Tari, we travel by four-wheel drive to Mt. Hagen, the capital of the highlands. This day-long drive that is not just another day on the road but a spectacular travel experience in its own right through a limestone landscape of incredible beauty. Finally, after exploring Mount Hagen, we fly to Madang on the coast, where we unwind from our exotic trip by indulging in all the pleasures of a tropical island paradise—coconut cocktails, coral diving, people watching, and hiking to nearby points of interest.

ITINERARY:

Day 1: Port Moresby to Tari.

Days 2-4: Tari Basin trek.

Day 5: Ambua Lodge.

Day 6: Drive to Mount Hagen.

Day 7: Rafting.

Day 8: Fly to Madang.

Days 9-10: Exploring north coast; overnights in village guest houses.

Day 11: Malolo Lodge.

Day 12: Return.

MEDIUM

February-April, June, October, December

Trans Niugini Tours

Kokoda Trail (OC 53) ⚡⚡⚡

DIFFICULT JUNGLE
TREK—CLASS IV

➤ *World War II battle zone*

➤ *84 miles of jungle trail*

➤ *Peaceful native tribes*

One of the world's great walks is the challenging Kokoda Trail, a beautiful rain forest path still haunted by a bitter and bloody struggle that took place in World War II. The trail was the scene of a prolonged and deadly conflict between Australian troops and the Japanese army, but the strongest force was clearly the force of nature: tropical rains flooded the paths and snatched victory from the jaws of the Japanese, leaving behind the rusted hulks of war machinery.

Our 84-mile trek route is littered with these vivid reminders of battle, but the images that last are our encounters with the gentle Papuan people of this region: the Kaoiri tribespeople of the deep jungle highlands surrounding Mount Victoria (13,450 ft.). Eight days on the trail allow us time enough to pursue individual interests such as photography, lolling in mountain pools, searching for rare birds and butterflies, or contemplating the decay of iron weaponry—rusting guns, worn helmets, spent ammunition, plane wreckage, and truck chassis. We spend each night in the comfortable houses of the Kaoiri, who treat us with friendly smiles, fresh fruit, and maybe even some tales from elders who were young when the war raged about them. Although ours is a peaceful mission, in the end we will do what the mighty armies of World War II failed to do—conquer the Kokoda Trail.

ITINERARY:

Day 1: Port Moresby.

Day 2: Fly to Kokoda; begin hike.

Days 3-10: Hike Kokoda Trail.

Day 11: End hike at Owens Corner; bus to Port Moresby.

Day 12: Return.

MEDIUM

February, April-May, July, October, December

Trans Nuigini Tours

Rivers and Rain Forests (OC 62)

ADVANCED RAFTING—
CLASS IV

> ➤ *Raft the Tully and the Johnstone*
> ➤ *Tropical Atherton Tablelands*

This is an Australia few have ever seen— the tropical rain forest of Queensland's Atherton Tablelands where some of the world's most oddball life-forms can be found. Here are giant trees of world heritage significance because they are the only living remains of groves that disappeared from the rest of the earth millennia ago.

And here are birds and butterflies in color combinations so crazy you have to laugh out loud at the sight of them.

We discover this fascinating world on two of Australia's finest whitewater rivers—one of them, the Tully, a technical run and the site of Australia's slalom championship; the other, the Johnston, an exciting gorge run where we take on some Class IV rapids. We begin our run on the Tully with five hours of nonstop action, negotiating rapids like Alarm Clock Falls, Scales of Justice, The Full Stop, and the bewildering Corkscrew. The river drops 40 feet (120 m) from start to finish, assuring us a day of excitement.

After an overnight stay in rustic cabins above the Johnston River Gorge, we spend a day walking in the rain forest with a wildlife guide, taking plenty of time for a midstream swim. More than 400 kinds of animals and 700 kinds of birds are found in Australia, and many of them thrive in this rich ecosystem.

The next day we helicopter into the gorge and start our five-day run of the Johnston, which roars down from its birthplace in the Great Dividing Range. We thunder along with it, through a variety of its rapids, portaging one Class VI called the Berlin Wall. Here, wildlife from crocodile to duck-billed platypus dot the riverbanks, and flashing birds fill the clear air with their songs—the laugh of the kookaburra, the chatter of parrots, the mimicry of the lyrebird. We spend one rest day on the river, during which we swim, fish, trek through the rain forest in search of cassowaries and the rare giant Ulysses butterfly, or just relax in camp. There's also a chance to shower under a waterfall, to climb a mountain (Mt. Poorka), and to pan for gold.

On our last day on the Johnston we bounce down through rapids with names like the Mushroom and Lookout until the river widens, the rapids give way to calm pools, and we finally come to a road. We drive back to Cairns having had the best of both worlds: a close-up look at a strange, isolated ecosystem and a thrilling whitewater run.

ITINERARY:

Day 1: Cairns to Tully River.

Day 2: To Atherton Tablelands.

Days 3-5: Rafting the Johnston.

Day 6: Hiking the rain forest.

Day 7: End rafting, return to Cairns.

MEDIUM

January-October

Raging Thunder

New Zealand Cycling (OC 69) ◣⋀⋀⋀⋀⋀

MODERATE BICYCLING— CLASS III

➤ *Grandeur of the southern Alps*

➤ *Maori culture*

➤ *Choice of itineraries*

New Zealand is nature's improbable masterpiece: a world of beauty and wonder jammed into three unforgettable islands; a gem of breathtaking brilliance, its attraction startlingly brilliant and lingering far beyond journey's end. And what better way to experience this panorama of natural wonders than by bicycle? These 6- to 18-day trips cover an astonishing amount of territory, running the gamut of terrain and town, seashore and mountain, river, gorge, and glacier, and stopping at small inns for overnight stays.

On the North Island we can see the Coromandel Peninsula, a microcosm of New Zealand, with mountains tumbling right down to the sea, or pedal along the

East Cape, with its Maori people and the remaining trimmings of their culture, including carved churches. We can visit the area of the Waikato with thermal activity and hot springs; or the Volcanic Plateau, or Lake Taupo. The roadside attractions here are endless.

On the South Island all we have to do is look around us to see sweeping vistas including the southern Alps, a spectacular range of peaks with views to rival any mountains in the world. Here we ferry across the Marlborough sounds, raft through Buller Gorge, ride along the coast to the glaciers, and then pump over the pass to Wanaka and Queensland. In this uncrowded country where almost all the roads are beautiful, bicycle trips to fit each person, each need, can be arranged.

SAMPLE ITINERARY,
Grand Tour:

Day 1: Meet at Wellington, ferry to Picton.

Day 2: Ride to Canvastown.

Day 3: To Nelson.

Day 4: To Murchison.

Day 5: To Westport.

Day 6: Coast route to Greymouth.

Day 7: To Lake Ianthe and Franz Josef Glacier.

Day 8: Fox Glacier.

Day 9: Rest day, Gillespies Beach.

Day 10: Forest route to Lake Moeraki.

Day 11: To Makarora.

Day 12: Mt. Aspiring National Park.

Day 13: To Queenstown.

Day 14: Lake Wakatipu.

Day 15: Omarama.

Day 16: Mount Cook Village.

Day 17: To Fairlie.

Day 18: To Christchurch.

MEDIUM

Grand Tour: *January-March, December*

Southern Alps: *January-April, October-November*

Highlights Tour: *January-February, November-December*

East Cape: *February-March*

Coromandel: *February, November-December*

New Zealand Pedaltours

Sepik and Highlands Odyssey (OC 74)

VARIETY PACKAGE—
CLASS III

➤ *Three days river canoeing*

➤ *Three days highlands trek*

➤ *Two days jungle hiking*

Discover one of the most artistically interesting primitive cultures on earth on this two-week camping and lodge expedition through the remote regions of Papua New Guinea. Here, men wear intricately designed hats, masks, wigs, necklaces, bracelets, and body paint as they work, play, go to market, and in general, hang out. On this large, densely forested island, entire regions and peoples lived unknown to the outside world until the 1930s and even the late 1950s. We visit some of them, as well as some of the best spots on the island for viewing the country's amazing tropical flora and fauna.

Our first adventure is three days of canoeing on the Sepik River in a motorized crocodile-prowed dugout. This takes us through the richest region of the Sepik cultural area, where primitive carved art,

and mask-making in particular, is abundant. Then it's a day's ride up the Karawari River, a major tributary of the Sepik, to go ever deeper into the rain forest of parrots and cockatoos to the famous Karawari Lodge, headquarters for two days of jungle walks. But that's not all. Another adventure awaits us in the highlands of the Tari Basin, an inhabited valley surrounded by towering mountain ranges where we'll find Huli tribespeople, known for their brilliant adornment. Here, also, are mountain orchids and a dozen species of the rare and endangered birds of paradise that give the Papuan men their plumage. Our highlands trek is scheduled to coincide with market day, so we'll have plenty of opportunities to encounter the Huli and other highlands people and perhaps even stumble upon sing-sing. This is a trip to take now, before a rare and beautiful culture is lost to history books.

ITINERARY:

Day 1: Wewak.

Day 2: To Sepik River; begin canoeing.

Days 3-4: Sepik River.

Days 5-7: Karawari River.

Day 8: Fly to Mount Hagen.

Day 9: Drive to Tari.

Days 10-12: Tari Basin trek.

Day 13: End trek in Ambua.

Day 14: Fly to Port Moresby and return.

MEDIUM

January, March, May, June-September, November

Trans Nuigini Tours

Rain Forest Cycle (OC 76)

MODERATE BICYCLE TOUR—CLASS III

➤ *World heritage rain forest*
➤ *Historic hotels and plantations*
➤ *Leisurely cycling*

The royal way to see Queensland is by mountain bike, taking the time to see the sights and scenes that the motor age passes by. On this trip we pedal along Queensland's back roads, passing through enough ecosystems to last a lifetime: tropical rain forest, crystalline lakes, misty mountains, agricultural valleys, and majestic tablelands.

This week-long tour begins in Cairns with a two-hour train ride up the Barron Gorge to the village of Kuranda. Here we board our mountain bikes for a ride into the nearby rain forest. After a quick introduction to the endangered ecology of this world heritage site, we proceed leisurely, pedaling in the wake of a support vehicle through the rolling hills and pastures of the Atherton Tablelands.

Along the way we stop at historic hotels, provincial parks, and hospitable homesteads. The pace of the tour is suitable for those with minimal cycle touring experience, but fitness will make the trip more enjoyable. A special canoe trip down the Mulgrave River gives our legs a break en route back to Cairns, a refreshing cap to an extraordinary adventure.

ITINERARY:

Day 1: Cairns to Cassowary Lodge.

Day 2-3: Yungaburra.

Days 4-5: Honeyflow Homestead.

Day 6: Mulgrave Valley.

Day 7: Mulgrave River and return to Cairns.

MEDIUM

April-October

Go! Adventures

Islands in the Sun (OC 77) ▲▲▲▲▲

RELAXED TROPICAL
PADDLING—CLASS III

➤ *Snorkel the Great Barrier Reef*

➤ *Bushwalk Hinchinbrook Island*

➤ *Sea kayak touring*

The Coral Sea is a marine Garden of Eden. Its clear warm waters are decorated by a string of tropical islands, and its western edge holds the fantastical Great Barrier Reef just off the coast of Australia. Need we give any other reason why it is a perfect place to sea kayak? Here the offshore islands are all national parks, and some of them—such as the largest, Hinchinbrook—offer enough diversity to fill a guidebook with poetry and photos.

We begin our week's adventure with a training session in Mulligan Bay, then hone our skills in sheltered Zoe Bay,

which has been called "perhaps the most beautiful place on the entire east coast of Australia" by one avid literary yachtsman. And it is our base for several days of exploring. From Zoe we investigate Hinchinbrook's interior on foot, an Elysian fields of waterfalls, rain forest, mangrove trees, and sandy beaches; a protected habitat for wallabies, echidnas, goannas, and over 250 species of birds. Then we head across the open seas to the Brook Islands, a six-mile paddle away, where we explore the coral reefs.

Scientists refer to the Great Barrier Reef's "high order of internal organization" that is, they say, even greater than that of a tropical rain forest. The reef receives large amounts of solar radiation, the ultimate source of all ecosystem energy, and has more species per square foot than anyplace on earth. And just by putting on a snorkel and mask and floating lazily in the water, we can see it all. Here it becomes instantly clear that there is nothing new under the sun, no color combination created by man that was not first created by nature underwater, no pattern or design that was not drawn on this primitive landscape long before prehistoric people made scratchings inside a cave.

After seven days of relaxed drifting through this underwater idyll (we paddle our kayaks for only a total of eight hours), we return to reality in Cairns—maybe. This is the kind of voyage that can easily turn into a Hans Christian Anderson tale about a sailor being tugged down into the sea by a mermaid.

ITINERARY:

Day 1: Cairns to Hinchinbrook Island.

Day 2: Hiking Hinchinbrook.

Day 3: Cape Sandwich.

Days 4-5: Brook Islands.

Day 6: Family Islands.

Day 7: Dunk Island, return to Cairns.

MEDIUM

April–December

Raging Thunder

Pentecost Land Dive (OC 79) ◣◥◣◥◣◥◣◥

CULTURAL ADVENTURE— CLASS II

➤ *Daring divers of Vanuatu*
➤ *Visit the Outer Islands of Fiji*

Poised at the top of a tower, a solitary man stands nearly naked. Suddenly, with a cry, he spreads his arms wide and leaps, plummeting headfirst toward the earth below. Inches from the ground, his fall is halted by two thin lianas tied around his ankles, and he bounces up and away from certain death. The incredible ritual of the Land Dive of Pentecost Island has long been the subject of rumor and rare footage, but for the first time adventure travelers can witness this ceremony first-hand. The Land Dive is the culmination of an 18-day tour of the Outer Islands of Fiji, a tour that travels the distance between active volcanoes and cargo cults, coral reef snorkeling, and genuine Polynesian luaus.

From the moment we arrive in Fiji's capital of Nandi, we are transported into another world, a place where there's nothing new beneath the equatorial sun. As well as Pentecost and the large island of Vanua Levu, we visit Taveuni, Efate, Rabi, and Tanna, where we find a smoldering volcano and the cargo cult of John Frum, a mysterious white man who visited the island over fifty years ago and promised a bonanza of Western booty that the islanders still await. Fijian ponies will take us into the forested interiors, motorboats will take us beyond the coral reefs, and the brave Land Divers of Pentecost will take us to the edge of our seats.

ITINERARY:

Day 1: Departure.
Day 2: Lost to International Date Line.
Day 3: Arrive Nandi, Fiji.
Days 4-7: Vanua Levu.
Day 8: Taveuni.
Day 9: Nandi.
Day 10: Port Vila, Vanuatu.
Day 11: Tanna.
Day 12: Port Vila.
Days 13-16: Pentecost.
Day 17: Land dive.
Days 18-19: Nandi and return.

MEDIUM

March–May

SOBEK Expeditions

Whitewater New Zealand (OC 80) ⚡⚡⚡

CHALLENGING RAFTING— CLASS IV

➤ *Ten rivers in 18 days*
➤ *Paddle instruction included*

Rambunctious and rowdy are words used to describe both the rivers of New Zealand and the style of the "Kiwi" guides. While the rivers twist and turn through awesome gorge country, the guides navigate steep holes and narrow chutes to provide thrill after thrill, making the most of the action. Here is a complete tour of the country's rivers, both north and south, beginning with a one-day descent of the mild Class III whitewater of the lower Tongariro, one of the North Island's best trout streams. Then it's on to the Mohaka for a two-day trip, followed by the Motu's three-day run through Class IV rapids.

After this triad of tributaries we head for the exciting streams of the South Island, kicking off with the Gowan-Upper Buller run, a tough-as-nails section that ends, thankfully, at the Owen River Tavern. But your Kiwi guides aren't through with you yet. Ahead lies the "earthquake" section of the Buller, its beautiful gorge filled with Class IV rapids shaped by recent tectonic movement. And after that is the relatively tranquil Grey, a scenic wonder with Class III rapids. Our trip ends in Queenstown, for the Class V runs of the Shotover and Kawarau.

Still looking for the ultimate whitewater thrill? How about the Rangitaiki, with its steep, boulder-strewn drop powered by volcanic whitewater that can take your breath away. If river running was new to you before this trip, you'll be an old hand after 18 days in the capable hands of the masters of Whitewater New Zealand.

ITINERARY:

Day 1: Arrive Auckland.

Day 2: Tongariro.

Days 3-4: Mohaka.

Days 5-8: Motu.

Day 9: Ferry to South Island.

Day 10: Gowan-Upper Buller.

Day 11: Buller.

Day 12: Grey River.

Day 13: To Queenstown.

Day 14: Shotover.

Day 15: Kawarau.

Day 16: Rangitaiki; to Christchurch and return.

MEDIUM

December-January

Dvorak Expeditions

John Kramer/SOBEK photo file

Paddle Fiji (OC 82)

SEA KAYAKING—
CLASS III

➤ *Kayak Fijian islands*
➤ *Friendly villages and lonely isles*
➤ *Explore sea caves and coral reefs*

This tropical odyssey could be the adventure of your dreams, a trip by sea kayak to the Yasawa Islands of Fiji. Here, sixteen islands, fringed with white sands and azure seas, stretch over 50 miles of Fiji's waters, each its own little piece of paradise under the Pacific sun. After learning the strokes of our craft, we paddle among these islands for two weeks, mingling with the friendly native Fijians who live by fishing and smiling, and we spend time alone to relax and contemplate.

We travel for three or four hours a day, then make camp on one of the islands under majestic palms. In the afternoons, we snorkel and fish the rich coral reefs, take pictures of the unbelievable postcard scenery, or just walk around entire uninhabited islands in an afternoon. When we stay on inhabited islands, we are the guests of some of the most hospitable people imaginable, who may find our visit cause for celebration—to which, of course, we are invited.

Isolated coasts, picturesque islands, limestone sea caves, friendly villagers, convivial company—if Odysseus never had it so good, he should have come to Fiji.

ITINERARY:

Day 1: Nandi.

Day 2: To Yasawa Islands.

Day 3: Paddling instruction.

Days 4-11: Sea kayaking.

Day 12: Drive back to Nandi.

Day 13: Return.

MEDIUM

June-August

World Expeditions

Adventure Queensland (OC 83)

VARIETY PACKAGE—
CLASS IV

➤ *The Outback by mountain bike*
➤ *Rain forest trails on horseback*
➤ *Sea kayaking, hiking, and more*

The Australian state of Queensland is a surprise to most travelers. It is a huge land of tropical rain forests, rambling mountains, raging rivers, and inland meadows, with the Great Barrier Reef lining its eastern coast. Geologists find oil deposits and bauxite in Queensland; farmers raise sugarcane, cotton, and wheat; but adventurers discover a wealth of activities to erase forever the image of Australia as a vast, red, dusty Outback. This trip looks at it all from just about every vantage point: whitewater raft, sea kayak, mountain bike, horseback, and snorkel. At night we relax in comfort, mostly in inns and hotels.

Our trip begins in Cairns at the Colonial Club, a tropical resort set on eight acres of award-winning landscaped grounds, and then moves on to the Tully River for some whitewater action. The Tully is the sight of Australia's slalom championships and is a tight, narrow, highly technical Class III-IV run that we make in small, self-bailing boats with everyone paddling. After a day of thrills, we go to the coast for some less vigorous but equally sensual pleasures: a trip by sea kayak to some deserted islands on the edge of the Great Barrier Reef. On Dunk Island National Park and the smaller Family Islands, we do some serious tropical island paradise living: swim in the warm, clear water, snorkel or dive at the edge of the Great Barrier Reef, fish, and wander into the warm rain forests. At night we camp on deserted beaches.

After three days of island hopping, we return to the Cairns Colonial Club, and then take off the next morning for a ride through the Atherton Tableland to the rain forests of Kuranda. Here we get on mountain bikes and pedal for two days on rough forest trails through a world of rare orchids, ferns, butterflies and natural swimming pools. A van for nonbikers follows. Our destination is Lake Eacham, where we spend another two days in the middle of the rain forest at a unique, nature-oriented hotel, surrounded by pademelons, bandicoots, and rat kangaroos that come for nightly, lighted feedings. Here we kick back, take day hikes, and contemplate the strange life forms on the other side of the Wallace line. From Lake Eacham we penetrate even deeper into the rain forest on an overnight horse trail ride in the Cannabullen Forest, emerging on the second day into lush open dairy country.

Back at the Cairns Colonial Club, we head to the ocean again for what will surely be our most mind-boggling adventure: a trip out in a dive boat to the "Big Apple" of the snorkeling and diving world, the Great Barrier Reef. Here a truly alien and beautiful world awaits us. Just a few feet underwater, a kaleidoscope of bizarre shapes and colors and textures that make up what many say is the most splendid ecological niche on earth.

If you've always thought of Australia as a land of red rock and flies and scrub brush, this trip through a lush, natural playground will forever change your mind.

ITINERARY:

Days 1-2: En route.

Day 3: Arrive Cairns.

Days 4-6: Mountain biking; to Lake Eacham.

Day 7: Rain forest hiking near Lake Eacham.

Days 8-9: On horseback; return to Cairns.

Day 10: Rafting the Tully.

Days 11-12: Sea kayak Coral Sea.

Day 13: Cruise Great Barrier Reef; return to Cairns.

Day 14: Departure.

MEDIUM

April-December

SOBEK Expeditions

Freycinet Sea Kayak Expedition ▰▰▰▰▰▰ (OC 200)

KAYAKING — CLASS III

➤ *Tasmanian coastline exploration*
➤ *Spectacular sea kayaking*
➤ *Feast on fresh seafood*

Enjoy the fastest-growing water sport of North America on the beautiful and rugged east coast of Tasmania. After meeting and checking gear in Hobart, we drive to the tiny coastal town of Coles Bay and Freycinet National Park. Here our guides give us a thorough safety briefing and an afternoon's introductory paddle in the sheltered bay waters. Our extremely stable, two-person sea kayaks are easy to master and have storage space for personal gear.

From here we take off for six days of exploring the coastline of the Freycinet Peninsula, with its spectacular scenery and Moulting Lagoon, which is a breeding ground for black swans. Our itinerary allows time for side trips to the mountains, and we'll explore hidden sea caves in towering coastal cliffs, camp on isolated beaches, and feast on freshly caught seafood. If the weather permits, we'll visit Schouten Island. After a great week of paddling and exploring, we return to Hobart for a celebratory dinner.

ITINERARY:

Day 1: Hobart, Coles Bay, then Freycinet National Park.

Days 2-6: Explore the coastline of the Freycinet Peninsula.

Day 7: Return to Hobart.

MEDIUM

December-March

World Expeditions

Northern New Zealand Sea Kayaking (OC 201)

SEA KAYAKING—
CLASS III

➤ *Enjoy prime New Zealand summertime*

➤ *Warm water ocean kayaking*

➤ *Beachcomb offshore islands*

Northern New Zealand offers a wonderfully scenic and exhilarating ocean kayaking experience to both novice and experienced paddlers alike. The subtropical climate and warm water in this very northerly region of New Zealand provide for easy camping and confident paddling. Our 16-foot, Nimbus-designed Puffins are single-seat, rudder-equipped seal kayaks that are seaworthy, responsive, and comfortable. We'll practice and perfect paddling skills, group and solo rescues, and surf landings. We offer freshly caught and locally grown cuisine.

The ten-day Bay of Islands Tour is a journey through the heartland of old Maori civilization. Visit the seven major islands of this 100-square-mile Maritime Park. Spend one night in a decommissioned lighthouse. During the ten-day Northeast Coast Tour, we'll discover a sea kayaker's paradise: white sandy beaches, "surfyaking," snorkling, strange rock gardens and hidden coves, and night paddling under the the warm, starry sky.

BAY OF ISLANDS ITINERARY:

Day 1: Arrive Paiha, New Zealand.

Days 2-9: Sea kayaking (Moturoa, Cape Wiwiki, Motuarohia Island, Urupukapuka, Cape Brett, Deep Water Cove).

Day 10: Return to Paiha.

NORTHEAST COAST ITINERARY:

Day 1: Arrive Paiha, New Zealand.

Days 2-9: Sea kayaking (Matauri Bay, Motukawanui Islands, Mahinepua Peninsula, Stephenson Island, Whangoraa Harbor).

Day 10: Return to Paiha.

MEDIUM

December-April

New Zealand Adventures

South American adventures. Upper left: steps leading down from Machu Picchu, Peru (photo: Rex A. Bryrigelson/SOBEK photo file); bottom: the ancient ruins of Machu Picchu (photo: Rex A. Bryrigelson/SOBEK photo file); upper right: stone monuments on Easter Island (photo: Richard Bangs/SOBEK photo file); center: Jivaro Indian, Ecuador (photo: Jordan Coonrad/SOBEK photo file).

North American adventures. Background photo: caribou migration in Quebec (photo: SOBEK photo file); far left: Walker Glacier, Alaska (photo: Bart Henderson/SOBEK photo file); Kobuk Sand Dunes, Alaska (photo: Steve Hacksit/SOBEK photo file); osprey expedition, Alaska (photo: SOBEK photo file).

Rafting the Colorado in the Grand Canyon (photo: Bert Sagara/SOBEK photo file); river crossing near Mt. McKinley (photo: John Kramer/SOBEK photo file); hiking and loafing in the canyon country, Utah/Arizona (photo: SOBEK photo file).

Himalayan adventures. Background photo: Namche Bazaar in Nepal (photo: Kelly Bricker/SOBEK photo file); houseboat on Dal Lake, Kashmir (photo: Will Weber/SOBEK photo file); child in a basket, Nepal (photo: Bart Henderson/SOBEK photo file); carrying the kayak to the river, Nepal (photo: J. Suchowiejko/SOBEK photo file).

Big brother is watching—eyes on the stupa (temple) of Swayambhunath, Kathmandu (photo: Jack Hollingsworth/SOBEK photo file); trekking in Nepal (photo: Will Weber/SOBEK photo file).

Jungle and tropical adventures. Romancing the Okavango Swamp, Botswana (photo: James Pleyte/SOBEK photo file); hungry hippos in the Zambezi River, Zambia (photo: SOBEK photo file); mother, child, and house pig, Irian Jaya (photo: George Fuller/SOBEK photo file).

Top row: boys on stilts, Thailand hill country (photo: Michael Saint James/SOBEK photo file); children up the tree backwards, Sumatra (photo: George Fuller/SOBEK photo file); Pentecost Island land divers, Fiji (photo: Jim Slade/SOBEK photo file); bottom: welcoming committee in an Irian Jaya village (photo: James Polster/SOBEK photo file).

Upper left: Hawaiian island bicycle adventures (photo: SOBEK photo file); research expedition in Antarctica (photo: Jim Slade); bottom left: kayaking on the Agua Azul, Chiapas, Mexico (photo: Bill Sims); top right: St. Basil's Cathedral, Moscow (photo: Dave Edwards); schoolchildren in the Chatkal region, USSR (photo: Sharon Ahern); diving in the Dutch Antilles (2 photos: Joan Curtis); bottom right: Fiji native (photo: SOBEK photo file).

Asia

Everest / Arun Valley (AS 2)

EXTENDED TREK—
CLASS IV

- ➤ *Gurkha, Tibetan, and Limbu culture*
- ➤ *Sherpa villages and monasteries*
- ➤ *Everest Base Camp*

This is the less-traveled route to Everest, up a valley on the mountain's eastern flank carved by a river that flows from high in the Khumbu down to the Ganges plain. Few Westerners know about this valley, and yet it offers a chance to experience the entire scenic and cultural range of Nepal, from the game-rich jungles of the Terai to the glaciers of Everest.

We begin our trip in Dharan, a market town in easternmost Nepal, at 1,350 feet. From here we drive to Hile, at 6,200 feet, and then hike down to the Arun Valley floor, a hot, steamy place full of tropical flora and fauna—a naturalist's delight. The valley is peopled by ex-Gurkha soldiers and Tibetan expatriates as well as by its traditional Limbu inhabitants. Then we start up, rising through the wild and broken country of the middle hills to enter the first mountain villages, and finally we reach the Khumbu, homeland of the Sherpas.

We acclimate among the Sherpas under the spell of the earth's loftiest peaks, preparing for our final push to Everest Base Camp (17,712 ft.). From Namche Bazar, the bustling, spectacularly beautiful Sherpa town on the Tibet-India trade route, we follow the classic route to the Everest Base Camp. Those who wish to, may ascend Kala Pattar for an unparalleled view of The Big One. A dramatic flight back to Kathmandu from Lukla leaves a hawk's-eye view in our minds which lasts as long as the Himalayan snows.

ITINERARY:

Day 1: Arrive Kathmandu.

Day 2: Kathmandu.

Days 3-4: Bus to Hille.

Days 5-11: Cross Mahabharat Range; descend Arun River Valley.

Days 12-18: By Makalu and through Gurkha and Limbu area.

Days 19-24: Into Sherpa country.

Days 25-30: Everest Base Camp and Kala Pattar.

Day 31: Fly Lukla/Kathmandu.

Days 32-33: Kathmandu.

Day 34: Return.

MODERATE

January-May, October-December

World Expeditions

Classic Everest (AS 3)

RUGGED TREK—
CLASS IV

- ➤ *In the footsteps of Hillary*
- ➤ *Optional climb of Kala Pattar*
- ➤ *Unsurpassed Himalayan vistas*

We retrace the original expedition route to Everest on this classic Nepalese trek, walking east from Jiri through picturesque lowland villages and then turning north toward the destination of most trekkers in Nepal—the Solo Khumbu. Our journey ends with the experience of a lifetime—standing on Kala Pattar, at 18,192 feet, directly facing Mount Everest; a world of snow and rock where the ice sparkles with a crystal clarity and the stillness is broken only by the thunder of an avalanche. Although it's possible to fly into the Khumbu, this trek follows a historic and culturally fascinating route; it's also recommended for acclimatization at higher altitudes. We begin with a full day in Kathmandu, an entire city that's like an outdoor art museum with its many temples and pagodas. Then we drive to Jiri to begin the trek. For the next week we hike a well-worn trail, the main east-west "road" across the vast foothills, walking up and over passes, down through valleys, and up and down again. All around us are hills that would be called mountains in any other country, only these are terraced with rice fields.

This is the Buddhist Himalaya, and we walk by stone "mani" walls, monasteries set into cliffs, and prayer flags snapping in the wind. On the trail with us are children going to school, women going to market, porters carrying loads to and from Kathmandu, and traders from China and Tibet. In the teahouses, the Himalayan equivalent of the British pub, we meet other trekkers from all over the world as well as local people.

On our fifth day out we come to the Dudh Kosi River and turn north; on the eighth day we enter Sagamartha National Park and begin the steep climb to Namche Bazar (11,300 ft.) where we rest and acclimate for a day.

Namche is the largest town in the Khumbu and a center for the Sherpa people. For centuries it has been on the trade route from India to Tibet, and its setting in a large mountain cirque is stunning. We wander its rocky slopes, shop for Tibetan antiques, and prepare for the world of rock and ice ahead. On Day 10, we push on to Thyangboche Monastery, the beautiful "gompa" on the cover of just about every Nepalese trekking book. To everyone's great sorrow, Thyangboche burned down in January 1989, but it is being rebuilt. In fact, work may be in progress when we arrive.

In any case, the view from Thyangboche is stupendous, especially of Ama Dablam, an awesome mountain with an icy, needle peak that rises like a prayer flag directly overhead. We continue on, now in a world of milk-white glacial streams, yaks, and rocky paths and walls, stopping at Pangboche to visit a gompa, spending a day at Pheriche (14,000 ft.) to acclimate, and finally pushing on to Lobuche, at 16,200 feet, the highest town in the region. From here, those who want to can begin the ascent of Kala Pattar and and come face to face with Everest's south flank and Lhotse, fourth highest mountain in the world.

We take another five days to hike back to Lukla (8,500 ft.), where we spend the night and then fly to Kathmandu, still feeling a little unreal. Having experienced such overwhelming visual beauty and been immersed in a world so alien and yet so full of friendly people, not to mention a palpable spirit world, it will be sometime before we can assimilate it all.

ITINERARY:

Day 1: Arrive Kathmandu.

Day 2: Kathmandu.

Day 3: Drive to Jiri; begin trek.

Days 4-8: Trek over 9,000 feet to Dudh Kosi.

Days 9-13: To Namche Bazar; acclimate for one day.

Days 14-18: To Lobuche (16,200 ft.).

Day 19: Kala Pattar.

Days 20-24: Descend to Lukla.

Day 25: Flight to Kathmandu.

Day 26: Free day in Kathmandu.

Day 27: Return.

MODERATE

January-May, October-December

World Expeditions

Annapurna Circuit (AS 7)

RUGGED TREK — CLASS IV

➤ *Nepal's most scenic trek*

➤ *The world's deepest gorge*

This is the classic Annapurna trek, we spend a month circling the high peaks of the Annapurna Massif, one of Nepal's most spectacular regions. Our 22-day trek begins with leisurely days ambling up rhododendron-lined trails, following the ancient footpaths that wind beneath increasingly high peaks. The pace picks up as we cross the passes and reach new plateaus of altitude and splendor until, at the 17,700-foot level, we are surrounded by the wild and breathtaking landscape of Thorong La. Here the pass crosses between two twin 21,270-foot peaks. From here we descend into Mustang Province and the holy shrine of Muktinath, home to a devout colony of Tibetan Buddhists. Our return takes us along the precipitous Kali Gandaki Gorge, where Dhaulagiri, four miles above us, casts its shadow into the deepest secrets of Nepal. By the time we reach Pokhara and then drive back to Kathmandu, the splendor of Annapurna has penetrated our souls, even as we have pierced the cloud-draped curtains of the Himalaya.

ITINERARY:

Day 1: Arrive Kathmandu.

Day 2: Kathmandu.

Day 3: Drive to Gurkha.

Day 4: Begin trek.

Days 5-14: To Phedi camp (14,450 ft.).

Day 15: Over Thorong La; descend to Muktinath (12,500 ft.).

Day 16: Muktinath.

Days 17-23: Descend Kali Gandak Gorge trail.

Day 24: End trek at Yamdi Khola; drive to Pokhara.

Day 25: Drive to Kathmandu.

Day 26: Kathmandu.

Day 27: Return.

MODERATE

March-May, October-December

World Expeditions

Annapurna Sanctuary (AS 8)

MODERATE TREK— CLASS III

- ➤ *Into the heart of Nepal*
- ➤ *Incredible mountain vistas*

Picture a 360-degree vista of the icy summits of no fewer than nine massive mountains. All are over 21,000 feet and one of them, Machapucchare (22,958 ft.), is one of the most visually spectacular peaks in the world. This is the Annapurna Sanctuary: a three-by-five-mile pocket in the high Himalayas, a beautiful meadowed upland without parallel in the known world, a place undiscovered by Western man until 1956.

Our journey starts at Pokhara, a trekker's trailhead in the shadow of the Himalayan giants. From here we walk north into the mountains, going higher and higher as the views of Dhaulagiri, Machapucchare, and the Annapurnas grow ever closer. Through thickets of bamboo and forests of conifer we rise,

finally breaking into the alpine grasslands of the sanctuary at Machapucchare base camp. In this awesome interior we spend several days, wandering from view to vista to vision until our entire perspective changes from one of wonder and disbelief to one of acceptance, pure and simple. That's just the way it is in Nepal.

ITINERARY:

Day 1: Arrive Kathmandu.

Day 2: Kathmandu.

Day 3: To Pokhara.

Day 4: Begin trek to Panchase Lekh camp.

Days 5-9: Trek to Poon Hill (10,473 ft.).

Days 10-12: To Hinko Cave (10,400 ft.).

Days 13-16: Annapurna Sanctuary.

Days 17-19: Return trek to Pokhara.

Day 20: Flight to Kathmandu.

Day 21: Kathmandu.

Day 22: Return.

MODERATE

January-May, October-December

World Expeditions

Nepal Panorama (AS 12)

VARIETY PACKAGE— CLASS III

- ➤ *Nine-day trek to the Annapurnas*
- ➤ *Two days rafting the Trisuli*
- ➤ *Culture and creatures of Nepal*

The kaleidoscopic Himalaya is revealed in all its glory on this 20-day introduction to the heartland of adventure travel. Nepal is a land where time is mea-

Garry Bolton/SOBEK photo file

sured not in hours but in centuries, and distance not by hours on the highway but by how far you can walk in a week. Our test of time and space comes early, as we set out from Pokhara in central Nepal to take the less-traveled trails behind Phewa Lake across the foothills of the majestic Annapurnas. Nowhere in the Himalayas are the mountains so clear and impressive from relatively low trails. On ground level, the route winds among mountain villages that have not yet fully entered the twentieth century, while up above, Annapurna South and Machapucchare dominate the skyline, each with its own distinctive character.

Then the pace quickens with an exciting two-day descent of the Trisuli River, with its rapids and beach camps, a perennial favorite among Nepalese travelers. And finally we ride elephants through the high grass of Chitwan National Park in search of rare rhino, elusive leopard, and twilit tiger in the junglelike setting of southern Nepal. We end our adventure with two days in Kathmandu immersing ourselves in the art and culture of its unique Hindu and Buddhist culture, eating plenty of good food, and shopping for treasures.

ITINERARY:

Day 1: Arrive Kathmandu.

Day 2: Kathmandu.

Day 3: Drive to Pokhara.

Days 4-11: Trekking.

Day 12: Pokhara.

Days 13-14: Rafting the Trisuli.

Day 15: End rafting, drive to Chitwan.

Days 16-17: Chitwan jungle safari.

Days 18-19: Kathmandu.

Day 20: Return.

MODERATE

January-May, September-December

World Expeditions

Sun Kosi Rafting (AS 15) ∿∿∿∿∿∿

MODERATE TREK AND RAFTING — CLASS III

➤ *Eight-day trek to riverside*
➤ *Rafting the river of gold*
➤ *From mountains to jungle*

Nepal is more than just mountains. Ice and water carve the Himalayan peaks, and rivers adorn their flanks like pearl necklaces. The headwaters of the Sun Kosi, the river we run, are in the dramatic high Himalayas, and from there the river flows down to the broad tropical valleys of the Terai, making it an awesome way to see a broad cross section of Nepal. Besides watching the riverside ecology change from ice and snow to palm trees, we will see the isolated retreats of *rishis* (Hindu sages), the cobbled squares of Newari villages, and suspension bridges that seem to be an eon old, and the raging rapids of the river itself.

To reach this whitewater highway we trek for a full week to over 12,500 feet where we will have memorable views of several major peaks—Himalchuli, Gaurisankar, and perhaps 27,000-foot Cho Oyu in far Tibet. Then we descend the Tamba Kosi, tributary to the River of Gold, and begin our Sun Kosi river run. Whitewater, scenery, and culture fill to bursting the next six days, with Class III-IV rapids and, in the lower gorges, tropical vegetation. Traveling by river is always exciting, but it is especially so when, as on the Sun Kosi, we see at every turn another view of towering mountains. On this trip, as on almost all trips in Nepal, the presence of the Himalayas turn every day into eternity and put infinity into every flower.

ITINERARY:

Day 1: Arrive Kathmandu.

Day 2: Kathmandu.

Day 3: Drive to Charikot (9,000 ft.); begin trek.

Days 4-8: Trek to Tamba Kosi.

Days 9-11: Trek to Sun Kosi confluence.

Days 12-16: Rafting.

Day 17: Return to Kathmandu.

Day 18: Kathmandu.

Day 19: Return.

MODERATE

March, October-November

World Expeditions

K2 Base Camp (AS 18) ▲▲▲▲▲▲

DIFFICULT TREK — CLASS V

➤ *The world's penultimate peak*
➤ *Three weeks of glacial wilderness*
➤ *Throne room of the mountain gods*

Spectacular is the word for this expedition to the base of the world's second highest peak, K2, in Pakistan's Karakoram Range. Just as 28,252-foot K2 presents a more difficult challenge to climbers than its taller cousin Everest, the trek to the K2 Base Camp is far more demanding to the adventure traveler. It takes over three weeks of hard walking to get there, through some of the remotest regions of the Himalayas. We will be far from home, hearth, and other signs of human habitation, often over 16,000 feet in elevation. But the rewards are correspondingly greater, too: a mind-blowing realm of towering mountain giants, including Masherbrum, Gasherbrum, Broad Peak, Hidden Peak, and K2 itself, all converging on a high realm called Concordia.

The magic journey begins in Pakistan's new capital of Islamabad, and from here we drive to Skardu on the banks of the Indus River to begin our trek. This trek is not one for the faint of heart: prior trekking or extensive hiking experience is essential for the trails are far more rugged, higher, and more isolated than those in Nepal. But consider the joys: a night, for instance, camped beneath a solid canopy of brilliant stars and surrounded by moon-white snowscapes, hearing only the absolute stillness and the occasional sounds of living glaciers grinding the earth to dust. This is a trip promising an experience that only a few will ever know.

ITINERARY:

Day 1: Arrive Islamabad; Rawalpindi tour.

Day 2: Islamabad.

Days 3-4: Skardu.

Day 5: To Dassu and begin trek.

Days 6-11: Trek to Piaju; acclimate.

Days 12-15: Trek to Condordia.

Days 16-18: Concordia.

Days 19-28: Return trek to Dassu.

Day 29: Skardu.

Day 30: Drive to Gilgit.

Day 31: Drive to Islamabad.

Day 32: Return.

MEDIUM

August-September

Adventure Pakistan

Kashmir/Ladakh Panorama (AS 27)

RAFTING AND TREKKING—CLASS III

➤ *Fabled monasteries of Ladakh*
➤ *Eight-day trek in idyllic Kashmir*
➤ *Rafting the Indus River*

It would be difficult to imagine two neighboring areas more different than the virgin mountains of Kashmir, the Switzerland of Asia, and the stark terrain of Ladakh, known to seasoned travelers as "Little Tibet" a land of treeless, rocky plains, hilltop Buddhist monasteries, prayer walls, and flags. Yet we become intimate with both on this three-week trip.

We begin in Delhi and fly to Srinagar in Kashmir, a nearly mythical land of rich farmlands, quiet lakeside villages, and pine-scented forests, a fabulously fertile province with a long tradition of generous hospitality. We experience it all on a week-long trek to the Kolahoi Glacier. Starting at 7,000 feet we hike through forests, across alpine meadows, and up to the high country where the forests thin and we are surrounded by views of glacier-covered Himalayan peaks. On the third day we reach the glacier (10,900 ft.) and stop to take in the scenery, including the striking Kolahoi Peak that looms directly overhead. Then we walk even higher to the alpine meadow of Seikwas (11,300 ft.), an extremely peaceful spot where we spend a day acclimating and exploring. Seikwas is everyone's favorite meadow and is usually full of alpine flowers. From here we hike up to Sanamous Pass (13,501 ft.) and stop to take in its awesome views of jagged, snowy peaks before heading down to the hair-raising road that goes up from Srinagar to Ladakh.

For the next three days we drive through stark, brown, desolate mountains of sand and rock capped by snow and ice to Leh, Ladakh's high capital. Monasteries and monks provide unworldly color; prayer wheels and prayer flags lead the way. Leh is the heart of this isolated Buddhist kingdom, as yet unconquered by more powerful cultures. The smiles of a hundred monks at Hemis, a sixteenth-century gompa surrounded by jagged peaks, welcome us to a living Shangri-La.

Our voyage of discovery is not over until we board inflatable rafts for the highest river trip in the world, down the swirling waters of the "Lion River," the Indus. Our two-day descent takes us through gorges where even the hearty Ladakhi monks have been unable to construct trails, and we end our quest for new experience with a thrill. This is a trip for those who want to experience a variety of both natural and cultural wonders in some of the most beautiful places in the world. By the time we return to Srinagar and relax on its luxurious houseboats, our hearts and souls will have grown by several dimensions.

ITINERARY:

Day 1: Arrive Delhi.

Days 2-3: Srinagar.

Day 4: Drive to Pahlgam, begin trek.

Days 5-10: On trek.

Days 11-12: End trek, drive to Leh.

Day 13: Leh.

Day 14: Hemis.

Days 15-16: Rafting the Indus.

Day 17: Leh.

Day 18: Fly to Srinagar.

Days 19-21: Srinagar.

Day 22: Delhi and return.

MEDIUM

June-September

World Expeditions

Himalayan Traverse (AS 29) ▲▲▲▲▲▲▲

RUGGED TREK—
CLASS IV

➤ *Across a triad of ranges*
➤ *Share nomadic campfires*
➤ *The lunar landscapes of Ladakh*

This classic trek crosses no fewer than three named mountain ranges: the Pir Panjal, the Great Himalaya, and the Zaskar. From rich alpine regions and the isolated farming villages of Kashmir, through the rugged homeland of nomadic herdsmen and into the stark, rarefied atmosphere of of Ladakh, or "Little Tibet", this trip has a little bit of everything and a great deal of the best. We begin at Lehinvan and trek through pine forests, across the Pir Panjal, and end up in the verdant Warvan Valley, one of the most picturesque farmlands in Asia. Then we go farther back in time to the pasturelands of the Bakharval herdsmen who point the way over the Great Himalaya via 15,093-foot Boktol Pass. The glaciers and icefalls of Nun Kun (23,410 ft.) greet our passage into the lunar landscapes of Ladakh, whose first citizens are Balti farmers from far Baltistan.

Finally we surmount our highest pass, Kanji La at 17,234 feet, and enter the heart of Ladakh, a region of startling shapes and colors like nowhere else on earth. We take tea with the monks in hidden monasteries, look down on starkly beautiful but uninhabitable landscape, and wonder if we're naturally high or if there's some extra chemical in the thin air we breathe.

ITINERARY:

Day 1: Delhi.

Days 2-3: Srinagar.

Day 4: To Leh in van, begin trek.

Days 5-21: On trek.

Day 22: End trek, drive to Leh.

Days 23-24: Leh.

Day 25: Fly to Srinagar.

Days 26-28: Srinagar.

Day 29: Delhi and return.

MODERATE

June-October

World Expeditions

Kashmir Adventure (AS 31) ▰▰▰▰▰▰▰

MODERATE TREK—
CLASS III

> *Eight-day trek in alpine Kashmir*
> *Three days of Srinagar houseboats*

This adventure gives a short and serene survey of the charms of Kashmir and covers the same area as the Kashmir Alpine Trek (AS 95) does. We spend eight days trekking to a mountain lake and three days relaxing in the well-appointed houseboats of Srinagar. We take this trip in the green seasons of spring and summer, when the colors and warmth of Kashmir are at their best.

The trek starts from Pahlgam and follows the Lidder Valley to its source at Mount Kolahoi, the impressive peak that dominates Kashmir. A climb up its verdant foothills to Tarsar Lake gives us the essential trekking experience with unrivaled views and mirror-clear glacial lakes. The trip climaxes with our crossing

of Sonamous Pass, just a tall man short of 13,000 feet. Our return route through the Sindh Valley takes us back to Srinagar, where three mind-numbing days in luxurious houseboats offer the delights of true civilization, our just reward for accepting the challenge of an introductory trek in Kashmir.

ITINERARY:

Day 1: Delhi.

Day 2: Fly to Srinagar.

Day 3: Srinagar.

Day 4: Drive to Pahlgam; begin trek.

Days 5-7: To Tarsar Lake.

Day 8: Sonamous Pass (12,993 ft.).

Days 9-10: Sindh Valley trekking.

Day 11: End trek; drive to Srinagar.

Days 12-14: Srinagar.

Day 15: Delhi and return.

MEDIUM

May-September

World Expeditions

South India Adventure (AS 37) 〰〰〰〰

VARIETY PACKAGE—
CLASS III

> *Trek the Nilgiri Hills*
> *Cycle the southern plains*

Where India's two coastal ranges, the Eastern and Western Ghats, converge, is a forgotten landscape of villages, fields, and misty mountain valleys. Two weeks exploring this part of the subcontinent by bicycle and foot gives us a good look at the part of India that survives in its most ancient and purest form. From our meeting place in Madras, we fly on to Bangalore and then drive to Mysore, spending a full day exploring the city's famous palace and bazaars.

This brief acculturation prepares us for a four-day bicycle tour of the rural villages of Mysore Province that ends in Ootacamund, "Queen of the Hill Stations" of the British Raj. A day here allows us to savor the fine mountain air and to gaze across the misty valleys of our trek route. For the next five days we hike these regions, in the heart of the Nilgiri Hills, across high forested ridges above the plantations and plains of southern India. Finally, our trail returns to "Ooty" and, after a last night in the hills, we return to Madras.

ITINERARY:

Day 1: Madras.

Day 2: To Mysore.

Day 3: Mysore.

Days 4-6: Cycling.

Day 7: Arrive Ootacamund.

Day 8: Ootacamund.

Days 9-12: Trekking.

Day 13: Return to Ootacamund.

Day 14: Cochin.

Day 15: Madras and return.

MEDIUM

October-March

World Expeditions

Maldives Sailing (AS 39)

SAILING AND DIVING—
CLASS II

➤ *1,200 islands of paradise*

➤ *Rich Islamic and Buddhist cultures*

➤ *A visit to Sri Lanka*

Sailing and diving in the Maldives is an aquatic odyssey of pleasures—from snorkeling among what many divers consider the world's most beautiful coral reefs to catching barracuda and collecting coconuts for fresh exotic meals to just soaking up the sun. The Maldives are a paradise of more than 1,200 coconut-covered atolls scattered across the Indian Ocean off the southwest tip of India. Shallow coral surrounds every island, creating a reef fantasia of color and texture; Arabic dhonies slice across the waters, their triangular sails arched in the wind; white coral sand beaches delight the most discriminating of sunbathers. The islands were settled by Asians, who converted to Islam in the twelfth century and were influenced by Europeans from the sixteenth century on. This unique heritage adds a note of cultural resonance to our 12-day seafaring adventure in this remarkable part of the world.

From these isolated, often uninhabited islands, we go to Sri Lanka, formerly Ceylon, for a 12-day tour of a remarkable culture; the tour includes a visit to Buddhist temples, Portuguese churches, Dutch forts, and British tea gardens. Along with socialites arriving from all over the world to stay at the sophisticated beach resorts, we will see some glorious botanical gardens and the exotic wildlife of Yalla National Park as we hike and bike our way around the island in search of its many treasures.

ITINERARY:

Day 1: Colombo.

Day 2: Colombo to Male, commence sailing.

Days 3-15: Sailing.

Day 16: Male to Colombo.

Day 17: Colombo.

Days 18-27: Sri Lanka safari.

Day 28: Colombo and return.

MODERATE

November-June

Voyages Maldives

Japanese Alps (AS 41)

ALPINE TREKKING— CLASS IV

➤ *The "Swiss Alps" of Japan*
➤ *Nightly hot spring soaks*
➤ *A visit to the temple city of Kyoto*

The jewels of Japanese mountains are the Kita Alps, rising more than 10,000 feet from sea level in the northern reaches. We trek for nine days through this mountain marvel, climbing steeply through low-elevation forest along rocky, narrow trails to the peaks themselves. To ease the strain of our daytime exertions, we relax at night in Japanese-style mountain huts, soaking weary bones in communal hot springs. Here our only companions are likely to be Japanese mountain enthusiasts, since few Westerners are familiar with these Alpine trails.

In addition to exploring the beauty of a remote and wild part of Japan, we also spend three days in Kyoto, the country's ancient capital, where we explore the many temples and museums that make the city a living museum of Japanese culture, art, and history.

ITINERARY:

Day 1: Departure.

Day 2: Arrive Tokyo.

Day 3: Tokyo.

Day 4: Train to Nakabusa.

Days 5-7: Kyoto.

Day 8: Train to Nagoya.

Day 9: Mt. Ontake.

Day 10: Takayama.

Days 11-18: Trek.

Day 19: Tokyo.

Day 20: Return.

MEDIUM

August

A Guide For All Seasons

Japanese Country Inns (AS 42)

CULTURE—CLASS I

➤ *Culture, food, and life-style*
➤ *Nights in family inns*
➤ *National Parks and Mount Fuji*

The objective of this trip is to provide an introduction to Japanese culture, food, and life-style. We travel, eat, bathe, and sleep as the Japanese do. Except in Tokyo where we stay in a modern hotel, all lodging will be in Japanese-style inns, called *ryokans*, where we will be treated as honored guests, as the outfitter has known some of the families who operate them for a number of years.

We'll spend a full day at the lovely Nikko National Park, filled with memorials to the first of the Tokugawa Shoguns, and then travel halfway up Mount Fuji by bus. Later we'll travel across the central Honshu and into the mountains, where we'll stay at a hot springs (*onsen*) resort. Then we'll take a tour of the Chubu-sangaku National Park, in the ''Alps of Japan,'' and finally spend three days in Japan's capital of culture, Kyoto, where we'll visit farmer's markets, Samurai houses, castles, shrines, and folk art palaces. Our hosts take special care to see that the food is tasty and served with style. Activities are loosely structured to allow plenty of time for exploring, day hiking, and shopping. Travel is at a leisurely pace, which allows us to enjoy the benefits of group travel without its regimentation.

ITINERARY:

Day 1: Depart USA.

Days 2-3: Tokyo.

Day 4: Nikko National Park.

Day 5: Free

Days 6-7: Mt. Fuji/Kawaguchiko.

Day 8: Mt. Onsen.

Day 9: Kamikochi.

Days 10-11: Takayama.

Days 12-14: Kyoto.

Day 15: Return via Osaka.

MEDIUM

October, May, August

A Guide For All Seasons

Thailand Adventure (AS 47)

VARIETY PACKAGE— CLASS III

➤ *Hill tribes of Thailand*
➤ *Trek the Golden Triangle*
➤ *Snorkel the Gulf of Thailand*

The crown of Southeast Asia is Thailand, once ruled by the wealthy kings of Siam. Never colonized by Western empires and closed to foreigners for over one hundred years, modern Thailand has been created only in this century, thus ensuring that many of its secrets and treasures are still preserved. We will unveil some of them on this three-week tour of Thailand's most exotic sites, including the fabled Golden Triangle in the north.

The trip begins in Bangkok, continues on to Chiang Mai, and from here we head into the hills to spend almost two weeks traveling through the isolated towns near the Burmese border, making our way by bus, truck, and boat until we must strike out on foot, spending the night as guests of the village headman. Luckily, the lush landscape seems to have been tailor-made for trekking, and we pass through the villages of very distinct tribes of people including the Lahu, Lisu, Meo (Hmong), Akha, Yao, and Karen, all of whom preserve traditional costumes and crafts and maintain an ancient way of life that predates most others in Asia. We walk from three to six hours a day, following trails that vary from dirt roads to small jungle tracks, and in the afternoons are free to explore the villages and closely observe the daily life of the people. Meals are prepared by our Thai guide from Chiang Mai who accompanies us throughout the trek, and we sleep on locally made grass sleeping mats in guest rooms attached to the headman's house. At one point on our trek we board elephants for a jungle ride; and toward the end of the trip we build bamboo rafts and float downriver.

After returning to Chiang Mai for some shopping and sightseeing, we take an overnight train to Bangkok and then a bus ride to Kanchanaburi where we visit the Allied Cemetery and the "Bridge on the River Kwai." Here we transfer to River Kwai Jungle Rafts and paddle to the "Floatel," where we spend a luxurious day and night swimming and relaxing.

The final, "tropical-island-paradise" portion of our adventure is a four-day voyage around the islands of the eastern gulf on a Thai sailing junk. The Gulf of Thailand is usually calm in this area, and we travel between many small islands in almost no open water (although there may be very brief squalls). Our days here are leisurely: we sail for two to three hours in the morning and then moor off an island to swim, snorkel, fish, and even windsurf. In the afternoon we sail on a little farther, stopping at local fishing villages to restock fresh provisions and meet people. The food our Thai cook prepares is fresh and delicious, and we sleep in shared cabins or on mattresses spread out on the deck, under the stars. By the end of our trip we have spent our days enjoying charms so numerous that, like the King of Siam himself, we are reduced to listing them in Latin: "Et cetera, et cetera, et cetera."

ITINERARY:

Day 1: Arrive Bangkok.

Day 2: To Chiang Mai.

Days 3-6: Hill tribe trek.

Day 7: Golden Triangle.

Day 8: Fly to Mae Hong Son, begin combined trek.

Days 9-12: Rafting, elephant riding, trekking.

Day 13: Chiang Mai.

Days 14-15: Bangkok.

Day 16: To Pattaya.

Days 17-20: Sailing tour.

Day 21: Bangkok and return.

MODERATE

November-February

World Expeditions

Thailand Hill Trek (AS 49)

CULTURAL TREKKING— CLASS III

➤ *Explore the ancient temples of Chiang Mai*

➤ *Trek the Golden Triangle*

➤ *Observe hill tribe artists at work*

This week-long trek through the tribal villages of Thailand is the perfect way to see the "Golden Triangle," where life goes on much the way it did hundreds of years ago. The tribes are shy and clannish, but our guides are their friends and we have an opportunity to sleep in village houses and to participate fairly intimately in their lives.

From Bangkok, we bus to the hill city of Chiang Mai, famed for its crafts and antiques, and from here begin our trek through beautiful rolling country to the villages of the Lahu, Lisu, and Akha tribes. The Lahu are famed for their hunting skills; the Lisu have strong animist beliefs (each village has a folk healer and exorcist); and the Akha are known for their beautiful embroidery.

The trekking in Thailand is moderate in terms of the length of days walking, but it is considerably rougher than in Nepal in terms of the standard of service. We sleep in communal guest rooms of village houses, which are less comfortable than the tents in Nepal, and carry our own personal clothing, though this need not exceed 25 pounds. The trade-off is that we return from this trek having experienced a genuine and fascinating cultural experience.

ITINERARY:

Day 1 (Sat.): Meet in Bangkok.

Day 2: Bus to Chiang Mai.

Days 3-5: Trekking

Day 6: Return to Chiang Mai.

Day 7: In Chiang Mai.

Day 8: (Sat.) Fly Chiang Mai/Bangkok.

MODERATE

May-October

World Expeditions

Coruh River (AS 50) ∿∿∿∿∿

CULTURAL RAFTING— CLASS IV

➤ *World-class whitewater*

➤ *Lush gorges and snowy peaks*

➤ *Castles and hidden villages*

The average American thinks of Turkey as a land of camels, sand dunes, and vast expanses of desert—the landscape of much of the Middle East. But just 9 percent of Turkey's land is level or gently sloping; most of it is over 6,500 feet and is made up of lofty mountains, high plateaus, and plenty of exciting river runs. And the Coruh is one of the best. It is a whitewater delight, with fast and furious rapids and all the hydrotechnics that make river running such a thrilling sport.

What makes the Coruh unique are the villages and people we run into alongside its banks. Many of the villages are truly untouched by the outside world, and their inhabitants are extremely friendly and curious.

We begin our trip on a chilly plateau in the northeast of Turkey, not far from Mount Ararat. Here, in the town of Erzurum, we see traditionally fez-topped white-whiskered men and fully wrapped women walking noisy, narrow streets at the foot of snow-covered mountains. After a day in Erzurum, we drive north to Bayburt for our put-in. We are now in a world where streams weave and funnel into rivers, old Roman roadbeds and irrigation aqueducts wind along the water's edge, and the 10,000-foot snow-touched peaks of the Kara Deniz loom overhead. Mallards, storks, herons, and egrets stalk the riverbanks, and flocks of ankaz, red-breasted geese that migrate from the Arctic, wheel overhead. This is the most gnarled and rough-hewn part of Turkey, and its most thinly populated region with just thirteen people per square mile: a true wilderness where wildlife still roams free. In some of the remote river canyons we careen past cattle, water buffalo, sheep, and gaily dressed Black Sea children with almond eyes. Much of the land here is farmed, and we are rarely more than a few deft strokes from peaches, cherries, peas, and other fresh fruits and vegetables.

Perhaps the most amazing sight on the river is a huge, buff-colored, twelfth-century castle, pointing to the clouds and perched on a crag overlooking a gray-brown village. We stop to visit it and discover the town of Isper, which is a very special pleasure, all but unknown until the first SOBEK rafters discovered it over a decade ago. Here is a living tableau torn from the Crusades: veiled women padding past crowded, smoke-clouded coffee-houses where the men feverishly pitch *tavla* (backgammon) dice between swigs of tea. In the small back rooms of this town we can watch young women painstakingly weaving the traditional silk rugs for which Turkey is so famous. And from the top of the castle we can hear the *Adhan*, or Moslem, call to prayer.

Throw in a hot springs, some Armenian ruins, and the usual thrills of an unusual river that includes a 14-mile-long Class IV rapid near trip's end, and our ride down the Coruh ends up being a combination of culture and sport that is just about perfect.

ITINERARY:

Day 1: Arrive Ankara.

Day 2: Fly to Erzurum.

Day 3: Drive to Bayburt; begin river trip.

Days 4-12: On the Coruh.

Day 13: Take-out, drive to Erzurum.

Day 14: Afternoon return to Ankara.

Day 15: Return.

MEDIUM

June, June-July

SOBEK Expeditions

Turquoise Coast Sail (AS 51)

SAILING — CLASS II

➤ *Explore ruins of empires past*

➤ *Motor-sail yachting*

➤ *Swim, snorkle, fish*

The Turquoise Coast of Turkey, with its wooded inlets and islands, beautiful Greek and Roman ruins, and charming villages, is one of the few places left in the modern world that is at once both unspoiled and civilized. We begin our trip on the quintessentially Greek island of Rhodes, where we board the *Kaptan*, our 65-foot motor-sail yacht, and set sail on the blue-green waters of the Aegean and Mediterranean. On the water we swim, snorkel, windsurf, and fish; when we drop anchor in any of the many isolated coves that decorate the region, we hike up pine-scented hills to wildflower meadows and clamber around the great stone ruins of long-eclipsed empires: Lycian, Carain, Greek, Roman, Byzantine, and Ottoman.

Turkish villages on many of the islands extend their hospitality when we shop for locally crafted carpet, brass work, and embroidery. Finally, we return to the fabled Isle of Rhodes, passing through the harbor mouth the great Colossus once straddled, back to the modern world that has descended from this Aegean heritage.

ITINERARY:

Day 1: Athens.

Days 2-3: Rhodes.

Days 4-13: Sailing.

Day 14: Return.

MEDIUM

May, September

SOBEK Expeditions

North Yemen (AS 52)

CULTURE — CLASS I

➤ *A visit to the past*

➤ *Richly costumed people*

➤ *Ancient architecture*

The Tibet of the Middle East is a mountainous marvel with a history stretching back 2,500 years. Here we see stone castles up to ten stories high perched on mountaintops, miles of stone terraces surrounding medieval walled castles, and friendly people, in robes and turbans and with bejeweled daggers, preening and posing for the cameras.

The principal cities and sites of North Yemen are accessible by car, but to see the more remote castles and mosques we take day-long hikes into this ancient land, discovering an entire country and culture that has been mostly hidden from the modern world. We also explore both the semiarid plains and the ancient ruin-filled ports of the Red Sea. This trip offers a chance to explore one of the best-kept secrets of the travel world—a country that is, many believe, unsurpassed in natural and architectural beauty.

ITINERARY:

Days 1-3: Sanaa.

Day 4: Wadi Dahr.

Days 5-6: Sadah, Bhamas hot springs.

Days 7-8: Ibb, Taiz.

Days 9-11: Red Sea coast.

Days 12-13: In the mountains.

Days 14-15: Sanaa.

Day 16: Return.

MEDIUM

January

Exodus Expeditions

China Bicycle (AS 63)

CULTURAL TWO-WHEELING—CLASS III

➤ *See China from a bicycle seat*
➤ *Rural Guangdong Province*
➤ *Highlights of Beijing*

Bicycling through China is the way to experience daily life much the way the Chinese do. Clusters of village children gather and giggle wherever we go as we dodge shoulder poles and lumbering buffalo and pedal through the land of a billion people into the twenty-first century.

Our adventure begins in Hong Kong, commercial capital of Asia, then changes abruptly as we boat up the Pearl River to Guangzhou (formerly Canton), one of the liveliest cities in China. At the city gates we begin our bicycle loop tour of Guangdong Province, whose people spearheaded the emigration to America, Australia, and South America in the nineteenth century, following the gold rushes. Here we see ancient pagodas rising over misty lakes and limestone crags looming in the pale gloom and visit schools, factories, ancient temples, and local bazaars. We stay in comfortable local hotels and feast on the famous banquets of southern China nearly every night. Following the bicycle tour, we all board the northbound train and watch the wheels spin us cross-country to Beijing, where we make pilgrimages to the Ming Tombs, the Forbidden City, and the Great Wall. Then it's back to Guangzhou and Hong Kong with a satchel full of memories from our immersion in China's sea of life.

ITINERARY:

Day 1: Hong Kong.

Day 2: Evening steamer on Pearl River.

Day 3: Guangzhou.

Days 4-15: Cycle tour.

Day 16: Guangzhou.

Day 17: Board train.

Day 18: Arrive Beijing.

Days 19-20: Beijing.

Day 21: Fly to Guangzhou.

Day 22: Hong Kong and return.

MEDIUM

January-May, September-December

World Expeditions

Alas River (AS 77) ∿∿∿∿

RAFTING AND WILDLIFE—
CLASS III

➤ *Run Sumatra's River of the Red Ape*

➤ *Orangutans, gibbons, and macaques*

➤ *Traverse the endangered rain forest*

The River of the Red Ape is the Alas, sliding through the world's largest orangutan reserve in northern Sumatra's Gunung Leuser National Park. First explored by SOBEK in 1984 and showcased in the television documentary "River of the Red Ape," the Alas has since vaulted to the top of the list of things to do in Southeast Asia. Not only is it a beautiful river in a tropical rain forest but it runs a journey through the homeland of the rare "man of the forest," the wild orangutan.

Our trip begins in Medan, the largest city in Sumatra and a morning's drive through palm oil and rubber tree plantations to the Bohorok Orangutan Rehabilitation Station. Here tame orangutans, once kept as household pets, are being induced to return to their native environment. These large apes are believed by some to be among the closest relatives of humans living on earth, and they are found in Gunung Leuser Park in numbers unmatched anywhere else in the world. At Bohorok we stay in small guest houses on a beautiful, clear, fast-running river and go for morning and afternoon walks to see the formerly captive orangutans come down from the treetops to feed.

The next afternoon we drive back through Medan and up into the crisp mountain air of the Karo Batak Highlands where we stop in Brastagi at a charming hotel, formerly a Dutch colonial mansion, set on a rolling green hilltop that doubles as a golf course. The next day is put-in for our four-day rafting trip down the Alas. At first we drift through agricultural valleys, noting both the timeless beauty of the ecosystem and the mounting pressures that threaten it. We float by four remote villages, waving greetings and exchanging smiles, but we also see and hear the signs of logging. The next day we enter the park, which is sometimes called the East Africa of Asia for the number and variety of wildlife it harbors. Here we float through a beautiful gorge where vine-draped trees of the rain forest press close and the air seems still and expectant. We run a couple of mild rapids and have an excellent chance of seeing gibbons, macaques, or leaf monkeys playing in the trees and hornbills sailing across the sky. At night we camp on a sandy beach and feast on some of the best food offered on any river trip, with candlelight, hors d'oeuvres, and wine included.

The next day we leave the steep-walled mountains of the gorge and drift through the preserve, occasionally floating alongside the boat in our life jackets, stopping to shower under waterfalls, relaxing, and looking and listening for wildlife. Five-foot monitor lizards, wild boars, deers, orangutans, even elephants live in the park, though it takes luck to spot them.

The last night we camp on the lowland plains above the Indian Ocean and the next morning, just before take-out and the return to Medan and then Jakarta, we listen to the monkeys calling to each other from the trees as we glide beneath them in the dark green river canyon.

ITINERARY:

Day 1: Arrive Medan, Sumatra.

Day 2: Bohorok.

Day 3: Bohorok to Alas River.

Day 4: Begin river trip.

Days 5-6: River safari.

Day 7: End river trip, return to Medan, flight to Jakarta; hotel overnight.

Day 8: Return.

MEDIUM

January-July, September-December

SOBEK Expeditions

Gateway to Nepal (AS 78)

POPULAR INTRODUCTION TO PARADISE—CLASS I/III

➤ *Overflight of Mt. Everest*

➤ *Wildlife of Chitwan*

➤ *Optional three-day trek*

From the markets of Kathmandu through the skies of Mount Everest to the fabulous wildlife of Chitwan National Park, this introductory package highlights the features that have made Nepal synony-mous with "Paradise Found." We begin in Kathmandu, a city that is truly an outdoor museum. Here we immerse ourselves in the art and architecture, walking streets that still seem medieval despite the tourist invasion. On our second day we take a spectacular early morning flight to see Mount Everest and other peaks (weather permitting) and in the afternoon visit the massive Buddhist stupa at Bodhnath and the ancient capital town of Bhaktapur, an exotic city out of another time.

Then we take a spectacular flight alongside the Himalayan massif to Pokhara, Nepal's "second city," situated in a low valley even closer to the immense Himalayan peaks than Kathmandu. From here we begin a three-day trek that has all the extras of a classic expedition—porters to carry our gear, Sherpas to lead the way, morning tea in tents, and views of the world's crowning summits. We stay below 6,000 feet, but the big mountains are all around us—Annapurna, Dhaulagiri, and Machapucchare. We'll also see a cross section of Nepali peoples, including the Gurungs (the famous British army Gurkhas), Magars, Chettris, and, if we're lucky, we'll see a pony caravan coming down from Tibet.

After relaxing at a first-class hotel back in Pokhara, we drive south to the tropics and a completely new world. Based in a jungle lodge in Chitwan National Park, we explore the park on the back of an elephant, moving through tall elephant grass in search of the oft-sighted rhino and deer and maybe even a leopard or tiger. The birdlife here is fantastic—some 450 species have been sighted within the park—particularly during winter when migrants from northern Asia come this far south. We'll also take dugout canoe rides to see crocodiles and waterfowl.

Back in Kathmandu we have time to shop and explore this distinctive city: dirty, sparkling, ancient, modern, Hindu, Buddhist, teeming, private, extremely memorable. If we missed the early morning mountain flight earlier on, we can catch it now. Then it's back to Bangkok and a flight home.

For the nontrekker, an extended tour of the Kathmandu Valley is offered, with visits to the ancient capital of Bhaktapur and the golden-roofed temple of Pashupatinath, plus, in Pokhara, a dugout canoe ride on nearby Phewa Lake, with views of Machapucchare, the Fishtail Peak. Either option assures all travelers of memorable views of the Himalayan giants and lasting memories of a country whose wealth is in its beauty and its magic.

ITINERARY:

Days 1-2: En route.

Day 3: Arrival in Kathmandu.

Day 4: Everest overflight (weather permitting); city tour.

Days 5-7: To Pokhara and trek, or nontrekking option.

Days 8-9: Chitwan National Park.

Day 10: Return to Kathmandu.

Day 11: Everest overflight makeup day or free day in Kathmandu. Day 12: Fly to Bangkok.

Day 13: Bangkok.

Day 14: Return.

MEDIUM

January-May, August-December

SOBEK Expeditions

Nepal Options (AS 80/88/136)

ADVENTURE ADD-ONS—
CLASS III

➤ *Instant Everest (AS 80)*

➤ *Nepal Rivers and Wildlife (AS 88)*

➤ *Instant Annapurna (AS 136)*

Once you've reached paradise, why not enjoy a little more of it? Three short adventures offer a chance to make quick but fulfilling trips to parts of Nepal no one should miss. The "Instant Everest" trek is a moderate week-long journey to over 13,000 feet. We fly into the mountain station of Lukla at over 9,000 feet, in the heart of the Sherpa region. From here we trek along the Dudh Kosi River, through Namche Bazar, to the site of recently burned and soon-to-be-rebuilt Thyangboche monastery with its justly celebrated view of Everest. Thyangboche is directly beneath Ama Dablam ("Mother's Charm Box," 22,494 ft.), a snowy, needle-peaked mountain that some say is the most beautiful of all in the Everest region.

For river lovers, the "Nepal Rivers and Wildlife" combination links three days on the Trisuli River, featuring mild whitewater and mountain views by day and moonlit riverside camps by night, with two full days at Chitwan National Park. In the park we view game from the back of an elephant or a dugout canoe or take birdwatching walks and excursions into the backcountry by jeep.

The "Instant Annapurna" itinerary is another week-long trek, this one starting in Pokhara, the crossroads town of central Nepal. It follows the middle hill ranges in the shadow of the Himalayan giants, offering impressive views of the "Fishtail Peak," Machapucchare, and other summits such as the Annapurnas and the Lamjung Himal.

ITINERARY, ''Instant Everest'' (AS 80):

Day 1: Fly Kathmandu to Lukla; begin trek.

Days 2-3: To Namche Bazar.

Days 4-5: Thyangboche.

Days 6-7: Return to Lukla.

Day 8: Fly to Kathmandu.

Day 9: Kathmandu.

MEDIUM

January-May, September-December

ITINERARY, ''Nepal Rivers and Wildlife'' (AS 88):

Day 1: Kathmandu to river; begin rafting.

Day 2: On the river.

Day 3: End rafting; drive to Chitwan.

Day 4: Chitwan.

Day 5: Late evening return to Kathmandu.

MEDIUM

Year-round

ITINERARY, ''Instant Annapurna'' (AS 136):

Day 1: Kathmandu to Pokhara; begin trek.

Days 2-7: On trek.

Day 8: Lukla.

Day 9: To Kathmandu.

MEDIUM

January-April, November-December

Regal Excursions

High-Altitude Trek (AS 85) ▲▲▲▲▲▲▲

MOUNTAIN TREK— CLASS V

➤ *High passes and legendary peaks*

➤ *Optional climb of Island Peak*

For an insider's view of the Everest region, this trek is unsurpassed. It is a long journey over some of the world's loftiest Himalayan passes and offers vistas few will ever see as well as a fair share of moraine, rocks, glaciers, and the sublime and distinct colors of high altitude. Since we will be doing some rock and ice climbing, participants are required to have extensive outdoor experience and to be in excellent physical condition.

Setting off on the classic Everest expedition route, we climb in the shadow of the northern peaks to Namche Bazar, our point of departure for the ascent to the beautiful Gokyo Valley and its glacial lake. Traversing Ngozumpa glacier's toe, we negotiate Chugima La Pass (17,777 ft.), under the north face of Cholatse, with encompassing views of the legendary Himalayan peaks. Descending to Thosia, we rejoin the Everest Base Camp route, trekking on to Gorak Shep. From here, we follow the Khumbu glacier, climbing Kala Pattar for the classic view of Everest. The final pass on our journey is Kongma La (18,171 ft.), which few trekkers attempt. Beyond this pass are beautiful isolated high valleys, the Imja Khola River, and our base camp (17,056 ft.) below Island Peak.

Those climbing Island Peak (20,300 ft.) will move to a rock shelf camp at 18,328 feet and from there begin the ascent. The knife-edged summit ridge of Island Peak gives an unforgettable glimpse into the heart of the highest peaks on earth—a full circle panorama including Lhotse's south face and Makalu, the fifth highest mountain in the world.

ITINERARY:

Days 1-2: Kathmandu.

Day 3: To Lukla, trek to Phakdingma.

Days 4-5: Namche Bazar.

Day 6: Thame.

Days 7-8: Sanasa and training.

Day 9: Dole.

Day 10: Machherma.

Days 11-12: Gokyo.

Days 13-14: Ngozumpa.

Day 15: Dragnag.

Day 16: Chugima La.

Day 17: Dzongia.

Days 18-19: Gorak Shep, climb Kala Pattar.

Day 20: Kongma La Base Camp.

Day 21: Chhukung.

Days 22-23: Island Peak Base Camp.

Day 24: High Camp.

Day 25: To Island Peak and back to Base Camp.

Day 26: Base Camp.

Day 27: Debuche.

Day 28: Namche Bazar.

Day 29: Phakdingma.

Day 30: Lukla.

Days 31-34: Kathmandu.

MODERATE

September-November, March-April

World Expeditions

Introduction to Expedition Travel (AS 89)

VARIETY PACKAGE— CLASS III

➤ *Trekking the Annapurnas*
➤ *Bicycle to Jaipur*
➤ *Elephants, camels, and whitewater*

If your thirst for adventure is tough to slake, consider a draught of this "try everything" trip through northern India and Nepal. Our multifaceted journey takes us over a wide area, but always we

Kebos/SOBEK photo file

explore a particular sight slowly, by foot, bike, camel, and raft, with time to savor the experience.

The trip begins with a four-day camel ride across the vast and empty deserts of Rajasthan and ends in Jaisalmer, an otherworldly fortress city built of rock and sand. Next we mount bicycles to wheel along the relatively flat 150-mile route from the Pink City of Jaipur to Agra, site of the fabled Taj Mahal. From here we head for Nepal by train and plane and take an eight-day trek in the untouristed foothills of the Annapurnas. After that it's a two-day whitewater voyage down the Trisuli River, and finally, in Chitwan National Park, elephants take us high and deep into the jungles for some wildlife viewing—our last exotic ride before two days of the eye-opening, art-filled market-places of Kathmandu. After all this, simple locomotion will never be the same.

ITINERARY:

Day 1: Delhi to Bikaner.

Day 2: Thar Desert.

Days 3-6: Camel caravan.

Day 7: Jodhpur.

Days 8-9: Jaipur.

Days 10-13: Cycle tour to Agra.

Day 14: Taj Mahal; on to Delhi.

Days 15-16: Kathmandu.

Day 17: Drive to Pokhara.

Days 18-26: On trek.

Days 27-28: Trisuli rafting.

Day 29: Drive to Chitwan.

Days 30-31: Chitwan.

Days 32-33: Kathmandu.

Day 34: Return.

MEDIUM

January-March, October-December

World Expeditions

Trans-Zanskar Trek (AS 94) ▲▲▲▲▲▲▲▲▲

RUGGED TREK—
CLASS IV

➤ *World's highest monasteries*
➤ *The culture of Little Tibet*
➤ *Finest scenery of the Indus watershed*

This trek in the stark and awesome Zanskar Mountains is not for the fainthearted, yet the compensations are many for those keen to explore a landscape and culture similar to Tibet. After luxuriating on a houseboat in Kashmir, we drive for two days on the spectacular highway to Leh, the high mountain capital of Ladakh where traditional Buddhist culture still remains intact. Then we drive to Lamayuru and begin our trek.

Ladakh means the land of high passes, and true to form we cross several ridges of the Zanskar Range on our first few days on the trail. Along the way we constantly pass mani walls and chortens that testify to the rich Buddhist culture of the region. At night we camp beside small settlements where the barley fields are irrigated by the snowmelt from the top of the highest ridges. Crossing the Singi La, the Lion Pass, we descend to the village of Lingshet, famed for its medieval Tibetan monastery. And two passes later, we reach the Zanskar Valley where we visit Zangla, home of the king of the Zanskar, who, if we're lucky, may give us an audience. The monastery at Karsha, near Zangla, is also an attraction: it is the largest in the Zanskar region and home to over a hundred Buddhist monks.

We continue trekking high above the river gorges until we reach the impressive Phugtal Monastery, whose main temple is carved out of a huge limestone cave high above the valley floor; and finally we make our way to the main Himalaya and cross the Shingo La. Here the huge snow-capped peaks stretch across the southern horizon, a fitting finale before we descend to the roadhead and a well earned rest in the picturesque, green Kulu valley.

ITINERARY:

Day 1: Meet Delhi.

Day 2: Fly to Srinagar.

Day 3: Srinagar.

Days 4-5: Drive to Leh.

Days 6-7: Leh.

Day 8: Drive to Lamayuru and commence trek.

Days 9-25: Trek.

Day 26: Complete trek and drive to Manali.

Day 27: Manali.

Day 28: Fly to Delhi.

Day 29: Trip ends, Delhi.

MEDIUM

June-September

World Expeditions

Kashmir Alpine Trek (AS 95) ▲▲▲▲▲▲▲

MODERATE TREK—
CLASS III

➤ *The Switzerland of Asia*

➤ *Two-week flower-strewn trek*

➤ *Srinagar houseboats*

Imagine the lakes, valleys, and peaks of Switzerland on a Himalayan scale and you have an idea of what Kashmir has to offer: clear streams, awesome peaks, and brilliant wildflowers erupting from ver-dant alpine meadows. It is this high landscape that has beckoned to the Gujar shepherds for uncounted generations, and this area is where we set our sights when we leave lake-lovely Srinagar for the trailhead at Sonamarg near the remote Indian station of Pahlgam. After a slow ascent through piney woods, we spend a day at lakeside in Vishensar, feasting on trout and enjoying superb views of Nanga Parbat, the world's tenth highest mountain at 26,660 feet.

Then, crossing a 14,000-foot pass, we reach the Sindh Valley and join the Gujar in their flower-strewn summer encampments. Our trek climaxes with an early morning hike to the ridges above Lake Gangobal, whose mirrorlike surface reflects the intensified sense of reality we have come to expect in this alpine world. A trilogy of days in Srinagar, relaxing in opulent houseboat accommodations, completes our trip.

ITINERARY:

Day 1: Delhi.

Day 2: Fly to Srinagar.

Day 3: Srinagar.

Day 4: To Pahalgam; begin trek.

Days 5-8: To Vishensar.

Days 9-11: To Lake Gangobal.

Days 12-18: Return trek.

Days 19-21: Srinagar.

Day 22: Delhi and return.

MEDIUM

June-September

World Expeditions

Tibet Overland (AS 108)

CULTURE—
CLASS II

➤ *Cross from Nepal to Tibet*

➤ *Everest view*

➤ *Two ancient capitals*

It has been decades since the ancient trade route between Tibet and Nepal was open to the adventurous traveler. Certainly in our lifetime, this is one of the first opportunities to cross this last frontier, the lost border between these two Himalayan kingdoms. Be among the first granted a permit to venture into these forgotten landscapes, to explore this world of lamas and mystery, with its treasures of tradition and its virgin vistas.

Our route begins in Kathmandu, where we poke and probe this fascinating city for two days. Then we either fly directly to Lhasa or board a bus to follow the age-old trading paths across the rarefied passes of the Himalaya to the Tibetan plateau, trundling by magnificent vistas of the northern flanks of Mount Everest along the way. We are now in the once-forbidden frontier of Tibet. After reaching Tibet, we explore the Buddhist capital of Lhasa, with its fabled Potala Palace, former winter residence of the Dalai Lama; and Xigaze, the beautiful second city of Tibet, and home to the Panchen Lama.

By the time we have finished our trip, we have crossed over more than the mightiest mountain range on earth: we have ventured across centuries of tradition, ages of history, and eons of geology. Don't miss this unique window in time. Be among the first to journey from Nepal to Tibet, across the greatest mountain range on earth.

ITINERARY:

Days 1-2: Kathmandu.

Days 3-7: Drive to Lhasa.

Days 8-10: Lhasa.

Day 11: Fly to Kathmandu.

Day 12: Kathmandu.

Day 13: Return.

MEDIUM

July-October

Regal Excursions

Ganges River (AS 109)

WHITEWATER
RAFTING—CLASS IV

➤ *Explore a most sacred river*

➤ *Search for Bengal tigers*

➤ *The exotic magic of Delhi*

The people in India call it "Ganga," one of the most celebrated of all the world's waterways, and on this trip we bathe in its waters—in Shiva's dripping hair, as they say. From its headwaters in the Garhwal region, where its source is honored by the devotion of pilgrims, to its outflow at the enormous delta on the Bay of Bengal, the Ganges is the major artery for northern India's millions. We explore its upper reaches along the Bhagirathi tributary, which links with the Alaknanda at Devaprayag to form the great Mother River. Then our route continues through narrow canyons, down 50-foot-per-mile drops, into the land of the Bengal tiger beyond our sandy beach camps. There's time, too, to see the cultural highlights of the Indian mountain communities we travel through as well as Delhi, the fascinating capital of ancient India.

ITINERARY:

Days 1-2: Delhi.

Day 3: Rishikesh.

Day 4: Devaprayag.

Day 5: Tehri.

Days 6-12: On the river.

Day 13: Rishikesh.

Days 14-15: Delhi.

Day 16: Return.

PREMIUM

October

Wild Life Adventure Tours

North India Adventure (AS 111)

VARIETY PACKAGE—
CLASS III

➤ *Cycle tour of India's villages*
➤ *Camel safari in Rajasthan Desert*
➤ *Temples, forts, palaces, and bazaars*

"Go to the villages, that is India; therein lies the soul of India." Mahatma Gandhi's dictum for discovery holds as true now as it did in his own time, but we put a spin on it with a companion camel caravan in the far desert of Thar. We begin by taking the night train from Delhi to the desert town of Bikaner, and then driving deeper into the desert where we meet our guides and our humped mounts. For four days we live in a lost age of cacaphony and color, Rajputs and

Maharajahs, carried back in time by our ghostly caravanserai. We see the desert close up and, atop our camels, peer over village walls into the timeless world that goes on inside them.

After exploring the architectural wonders and bazaars of Jodhpur, the bustling tourist city of Jaipur, and the desert fortress town of Jaisalmer, we begin the second stage of our adventure, cycling through Gandhi's villages along classic bike paths. We peddle past rice paddies and mustard fields, from village to town, stopping for food and drink and talk (someone speaks English in even the smallest villages in India), and end our bicycle tour in Agra, site of the fabulous Taj Mahal. From there we fly back to Delhi—back to the future and our own karmic destiny, riding the Western wheel of life.

ITINERARY:

Day 1: Meet in Delhi; board train.

Day 2: Arrive Bikaner.

Days 3-5: Camel safari.

Day 6: End safari, drive to Jaisalmer.

Day 7: Jodhpur.

Days 8-9: Jaipur.

Days 10-12: Cycle tour.

Day 13: Arrive Agra.

Day 14: Delhi.

Day 15: Return

MEDIUM

January-March, October-December

World Expeditions

Source of the Ganges (AS 114)

CULTURAL TREK—
CLASS IV

➤ *Trek to the fountainhead*

➤ *Stunning Himalayan panoramas*

➤ *Touch the Holy Glacier*

The holiest of pilgrimages for Hindus is the trek to the source of the Ganges, Gaumukh, "the cow's mouth," the snout of the great Gangotri Glacier at 12,000 feet in the Garhwal Himalayas. Once bathed in these sacred waters, the pilgrim will achieve inner peace and a higher state in the afterlife. The 1,500-mile long Ganges, the river of life for India, is fed by two major tributaries, the Alaknanda and the Bhagirithi. The latter is considered the true source, and we will drive along its steep banks, above its cold churning waters, as far as a vehicle can travel. Then we take off by foot, joining the scores of pilgrims on the trail on any given day, slowly making their way to the heavens.

Back in the town of Gangotri, the site of the temple of the deity of Shiva, we'll visit one of the most sacred shrines in Hinduism, Kedarnath. This is a quest for higher ground, a trek through country as powerful as any in the corporeal world.

Note: A full Source-to-Sea Ganges Expedition, floating the length of the great river from the Himalayas to the Bay of Bengal, is available as a 49-day Class V expedition. Contact SOBEK for details.

ITINERARY:

Days 1-2: To Delhi.

Day 3: Rishikesh.

Day 4: Drive to Gangotri.

Days 5-10: Trekking.

Days 11-12: Drive to Gaurikand.

Days 13-16: Trekking.

Day 17: Drive to Dehra Dun.

Day 18: Delhi.

Day 19: Return.

MEDIUM

May, July, October

Exodus Expeditions

Mount Ararat Trek (AS 124)

DIFFICULT TREKKING—
CLASS IV

➤ *Trek to Turkey's top*

➤ *Ancient capital of Istanbul*

Journey up the slopes of the flood's first island, 16,804-foot Mount Ararat, and follow the footsteps of the original mountaineer, Noah, down from the summit. Located in eastern Turkey near the Russian and Iranian borders, Ararat is a dormant volcano whose last eruption was in 1840, but it continues to dominate the skies of the Middle East. The upper reaches of the mountain are covered with year-round snows and the last hundred yards to the summit have turned to ice, the birthing of a glacial system. The climb is a wondrous journey through a landscape ravaged by volcanic activity as well as by the ages, and, of course, it pulses with the lure of legend. It is a relatively simple climb by mountaineering standards, but the altitude demands stamina and endurance.

In addition to reaching the mountaintop, we visit the fabulous ruins and exotic castles at Van, once the capital of the Urartu Kingdom and later an important Ottoman city. Since no visit to Turkey is complete without time to visit Istanbul, we return to this true cultural crossroads—one of the centers of both Eastern and Western civilization.

ITINERARY:

Day 1: Istanbul.

Day 2: Van.

Day 3: Dogubayazit.

Days 4-7: Climb up Mount Ararat.

Day 8: Descend; drive to Erzurum.

Day 9: Afternoon flight to Istanbul.

Day 10: Istanbul.

Day 11: Return.

MODERATE

May-October

Trek Travel

Silk Road Explorer (AS 127)

OVERLANDING—
CLASS III

➤ *In the footsteps of Marco Polo*

➤ *From Pakistan to China*

➤ *The Gobi Desert, Xian, and Beijing*

They called him a fabulist because no one could believe the tales Marco Polo told. But it was true in the thirteenth century and it is true today: the Silk Road over the Roof of the World into the Celestial Kingdom is one of the great trade routes of human history.

Today, the romance of Polo's passage can be rekindled with a minimum of fuss and hardship and a maximum of scenic splendor. For three weeks we shop the bazaars of the Hunza, jeep above the precipitous gorges of the Karakoram, and ferry across high rivers and low deserts, sharing our space with nomads and comrades.

The Silk Road for us begins in Gilgit, a garrison town in a valley of great beauty on the banks of the Indus. From here we drive our expedition vehicles up the rough roads leading to Hunza, where some of the world's highest mountain peaks drop down to fertile valleys and people routinely live to be over 100. Our sole border crossing takes place at one of the most remote stations in the world: the Khunjerab Pass three miles high in the Karakorams. From here on we're in China, first its remote and barren Xinjiang Province, then ever eastward through the trading centers and historic sites of the distant past. Too soon we arrive in the modern era, with a million tales to tell our disbelieving friends.

ITINERARY:

Day 1: Arrive Islamabad; flight to Gilgit.

Day 2: Gilgit.

Day 3: Begin overlanding to Karimabad.

Days 4-6: Over Khunjerab Pass to Kashgar.

Days 7-8: Kashgar.

Days 9-11: To Urumqi.

Day 12-13: Urumqi.

Day 14: Train across Gobi Desert.

Day 15: Dunhuang.

Day 16: Fly to Lanzhou.

Days 17-18: Xian.

Day 19: Fly to Beijing.

Days 20-21: Beijing.

Day 22: Return.

PREMIUM

July

Adventure Pakistan

Irian Jaya (AS 129)

CULTURAL TREK— CLASS IV

➤ *The equatorial Shangri-La*
➤ *Stone Age warriors of the highlands*
➤ *Guided hikes between mountain villages*

The last frontier of adventure is New Guinea, the largest island in the world next to Greenland and a place where the twentieth century is colliding headlong with the Stone Age. The western or Indonesian half of this island undoubtedly ranks as the most isolated and primitive region on earth today. Roads are almost nonexistent, and most villages in the interior can be reached only be walking up and down treacherous paths, sometimes for weeks. Naturally, a remarkable flora and fauna thrive on this last frontier, but so do some remarkable tribes of people. When Western explorers first stumbled upon the Baliem Valley in the hidden highlands of Irian Jaya in the 1930s, they thought they had discovered the lost paradise of Shangri-La. It is a mile-high, 45-mile-long corridor formed by the Baliem River—a beautiful green valley full of epyphitic ferns, wild orchids, climbing lianas, and the towering canopy of the lowland rain forests. About 700 species of birds live here including the huge, flightless cassowary and the fabled bird of paradise.

About 200,000 Dani tribesmen populate the area—people who have been slash-and-burn agriculturalists for centuries and now raise pigs, sweet potatoes, ginger, cucumbers, and bananas in checkerboard gardens surrounded by neat stone fences. Their homes are domed-roof huts clustered within womblike compounds, and their intricately constructed dwellings, elaborate suspension bridges, and extensive irrigation ditches display a high degree of engineering skill. Their dress is even more spectacular: basically they wear no clothing, even when the temperature drops to as low as 40° F. Girls wear reed skirts, married women wrap themselves with a braided cord, and men sport only long tubular penis sheaths made of dried yellow gourds. Armbands and throat patches fashioned from pigs' scrotums, bark cloth, or matted spider webs ward off evil spirits.

The Baliem Valley has begun to reflect the rapid expansion of Western influence on the primitive areas of the world, with the appearance of new roads in the valley and modern clothing and goods. In Wamena, the principal city of the Baliem Valley, we stay in a very comfortable hotel and walk to the local markets. But we soon leave the encroaching modern world by taking a charter flight out of Wamena to Korasik, a highlands village area to the east. Here we stay overnight in a guest house and witness a pit dance performed by the Yamilak tribesmen. And then we start our three-day trek, walking, with porters, on steep, slippery, jungle mountain trails from village to village, visiting people who may never have heard even a radio much less talked to a foreigner. When the area was discovered by aircraft in the 1930s, the Danis were engaged in a perpetual state of warfare. Today they are among the most friendly and welcoming people of Southeast Asia, treating foreigners as if they were valued guests worthy of a visit or a feast. On our trek, we spend the night at the houses of local teachers or other important villagers (or in tents if necessary).

Since Irian Jaya is being developed by mining and oil companies at an alarming rate, those who want to have a rare opportunity to stand with humanity's ancient social forebears on their own turf should make this trip soon.

ITINERARY:

Days 1-2: En route.

Day 3: Arrive Biak, Irian Jaya; connect to Jayapura.

Day 4: Flight to Wamena; tribal ceremony in Suroba.

Day 5: Fly to Korasik.

Days 6-8: Trek to Angguruk.

Day 7: Flight to Wamena, connect to Jayapura.

Day 10: Return to Biak for connections to Bali, Jakarta, or return home.

MEDIUM

March-October

SOBEK Expeditions

Islands of Fire (AS 130)

CULTURAL VARIETY— CLASS II

➤ *Bali, Asia's island paradise*

➤ *Volcanoes of Java*

➤ *Borobudur, world's largest temple*

Few of the world's islands are better known than Bali and Java. And with good reason: not only are they beautiful tropical paradises with white sandy beaches, impressive volcanoes, terraced rice paddies, and year-round fruits and flowers but they are centers of an extremely rich and visually beautiful culture. In Bali, Hindu and pagan gods inhabit everyday life, demanding peace and insisting on beauty. Every morning women make gorgeous sculptures of rattan and flowers to please unseen spirits; and men carve wood and stone to make the spirit world manifest. On this tiny island, art and religion flourish together as they must have during the Italian Renaissance, and tourists, so far, have only increased the artistic output. For some reason, Bali's extraordinary culture seems to surmount the onslaught of tourism.

Bali is also physically blessed, so lovely it seems unreal. It is a land of mossy temples and sweet hibiscus; of volcanoes and monkeys; of terraced rice paddies and handsome people. No wonder Jawaharlal Nehru, India's founding father, once declared Bali ''the morning of the world.''

Java is less renowned for its physical beauty, and, due to the sheer number of people on it, it has more social problems. But Java is nevertheless captivating: a tropical island with rich volcanic soil, a luxuriant rain forest, and some truly gorgeous volcanoes. We see the best of the island—its fabulous ninth century Buddhist monument, the view from the summit of a volcano at sunrise, and Yogjakarta, the city that is Indonesia's cultural capital.

Our trip begins on the beach in Bali, where we stay in the charming Surya Beach Cottages. Here, for two days, we relax, swim, and wander through nearby villages and rice paddies. We also visit a local market, a magnificent temple, and see a Ketchak (Monkey) Dance—a depiction of an ancient Hindu story accompanied by dramatic choruses and beautiful costumes. Then we drive up into the mountains to the region near Ubud for a walk through the picture-postcard scenery of terraced hillsides, swift-flowing rivers, and mountain vistas. In the afternoon we'll visit some of the nearby villages noted for crafts.

All too soon we leave Bali for Yogjakarta—a large, bustling city with some of the best shopping in the world. But here, also, our hearts and minds fill with wonder. Those who want to take one of the world's great hikes will leave after dinner for Mount Merapi to begin a nighttime ascent of the volcano. After spending the night at a village on the vol-

cano's high slopes, we get up early to climb to the summit by 5:30 a.m. Here, on the edge of the crater, we peer into the entrails of the earth and watch the sky and plains below us light up and change in color and intensity and mood until it seems nothing on earth can be more beautiful. Those who stay in Yogjakarta will visit an ancient Hindu temple, see the architecturally fascinating Kraton Palace, and browse central Java's largest market.

Everyone will want to visit Borobudur, perhaps the most impressive Buddhist monument in the world. Built in the eighth century, this elaborate temple in the shape of a mandala is composed of two million cubic feet of stone, nearly all of it elaborately carved with portraits of everyday life 1,200 years ago. It is designed to be experienced by spiraling counterclockwise up it, from bottom to top. At first the carvings are full of the richness and pain of human experience. They are lusty, greedy, and earthy. Then, gradually, almost imperceptibly, the carvings get more and more abstract until, at the top, we are in a world of stark, geometrical forms punctuated by half-hidden Buddhas—in other words, Nirvana.

From Borobudur we drive to the Dieng Plateau, a sacred spot with lovely mountain scenery, a cool climate, fascinating volcanic fissures and Hindu temples named after the heroes of the *wyang*, a puppet presentation of epic ancient mythology. Here we overnight and explore the area by foot before driving back to Yogjakarta for a flight back to Bali and a final taste of the warm breezes, rustling palms, and almost magical manifestations of beauty that bless these ancient islands of fire.

ITINERARY:

Days 1-2: En route.

Day 3: Arrive Bali; afternoon free.

Day 4: Balinese highlights, including Ketchak dance.

Day 5: Bali's highlands.

Day 6: Midday flight to Yogjakarta.

Day 7: Up at midnight to visit Merapi; afternoon return to Yogjakarta.

Day 8: Borobudur and Dieng Plateau.

Day 9: Dieng; drive to Yogjakarta.

Day 10: Return.

PREMIUM

Year-round

SOBEK Expeditions

Cycle Bali (AS 132)

CULTURAL TWO-WHEELING — CLASS III

➤ *Pedaling through paradise*

➤ *Glorious beaches, volcanoes, and temples*

➤ *Traditional dances and ceremonies*

Bali is heaven made for the lazy pace of cycling: the narrow roads guide you through continuous beauty, both natural and man-made. And the panoply of people, whether simple peasants bent in the rice fields or beach bums playing in the waves, are among the friendliest anywhere: the smiles are broad and real, the warmth as natural and as embracing as the tropical breezes.

The "real" Bali awaits inland—where we leave our Western way of thinking and immerse ourselves in traditional Indonesian life. We'll cycle through villages filled with ancient temples and visit the moated temple of Pura Taman Ayan before ascending into the cool, mountainous country toward Lake Bratan, perched on the edge of a live volcano. We'll see the famed Water Palace, snorkel in chablis-clear water, and feast on fresh fruit and spicy satay. For much of our trip, jade-colored rice terraces will descend the mountainsides like giant stairways for the gods. Each night's lodging is chosen for its magnificent setting, ranging from deluxe to more traditional Indonesian (all but one with a private bathroom). If you bring your skinny-tire bike, you can look forward to paved roads the entire distance (with occasional rough spots), while mountain bike aficionados might enjoy exploring some of the remoter villages.

ITINERARY:

Day 1: Depart USA.

Day 2: Arrive in Denpasar.

Day 3: Bali Oberoi.

Day 4: Bedugul.

Day 5: Lovina Beach.

Day 6: Penelokan.

Day 7: Rest.

Day 8: Tirtagangga.

Day 9: Balina Beach.

Day 10: Ubud.

Day 11: Rest.

Day 12: Denpasar.

MEDIUM

March-April

Backroads Bicycle

Turkish Odyssey (AS 135) ▰▰▰▰▰

RELAXED CULTURAL OVERVIEW—CLASS II

➤ *Hike the nomad's trails*
➤ *Three-day yacht cruise*
➤ *Hot springs and ancient ruins*

The gateway to Asia is Turkey, the focus of the great Ottoman Empire and one of civilization's birthplaces. Coupling day hikes with yacht cruises, hot springs with ancient ruins, this exploration of Turkey's extravagant attractions gives the curious traveler insights and adventures galore.

After a dizzying tour of Istanbul's mosques and markets, we fly south to Antalya on the Mediterranean, home of Roman ruins, Lycian temples, and the wilderness of Koprulu Canyon and the Kopru River. A two-day stay in Urunlu village allows us time to walk in the woods, explore the area's giant caves and subterranean lakes, and cajole our hosts into a lamb roast. Later we see the natural fires of the mythic Chimera, climb to over 8,000 feet for a sweeping view of the Mediterranean and the Taurus Mountains, and locate antique cities of Grecian lore. For many, the highlight of this adventure is a yacht cruise along the offshore islands of the Turquoise Coast, where we end our trip by visiting Byzantine monasteries, paying our respects at a Lycian temple, and snorkeling the cobalt lagoons of Cirali. There's much more to see on this odyssey into Turkey's illustrious past and much to remember once our Homeric journey comes to an end with a hot-spring soak beside the Mediterranean Sea.

ITINERARY:

Day 1: Arrive Istanbul.
Day 2: Istanbul.
Days 3-4: Antalya.
Days 5-6: Urunlu.
Days 7-8: Cirali.
Days 9-10: Yacht sail.
Days 11-12: Oludeniz.
Day 13: Dalyan.
Day 14: Miletos.
Day 15: Istanbul.
Day 16: Return.

MEDIUM

October-December, March

Exodus Expeditions

Karakoram and Kashmir (AS 138) ⋀⋁⋀⋁⋀⋁⋀

CULTURAL JOURNEY— CLASS I

➤ *The splendors of Lahore*
➤ *The spectacular Hunza Valley*
➤ *The houseboats of Srinagar*

Some of the most exotic sights on earth can be found straddling the border between Pakistan and India on this journey through the Karakoram and Kashmir. Here, glaciated mountain peaks drop down to green valley floors, and East meets West in the bizarre marketplaces along the Silk Route.

We begin our adventure in the twin cities of Rawalpindi, with its fascinating bazaars, and Islamabad, the modern capital of Pakistan built in 1961 with the assistance of world-famous architects including Ponti and Edward Durrell Stone. The next day we take a spectacular flight to Gilgit, weather permitting (if not, we will make the two-day drive on a tough but appropriately dramatic road). Gilgit, at almost 4,900 feet, is an ancient tribal town, now both cosmopolitan and friendly. Its people were originally fire worshipers before being converted to Buddhism, then Hinduism, and finally Islam. We tour the city and then drive north along the precipitous Hunza Gorge to Karimabad, the capital of Hunza and the inspiration for Kipling's "The Man Who Would Be King."

Eric Shipton, the famous British explorer, called Hunza "the ultimate manifestation of mountain grandeur. . . the most spectacular country I have ever seen," and soon we discover why. The neat, terraced fields of the valley are surrounded by literally hundreds of mountains over 20,000 feet. Rakaposhi peak, at 25,550 feet, rises almost 20,000 feet to the summit, probably the world's most sudden rise in altitude. Here, castles perch on crags above a gorge; glaciers shimmer down needle-shaped peaks, orchards grow on clifftops. Hunzakuts claim to be descendants of a lost part of Alexander the Great's army, and with their fair complexion and ginger hair, it's easy to believe. They are Moslem, but of a particularly mellow stripe—followers of the Aga Khan. Before returning to Karimabad, we take a short jeep ride to the Nagar Valley to sample the vitality of village life and visit the 500-year-old palace of the Mir of Hunza.

Next we drive north along the fantastic Karakoram Highway (built by Pakistan with the help of China), through snow leopard country and past tumbling glaciers to Passu, where the Batura Glacier meets the road. We scamper about on the glacier for a bit and then head back down to Gilgit. The following day we continue south on the Karakoram Highway, travel-ing the old Silk Route to Besham and pass-ing through the Kohistan district where villages perch on every available spur and houses are almost invisible against the rock. In the first two hours, the sheer flanks of Nanga Parbat (26,660 ft.), the western extremity of the Great Himalaya, intermittently protrude into the sky. We continue on to Rawalpindi, stopping en route at Taxila, one of the most important archaeological sites in Asia, literally on the cultural crossroads of the world where Alexander the Great discussed philosophy and where Buddhism flourished in the second century.

After a morning flight to Lahore, we explore this city of saints with its mosques, Moghul art, Shalimar Gardens, and markets, and the next day we fly to Delhi and then on to Srinagar in Kashmir, "the Switzerland of Asia." Here we spend two nights relaxing on a deluxe house-boat on Dal Lake, tour the Moghul Gardens built by Emperor Jehangir in 1616 for his wife, Nur Jahan, the "light of the world," take a boat ride, shop, and enjoy the scenery that has made this town legendary.

The final leg of our trip coincides with the full moon, which is the best time to see the Taj Mahal: its white marble seems luminescent in moonlight, and the shim-mering palace almost floats—hovering over the grounds and river that surround it in the warm, sensuous night. We stay overnight at the luxurious Hotel Moghul Sheraton and if we have time the next day, visit Fatehpur Sikri, a spectacular aban-doned city.

Karachi, the largest and most popu-lous city of Pakistan, is where our trip ends, and we reach the city with our minds and hearts still whirling from the exotic sights we have seen—palaces, mountains, entire kingdoms full of enough drama to last a lifetime.

ITINERARY:

Days 1-2: En route.

Day 3: Islamabad.

Day 4: Flight to Gilgit.

Day 5: Hunza Valley.

Days 6-7: Karakorams.

Day 8: Rawalpindi.

Day 9: Lahore.

Day 10: To Delhi.

Days 11-12: Srinagar.

Day 13: To Delhi and Agra.

Day 14: To Delhi; flight to Karachi.

Day 15: Return.

PREMIUM

June-October

Adventure Pakistan

Chitral and Swat (AS 139)

OVERLAND TOUR—
CLASS II

➤ *Ancient capitals of Pakistan*

➤ *High passes and hot springs*

➤ *The Karakoram and the Hindu Kush*

Crucible of ancient empires, Pakistan has a history so rich that most other countries don't even try to compete. Birthplace of the prehistoric Indus Valley civilizations, end point of Alexander the Great's eastward march, homeland of fire worshipers, Buddhist saints, and Moslem zealots, Pakistan still bursts with discoveries waiting to be made.

Beginning with Rawalpindi, we head northwest to the ancient sultanate of Swat, surrounded by the towering mountains of the Hindu Kush and the Pamir ranges. Here, among other marvels, we see the palace at Saidu Sharif and the museum of the artistic Gandhara culture. Then we go to Chitral, home of an independent-minded people who remained autonomous from both Pakistan and nearby Afghanistan into the 1960s. After a bath at a hot sulfur springs near Peshawar, we enjoy three days of tent camping in the mountains of the Hindu Kush and the Karakoram, capped by a drive over 12,210-foot Shandur Pass en route to the Gilgit River. If your cultural cravings are not yet satisfied by all this time travel, you can meet up with a tour of ''Karakoram and Kashmir'' (AS 138) for another two weeks of spectacular Pakistan.

ITINERARY:

Day 1: Islamabad/Rawalpindi.

Days 2-3: Swat.

Days 4-6: Chitral.

Days 7-9: Tour of Hindu Kush.

Day 10: Hunza; join AS 138 (Day 5) if arranged.

Day 11: Gilgit.

Day 12: Fly to Islamabad.

Day 13: Islamabad.

MODERATE

June-October

Adventure Pakistan

Inner Mongolia Horseback (AS 141)

HORSEBACK RIDING—
CLASS III

➤ *In the "hoof steps" of the hordes*

➤ *Across the giant steppes of mankind*

➤ *Lamaseries and yurts*

The horse has been an integral part of the nomadic culture of Central Asia for millennia. Whether herding sheep in Mongolia, yaks in Tibet, or conquering the known world as Genghis Khan did, horses have provided the mobility and speed needed to cross the grassy steppes of Asia.

Our ride through Inner Mongolia is exotic and remote and continually brings to mind the fierce mounted warriors who swept across Asia. At annual festivals, the skills of war can still be seen in contests of horsemanship, archery, and shooting. But even more enduring than this proud history is the hospitality the local people extend to travelers. As we ride through their country, we are treated like royalty. We are also surrounded by astounding scenery, whether we are crossing the endless sea of grass in Mongolia or fording a river in the Sichuan grasslands. In Inner Mongolia, the route reaches the edge of the Gobi Desert, and in Sichuan, snowy mountains and prayer flags ring our field of view.

We will ride on local stock with traditional tack, and local herdsmen will ride with us each day and tend the horses at night. A horse trip is not for everyone. We travel a 200-mile loop, averaging 25 miles per day, with up to eight hours in the saddle. We sleep in tents, communes, and yurts. There is very little running hot water, and the menu is dominated by mutton, yak, and noodles. For those who don't mind these inconveniences, however, this is a particularly thrilling and rewarding experience.

ITINERARY:

Days 1-3: To Beijing.

Days 4-5: Datong/Yun gang caves.

Days 6-7: Huhehot, capital of Inner Mongolia.

Day 8: Select, test horses.

Days 9-15: Riding across the steppes.

Day 16: Damiao Lamasery.

Day 17: Last riding day.

Days 18-19: Huhehot.

Days 20-21: Beijing.

Day 22: Return.

PREMIUM

July

Boojum Expeditions

Tibetan Highland Mountain Bicycle (AS 142)

CULTURAL TWO-WHEELING—CLASS IV

➤ *Cycle through the clouds*

➤ *Wind through the Wolong Panda Reserve*

➤ *Bike the borderland of Sichuan and Tibet*

In the remote perimeter region between Sichuan and Tibet lies the Great Corrugations, a series of massive mountain ranges and deep valleys created when the Indian subcontinent crashed into the landmass of Asia. Through these valleys, within a hundred miles of each other, run four of the continent's major rivers; and through the easternmost gorge of this almost impenetrable area, flanked by the 17,000-foot peaks of the Ta Hsueh Shan (Great Snowy Mountain) Range, runs the Dadu River. The areas we will visit are populated mainly by Tibetans, many of whom have never had any contact with "Foreign Devils"; they have much to learn about the weird ways of the West, from our rabid individualism to our penchant for fried eggs with salt instead of sugar. We will need to maintain an open and relaxed attitude to the inevitable inconveniences of travel in this distant and alien culture.

We mount our bikes in Chengdu, capital of Sichuan, and begin with a "sensorama" video game ride complete with thousands of people cycling and more walking, pushing carts, and driving small tractors, on our way to the zoo. Then it's off to the Dadu River, where we'll ride the rugged terrain along the banks for 150 miles. We'll finish our tour with a cycle to the Wolong Panda Reserve, a mile and a half high, and a visit to the Great Wall and the Forbidden City.

ITINERARY:

Days 1-3: To Hong Kong.

Days 4-5: Chengdu; prepare bikes.

Day 6: Drive to Wenchuan.

Day 7: Cycle through farmlands.

Day 8: Drive over pass and cycle along Samso River.

Day 9: Free day.

Days 10-14: Cycle along Dadu.

Day 15: Cycle to Zhilong.

Day 16: Descent to Wolong.

Days 17-18: Around Panda Reserve.

Day 19: Chengdu.

Days 20-22: Beijing.

Day 23: Return.

PREMIUM

August-September

Boojum Expeditions

Dadu River (AS 153)

RAFTING AND WILDLIFE— CLASS IV

➤ *Historic river of the Long March*

➤ *Challenging rapids in Sichuan's mountains*

➤ *See the pandas of Wolong*

Peter N. Fox/SOBEK photo file

In a nation of famous rivers—the Yangtze, the Yellow, the Mekong, and the Brahmaputra—one of the most significant is the relatively short Dadu. Here the people's army of Mao Zedong made its most succesful stand against the Nationalists, eluding almost certain capture in the wilds of Sichuan Province. But even more than that, the Dadu symbolizes the untamed side of China, the timeless side that can still be found far from its factories and universities. The Dadu Ho, en route to its confluence with the Min Jiang, a major tributary of the Yangtze, drains the eastern edge of the Tibetan Plateau and flows through deep canyons inhabited only by minority tribes who farm the terraced hillsides.

We begin our trip in Hong Kong and then fly to Chengdu, a 2,500-year-old city, capital of Sichuan Province and birthplace of Deng Xiaoping. Here artisans are back in the streets and there are markets everywhere—free markets, flea markets, black markets, peddler markets—all of which make this a great walking town. We also visit the ancient irrigation projects that give clues to China's profound innovative role in history.

The drive to put-in on the Dadu is through a remote part of China, a land of precipitous wooded canyons and steep limestone peaks covered with forest, countryside that looks first like a Chinese scroll and then changes tc open, cultivated slopes, dotted by prayer flags and yaks, countryside with roads climbing over snowy 14,000-foot passes. The people of this area are more Tibetan than Chinese—China having controlled the area only since the 1950s—and we may be treated to some Tibetan songs and drink.

Running the Dadu is five days of whitewater thrills. Challenging rapids are a virtual certainty, and Class IV and possibly higher drops may be found on the relatively isolated stretch we descend. We pass by some isolated villages during the day and at night, camping by the river. The skies are so black and full of stars they seem to suspend all mortal thought. And after the Dadu and the wild beauty of its setting, there's more: a part of China that's less grand but for some even more interesting. Just northwest of Chengdu is the Wolong Nature Reserve, and we spend two days here, viewing some of China's rare wildlife. Set up in the late 1970s for panda conservation, the reserve is estimated to have some 3,000 kinds of plants as well as some protected species such as the golden monkey, golden langur, musk deer, snow leopard, and the elusive bamboo-eating giant panda.

From wild waters to rare creatures, this is a China worth traveling half a world to see.

ITINERARY:

Day 1: Hong Kong.

Day 2: To Chengdu.

Day 3: Chengdu city tour.

Day 4: Drive to Li Shan.

Day 5: Begin river trip.

Days 6-10: Raft the Dadu.

Day 11: End river trip at Danba.

Day 12: To Zelun.

Day 13: Arrive Wolong.

Day 14: Wolong.

Day 15: To Chengdu.

Day 16: Chengdu.

Day 17: Fly to Hong Kong.

Day 18: Return.

PREMIUM

September-October

SOBEK Expeditions

Thai Elephant Trek (AS 154)

VARIETY PACKAGE—
CLASS II

➤ *Elephant safari in Golden Triangle*

➤ *Snorkel the Coral Bay*

Long isolated from the modern world by beautiful yet forbidding terrain, the hill tribes of northern Thailand retain a unique way of life, maintaining traditional costumes, crafts, and customs. What better way to penetrate their mysterious homeland than astride the broad back of the elephant, our mount for a three-day safari through the remote villages of the Karen tribes. We stay overnight at the homes of the White Karen people in simple but comfortable accommodations and watch the daily life along the Nam Mae Pon River.

After the elephant walk, we board a bamboo raft for a float down the Mae Yuam River en route back to Chiang Mai, "the flower of the north." Other highlights include a visit to the 500-year-old temple of bronze Buddhas at Cham Thong, and the Ob Luang Gorge, sometimes called Thailand's Grand Canyon. We end the trip with a three-day stay at the Coral Bay Resort in Koh Samui on the Gulf of Thailand, where we are housed like happy castaways in grass bungalows. All too soon we're back in Bangkok to say farewell with a special Thai barbecue.

ITINERARY:

Day 1: Arrive Bangkok.

Day 2: Bangkok.

Day 3: Chiang Mai.

Day 4: Mae Hong Son.

Days 5-7: Elephant trek.

Day 8: Bamboo float to Ban Mae Tia.

Day 9: Chiang Mai.

Day 10: To Bangkok and on to Koh Samui.

Day 11: Coral Bay.

Day 12: Afternoon return to Bangkok.

Day 13: Bangkok.

Day 14: Return.

MEDIUM

October, December-January

SOBEK Expeditions

Beyond the Great Wall (AS 156)

CULTURAL ADVENTURE
WITH RAFTING—CLASS II

➤ *Homeland of "The Last Emperor"*

➤ *Raft the San Tao Pai*

➤ *Hike the Bingyu Valley*

They built the Great Wall to keep the barbarian hordes at bay, to protect the palaces and riches of the Celestial Empire. But time has a way of vaulting all barriers, and the final dynasty of imperial China arose from beyond the Great Wall—in Manchuria, a vast region of fertile plains surrounded by rugged ranges. We begin our exploration of Manchuria by heading to Changbai Mountain, China's largest nature preserve and birthplace of Manchuria's three major rivers. Amidst the wildflowers and birch forests, we rig the boats for a rafting descent of the San Tao Pai, whose steep gradient promises Class III-IV rapids in virtually unexplored terrain. As the river gradually eases its drop, we encounter signs of human life and finally drift through a lush roadless valley inhabited by villagers sure to be charmed by the novelty of our arrival.

But the raft trip is only a warm-up for further explorations, and we continue on to Shenyang, second capital of the Manchus. Here we stop at Dalian, northern China's largest port with its fresh seafood and hand-blown glassworks, and visit a colorful locomotive factory where a dying industry still flowers. Finally, we drive to the Bingyu Valley, northeast China's scenic treasure, which we explore both by foot and in inflatable kayaks before heading back to Beijing, much as the barbarians did, laden with memories and dreams.

ITINERARY:

Day 1: Beijing.

Day 2: City tour.

Day 3: Fly to Changchung.

Day 4: Fly to Changbai Mountain.

Day 5: Tianchi Lake.

Day 6: Begin river trip.

Days 7-9: On the river.

Day 10: Fly to Shenyang.

Day 11: Fly to Dalian.

Day 12: Drive to Bingyu Valley.

Day 13: Hiking.

Day 14: River descent.

Day 15: Drive to Dalian.

Day 16: Locomotive factory; fly to Beijing.

Days 17-18: Beijing.

Day 19: Return.

PREMIUM

July-August

SOBEK Expeditions

Jim Slade/SOBEK photo file

Tsangpo River (AS 157)

CULTURAL RAFTING— CLASS III

➤ *Tibet's major waterway*

➤ *Monasteries and mountains of China*

➤ *Yak-hide coracles and neoprene inflatables*

The headwaters of the Brahmaputra, one of the largest rivers in Asia, are found in the magical region of Tibet. Here the river is known as the Tsangpo, and it runs due east from the sacred mountain Kailas toward Yunnan, then abruptly turns south to pierce the icy wall of the Himalayas. For centuries the mysteries of the Brahmaputra's source puzzled geographers, but for the Tibetans the Tsangpo has always been an eternal waterway.

We ride the river in two very different crafts, starting our journey near Xigaze—Tibet's second highest city and home to the country's largest active Buddhist monastery—in native coracles, traditional boats made of yak hide. As we drift across the high mountain plateau, snowcapped peaks encircle us, villages appear like daydreams along the seemingly fast-moving riverbanks, and our Tibetan boatmen sing ancient melodies.

Then, when the river's flow increases in both volume and gradient, we tie up our coracles, blow up the Avons, and challenge the Tsangpo through a steep and narrow gorge, relieved only by lonely villages. At the end of our trip a few days in Lhasa, the Vatican of Tibetan Buddhism, lets us round out our experience with appropriate thanks to Tibet's omnipresent deities. This is indeed a unique place to run a river—at nearly 12,000 feet in elevation, on the historic waters of one of the world's great streams, through a kingdom of magic and mystery.

ITINERARY:

Days 1-2: Kathmandu.

Day 3: Flight to Lhasa.

Day 4: Lhasa.

Day 5: Drive to Xigaze, begin rafting.

Days 6-13: Rafting the Tsangpo.

Day 14: Return to Lhasa.

Days 15-16: Lhasa.

Day 17: Flight to Kathmandu.

Day 18: Kathmandu.

Day 19: Return.

PREMIUM

June-July

SOBEK Expeditions

Into the Heart of Borneo (AS 158)

CULTURE TREK— CLASS III

➤ *Six-day circuit of a rain forest*

➤ *Travel by long-boat and footpath*

➤ *Cultural contact with remote Dyaks*

List the wildest places on earth, and Borneo may come out on top. It's a huge island—the world's third largest—and is home to orangutans, a rain forest, and, until the beginning of this century, headhunting tribesmen. Borneo has always evoked the dark side of humanity's collective psyche. The island represents a place people go to to disappear, like Lord Jim. But when we shed light on the Mahakam River rain forest we discover another side to the legend—a rich natural wonderland where flora and fauna thrive, a world of flowering bromeliads, tree ferns, rattan, and dripping broadleaf; a world where butterflies dazzle the eyes and adventures challenge the spirit. For almost two weeks we will immerse ourselves in this fascinating habitat, an inspiration to naturalists and novelists and a fertile field for anthropologists as well.

We begin our trip in Balikpapan in Indonesian Borneo, an oil and lumber boomtown on the island's east coast. From there we take a short bus ride to Samarinda and then a small plane up the major highway of the area, the Mahakam River. Now in deepest Borneo, we go by long boat to Tiong Ohang, a small jungle trading post of the kind Joseph Conrad wrote about, and begin our trek toward Mount Irih and some remote Dyak villages where people still live in longhouses and hunt with poison darts and blowpipes. Our circuit hike takes us through the thick undergrowth of primary rain forest where old trails disappear in weeks and have to be continually cut anew by Dyak hunters. We get intimately acquainted with insects of all descriptions, not to mention prickly plants, rotting vegetation, and plenty of slippery mud. This is the real thing: we experience a primary tropical rain forest firsthand. We feel its fecundity, see the life, smell the endless recycling of elements, and take joy in the surprises and small miracles along the way, such as dragonflies that look like UFOs, ferns that look like fetuses, bamboo as thick as a dinner plate.

The Dyaks along the way are a fascinating and friendly people. They are anxious to talk, even in sign language, and eager to laugh and have fun. As evidenced by the lumber boats that come up the Mahakam, these people are fast entering the twentieth century, but it's not too late to see and participate in the old traditions—to watch the woman with their beaded baby carriers, the men with their carved *parangs* (native machetes), the

immense longhouses where an outdoor veranda is as big as a main street. Back in Tiong Ohang, the Dyaks welcome us with a festive dinner and dance.

We end the trip with a couple of days in Bali—on the beaches and in the rice fields and temples and villages. On our adventure we may have gone to a place long considered one of the dead ends of the earth, but we will have seen its beauty just before it is destroyed and the hotels are built.

ITINERARY:

Day 1: Samarinda, Kalimantan.

Day 2: Fly to Mahakam River; by long boat to Tiong Ohang.

Days 3-7: On trek.

Day 8: Return to Tiong Ohang; welcome feast.

Day 9: Downriver to Data Dawai.

Day 10: Transfer to Samarinda and Balikpapan.

Day 11: To Jakarta and Denpasar, Bali.

Day 12: Bali.

Day 13: Return.

MODERATE

July-September

Colors of Asia

Trans-Siberian Express ∿∿∿∿∿ (AS 159)

RAILWAY JOURNEY— CLASS I

➤ *Beijing to Moscow by rail*

➤ *Complete tours of capital cities*

➤ *First-class hotels and sleepers*

There's something about a train to inspire the imagination and excite the poetic impulse, as rail travelers from Johnny Cash to Paul Theroux will attest. This is our chance to travel halfway around the world in romantic style. All aboard the Trans-Siberian Express for a two-week ride between the capitals of China and the Soviet Union.

Beginning with our arrival in Beijing, we spend two full days touring some of China's historic sites, including the Great Wall, the Forbidden City, and Tiananmen Square. Our hotel accommodations here are first-class, and we feast on Peking duck in anticipation of our two-day train ride across the Gobi Desert to Inner Mongolia.

In this remote part of the world, we take time to see the town of Ulan Bator, its lamasery, museum, and nomadic culture, and then board our cozy sleeper coaches for the train experience of a lifetime, crossing into Siberia at Naushki and heading toward the sunset for Lake Baikal. An overnight stop at Irkutsk on the shores of the world's ninth largest lake gives us time to sightsee in Siberia's major city, then we reboard the Express for the long two-day leg across Asia, over the Urals and into Europe, finally arriving in Moscow at rail's end. Saint Basil's Cathedral, Lenin's Tomb, and Red Square will seem anticlimactic to the clattering romance of rail travel across a landscape that seems at best timeless, at its most immediate, Old World.

ITINERARY:

Day 1: Arrive Beijing.

Days 2-3: Beijing.

Days 4-5: Rail to Ulan Bator.

Day 6: Ulan Bator.

Days 7-8: Rail to Irkutsk.

Day 9: Lake Baikal.

Days 10-11: Trans-Siberian Express.

Day 12: Arrive Moscow.

Day 13: Moscow.

Day 14: Return.

PREMIUM

Year-round

Speed Travel

Taste of Nepal (AS 201)

VARIETY PACKAGE— CLASS III

➤ *Trek to the Annapurnas*
➤ *Rafting*
➤ *Wildlife of Chitwan*

Nepal: short, sweet, and special. This action-packed itinerary includes a four-day trek in the Annapurna foothills, a raft down the Trisuli River, two days at the Royal Chitwan National Park, and time off in Kathmandu—all in just two weeks. There are few programs that offer so much in so little time.

We drive to Pokhara and commence our four-day trek amidst the lakes and the ridges of the Annapurna foothills. Annapurna and Machapucchare, two giant peaks, tower above us as we walk through the tropical foothills. We pass enchanting Gurung villages, where you can get an insight into a culture so different from our own.

Next comes two days of rafting down the Trisuli River. We all have the chance to paddle through the rapids: a great introduction for first-time rafters.

From the river we drive to the Royal Chitwan National Park. We ride elephants through the high bush keeping an eye out for rhino, leopard, and the elusive tiger. We also have time to appreciate the abundant birdlife in the park.

We return to the temples and palaces of the Kathmandu Valley, with time to reflect on the high points of this great journey.

ITINERARY:

Day 1: Meet Kathmandu.

Day 2: Kathmandu.

Day 3: Drive to Pokhara.

Days 4-8: Trekking.

Days 8-10: Drive to Trisuli River and raft.

Day 10: Drive to Chitwan.

Day 11: Chitwan.

Day 12: Return to Kathmandu.

Days 13-14: Kathmandu.

Day 15: Trip ends Kathmandu.

MODERATE

January-November

World Expeditions

Trek Nepal and Kashmir (AS 202)

MODERATE TREKKING— CLASS III

➤ *Two amazing treks*

➤ *Two extraordinary regions*

➤ *Houseboating in Srinagar*

This trip combines two very different treks, one beneath the spectacular Annapurna massif in Nepal, the other in the famed alpine region of Kashmir. The trip is timed to meet the change of the seasons, beginning in May, which is late spring in Nepal, and arriving in Kashmir just when the winter snows have melted.

From Kathmandu we drive to Pokhara to begin our nine-day trek across the foothills of the Annapurna Range. Nowhere are the mountain panoramas so impressive at elevations that rarely exceed 9,000 feet: the mighty Annapurna massif looms another 16,000 feet directly over the trail. As the views unfold, we wind through mountain villages that provide some scale to this vast Himalayan backdrop.

Then it's on to Delhi and Srinagar for a day of luxury houseboating before we begin the second stage of our adventure— an eight-day trek up the verdant Lidder Valley. In this alpine terrain we meet nomadic shepherds making their way up to the high pastures and immerse ourselves in the flowering of early spring in one of the most classically beautiful mountain settings on earth.

ITINERARY:

Day 1: Meet Kathmandu.

Day 2: Kathmandu.

Day 3: Drive to Pokhara.

Days 4-12: Trekking

Day 13: Return to Kathmandu.

Day 14: Kathmandu.

Day 15: Fly to Delhi.

Day 16: Fly to Srinagar.

Day 17: Srinagar.

Days 18-24: Trekking.

Day 25: Return to Srinagar.

Days 26-28: Srinagar.

Day 29: Fly to Delhi, trip ends.

MODERATE

April-June

World Expeditions

Thai Sailing
(AS 203)

SAILING—CLASS II

➤ *Golden temples and beaches*

➤ *A classy junk*

This opportunity to sail in tropical seas around the exotic islands in the Gulf of Thailand on an authentic Thai sailing junk is a once-in-a-lifetime experience. Our timber-hulled junk has four comfortable cabins and accommodates up to twelve guests. A crew of four (a European skipper, a Thai sailor, a Thai cook and his assistant) will cater to our every need and make our sailing and exploration of the islands a brief encounter with paradise.

Leaving Bangkok and driving south to Pattaya, we begin our idyll with two nights in a beach resort before boarding the junk. Then, for four days, we sail the warm waters of the eastern gulf, which enjoys good weather with plenty of sunshine and very calm waters for the greater part of the year. Among other islands, we visit to Koh Larn, Koh Pai, Koh Samae San, and Koh Samet. Most of the islands that we stop at along the way are uninhabited and we have ample time to laze away the hours in complete privacy— snorkeling the coral reefs, swimming in many lovely lagoons, fishing, sailing, and windsurfing to our heart's content.

ITINERARY:

Day 1: Meet Bangkok.

Day 2: Bus to Pattaya.

Day 3: In Pattaya.

Days 4-6: Sailing the eastern Gulf islands.

Day 7: Sailing and return to Pattaya, bus to Bangkok.

Day 8: Trip ends Bangkok.

May-October

World Expeditions

Journey into Kham
(AS 204)

CULTURAL RAFTING— CLASS IV

➤ *Churning Yangtze rapids*

➤ *Ancient Buddhist printing process*

➤ *Shooting stars*

This is a once-in-a-lifetime expedition: an opportunity to be one of the very first people into a region of Tibet closed to Westerners until 1986, when our guides made the first exploratory run of this fine whitewater section of the Yangtze River. This twenty-day adventure will span the range of technology and culture found in China today—from the hustle and bustle of rapidly growing southern China to the remote Qhingha-Tibetan Plateau, where the hands of time are turned back hundreds of years.

We begin in Hong Kong in one of the city's luxury hotels and then catch a flight to Chengdu, capital of Sichuan Province. In Chengdu, a melting pot of over fifty ethnic minorities, we have time to experience a great range of foods, dress, language, and peoples. Then the real adventure begins with a three-day drive in Toyota Land Cruisers through country that has only been seen by a few Westerners. We drive through the mountains into the remotest regions of China and enter a world of 20,000-foot peaks, crashing rivers, steep canyons, and passes almost 15,000 feet high. One pass is over 18,000 feet. People live and work here much as they did several centuries ago. In fact the road on which we travel did not even exist until twenty-five years ago.

Upon reaching the Yangtze River near Yushu, we set up camp. This is the largest river in Asia, the third longest in the world, and we are on the Chinese-Tibet border, about 400 miles from its source. Put-in is at 12,000 feet, and we spend a few days before we get in the rafts, relaxing, sightseeing, and acclimating to the altitude.

Our first stop is Yushu, a frontier city that is home to one of the few remaining active Buddhist monasteries in Tibet. Evenings in this camp are special, with skies so clear the stars seem magnified. Meteor showers are at their peak in summer, and stargazers may be treated to 100 or more shooting stars an hour.

When we finally put-in on the Yangtze, we will be running many Class II and III rapids as well as one churning Class IV that drops through a short rocky canyon, a perfect spot for picture taking. Camps are on sandy beaches and layover days are near friendly Tibetan villages, where we are often welcomed with chanting songs and boisterous dancing.

After eight days and 100 miles of river, we take out near the small town of Dege, where there is a monastery that prints 95 percent of the Buddhist Sutras (the Buddhist Bible) using hand-carved wood blocks, ink, and rollers. The monastery is filled with over 100,000 wood printing blocks, a king's treasure to the Tibetans. For a small donation, the monks will print prayer flags for us to take home.

We end our trip with another three-day ride through the spectacular mountain scenery, staying in local villages, sampling the local cuisine, and visiting monasteries that welcome us inside when we offer the monks a picture of the Dalai Lama. Back in Chengdu, and then Hong Kong, the twentieth century will take over, but our memories of this trip remain for a lifetime.

ITINERARY:

Days 1-2: Arrive Hong Kong.

Day 3: Fly to Chengdu.

Day 4: Chengdu.

Days 5-7: Scenic drive to Yushu.

Days 8-9: Yushu.

Days 10-16: Rafting on Yangtze River to Dege.

Days 17-19: Scenic drive to Chengdu.

Day 20: Fly Chengdu to Hong Kong.

Day 21: Depart Hong Kong.

PREMIUM

June-August

Steve Currey Expeditions

Kashmir and Ladakh Cultural Odyssey (AS 205)

CULTURAL TREK— CLASS II/III

➤ *"Roof of the World" odyssey*
➤ *Ruins of an ancient palace*
➤ *Houseboat stay on Dal Lake*

Remote, beautiful, and unchanging, the people and villages of Ladakh on the Tibetan plateau seem to inspire visitors to look deeply and optimistically at the human potential for survival and compassion. On this trip you will experience Ladahki society from the inside, hiking between isolated mountain villages and reflecting on ancient Buddhist monasteries.

The austere terrain of the western Himalayas of Ladakh, particularly around the northern Ladakh communities of Temisgam, Hemishakpatchan and Yangthang, provides a spectacular setting for learning and living the ancient traditions of Tibet. Led by JOURNEYS guides Norbu, Wangchook, and Phunchok, you will learn about traditional life-styles by staying in local homes and meeting the families of your guides. You will experience Tibetan Buddhism by visiting some of the most scholarly and traditional Buddhist monasteries in Asia, perhaps taking meditation advice from a lama. In effect, you will disappear from the twentieth century and find yourself in the capable care of friendly people who are proud of their culture and eager to create a comfortable context to explore and to learn. Expect food better than you could imagine possible in this remote place. While trekking you will hike three to eight miles per day at elevations ranging from 10,000 to 12,000 feet. We allow time for acclimatization before active trekking begins.

This trip includes a houseboat stay on Dal Lake in Srinagar followed by overland travel on the famous road across the Zoji La into Ladakh. Your itinerary also includes Delhi, the Taj Mahal, Kargil, Lamayuru, Alchi, Thikse, and Leh. This trip always includes a contribution to an environmental or community project. Past projects have included reconstruction of a village prayer wheel, resurfacing of a monastery courtyard, construction of trailside sanitary facilities, a solar heating project in a monastery, and repair of a long stone staircase leading to an ancient monastery. Land cost provides funding for the project. You may spend part of a day or two actually involved in doing such a project.

ITINERARY:

Days 1-2: En route.

Day 3: Delhi to Srinagar.

Day 4: Srinagar.

Days 5-6: Overland to Ladakh.

Day 7: Temisgam.

Day 8: Trek Temisgam to Hemishak-patchan.

Day 9: Trek Hemnishakpatchan to Yangthang.

Days 10-11: Trek Yangthang to Ridzong Monastery.

Day 12: Trek Ridzong to Alchi. Jeep to Leh.

Day 13: Leh.

Day 14: Fly to Delhi.

Day 15: Agra/Taj Mahal.

Days 16-17: Return.

MODERATE

June-October

JOURNEYS International, Inc.

Katun River (AS 206)

MODERATE RAFTING— CLASS IV

➤ *Whitewater Soviet-style*

➤ *Siberia's Altai Mountains*

➤ *Tour Moscow's historic sights*

Come along with us to promote glasnost in the way we understand best— by rafting the Class IV rapids of the Katun River with fellow rafting enthusiasts from the Soviet Union. This is a rare chance to meet the people whose smiles have been hidden by decades of propaganda— friendly folks who, like us, find thrills in the rush of glacial water between forested banks.

Siberia is a vast land of over five million square miles and occupies more than 60 percent of the territory of the USSR. Everything here, both natural and human, has sweeping dimensions, and the Katun is no exception. It runs through the Altai region of Siberia, about 70 percent of which is covered by mountain forests of conifers, birches, aspens, and larches. Small rodents populate its mountainous subdeserts and steppes, and in the forest Siberian animals such as bear, lynx, and musk deer can be found. High up in the mountains, many of which have glacial peaks, are snow leopards, goats, and mountain sheep. We run the Katun in the summer, which is the driest season of the year, and also the time when wild strawberries grow on the hillsides.

We begin the trip with a day of sightseeing in Moscow and then take a night flight to Barnaul, in Siberia. From there we fly to Ust-Koksa on the banks of the Katun, near the Mongolian border, and then take a helicopter to the launch site at the glacial source of the river near Mount Belucha, the tallest mountain in the region at 14,600 feet. From here it's seven days on the river, with both Soviets and Americans, paddling and oaring on some thrilling whitewater indeed. All groups include a Russian guide who is fluent in both Russian and English. We pass several villages populated not by dissidents and criminals but by highly nationalistic people with strong traditional beliefs and a deep cultural heritage. Most speak only the Altai language of the region, but we communicate as well as we can, and occasionally we're offered traditional yogurt, tea, and fresh fruit.

Our week-long float through this landscape of beauty and charm comes as a pleasant shock to those who imagine Siberia only as a land of gulags and tundra. And there's nothing like a huge wave or a recirculating trough to make Soviets and Americans understand that destiny lies in working together. This trip is not only a chance to ride some thrilling rapids but to be a citizen diplomat and promote further awareness for peace and environmental issues.

ITINERARY:

Day 1: Arrive Moscow.

Day 2: City tour.

Day 3: Fly to Barnaul, shuttle to put-in.

Day 4: Launch on the Katun.

Days 5-11: Rafting.

Day 12: End river trip, return to Barnaul.

Day 13: Fly to Moscow.

Day 14: Return.

PREMIUM

July-September

SOBEK Expeditions

John Tichener/SOBEK photo file

North America

Tatshenshini River (NA 1) ▰▰▰▰▰▰▰

SCENIC RAFTING—
CLASS III

➤ *Raft the river of ice*
➤ *The canyons of the St. Elias Range*
➤ *Wildlife and glacial wonders*

This is a trip for camera buffs as well as for river lovers: it may be the world's most beautiful river trip. The Tatshenshini slices south through the Yukon to the Pacific, cutting a course through the awesome St. Elias Range and a vast landscape of huge mountain peaks and meadows, churning, pewter-colored water, eerie blue-green glaciers,and sculptures of rock and ice and snow. Bald eagles soar overhead; grizzly bears and bull moose stalk the riverbanks; mountain goats, moose, and marmots roam the foothills, and salmon choke the tributaries. Nowhere exists a trace of civilization, of man's intrusion on nature, only wilderness in its wildest and most pristine state.

We begin the trip in Haines and drive for 110 miles to put-in at Dalton Post. Here the Tatshenshini begins as a fast, sparkling stream in the shadow of a nearly unbroken chain of 8,000-foot and higher summits, many of them unnamed, most unclaimed by climbers and explorers. As the river narrows into a constricted gorge, there are plenty of Class III rapids and eighteen hours of light to run them. Then the "Tat" widens out and joins with the Alsek River (see trip NA 100) to become a vast expanse of water moving at 60,000 cubic feet per second through an awesome landscape. Here the river is filled with silt off the flanks of the granite ranges surrounding it, and the carpets of wildflowers along its banks are interrupted by glaciers—frozen blue rivers of ice that have snaked down to meet the water. Skyscraper-sized chunks of ice calve off the glaciers and float alongside the boats, many of them breaking up into opaque sculptures that seem to have a deep blue core and a magical, prismatic glow. Occasionally, the ground shakes like an earthquake and the sound of thunder fills the air as pieces of ice, hundreds of feet thick and miles long, break loose.

To experience the world of ice close up, we stop for a day and scamper across a moraine onto the living face of a glacier—a billowing, serrated expanse of frozen crystal. We explore the ice, watching for cravasses and sinkholes, and listen to the sound of rivers tumbling under us like rolling empty oil drums.

At the end of the trip we meet up with the icebergs that have calved off the Alsek Glacier and make our way through an obstacle course. The river is a maze of shimmering ice flotsam, mammoth pointed polygons turning slowly in the current and sparkling like window display jewels. And then its a short hop by charter plane back to civilization.

Partly, it is the color and the light of this frozen world that is so spectacular. Partly, it is the sightings of grizzlies. But it is mostly the scale of the Tatshenshini that lasts in the memory. Its mountains and glaciers are awesome in a way that only those who have been to Alaska can know.

ITINERARY:

Day 1: Arrive Haines, Alaska.

Day 2: Drive to Dalton Post, Yukon; begin river trip.

Days 3-9: Rafting the Tatshenshini.

Day 10: Take-out at Dry Bay, Alaska; flight to Yakutat and return.

PREMIUM

June-August

SOBEK

Rivers of the Arctic (NA 3)

RAFTING/WILDLIFE— CLASS III

➤ *World's largest caribou herd*

➤ *Brooks Range backdrop*

➤ *Great fishing under the midnight sun*

The Porcupine River caribou herd is one of only two wild herds that survived the press of modern civilization. When the 100,000-strong herd masses for its annual migration from the barren northern slope of the Brooks Range across to the forests of Canada, its route leads up the Kongakut Valley. There can be no guarantee on the exact timing of this natural spectacle, but we time our Kongakut float to coincide with the normal early July migration. The midnight sun, Arctic wildlife, Brooks Range scenery, and fine whitewater produce a superb experience with or without the caribou. The Kongakut can have difficult or easy rapids depending on the spring melt, but it is always a winner.

We charter a bush plane to fly us and our river equipment to a gravel landing strip near the headwaters of the Kongakut. We float north through the mountains to the Arctic Ocean, and we hope to see the incredible spectacle of the caribou migration. The Porcupine River caribou herd migrates in late June or early July en masse from the north slope of the Brooks Range back to Canada. The river features fast and feisty whitewater and some of the best Arctic char fishing to be found.

As we float downriver we stop at interesting places for side hikes. The contrasting scenery as we drop out of the mountains and onto the tundra plains is fascinating. There will be plenty of time on this leisurely paced trip for all the hiking, resting and enjoyment that each person wants, and the midnight sun gives us 24 hours to do it. On the trip we may encounter Dall sheep, mountain goats, fox, wolves, brown bears, moose, and caribou, as well as a great variety of birds.

ITINERARY:

Day 1: Fairbanks to Kaktovik.

Days 2-11: On the river.

Day 12: Return to Fairbanks.

MEDIUM

June-July

Alaska River Expeditions

Talkeetna River (NA 10)

CHALLENGING RAFTING — CLASS IV

➤ *Exceptional and historic scenery*

➤ *High-class rapids*

➤ *Eagles, beavers, caribou, and more*

From alpine slopes to lush forest, the Talkeetna River whistles its way toward its confluence with the Susitna in the shadow of Mount McKinley. For six days we join in the whistling with whoops of our own as we descend this classic Alaskan river. Besides running the most thrilling wilderness whitewater in the North, we'll see gold miners, grizzly bears, wild moose, running salmon, and wolves stalking caribou herds—the whole gamut of Alaskan attractions.

Highlighting the rafting adventure is a two-day whoosh through the Talkeetna's central gorge, where the river drops 60 feet per mile for exhilarating Class IV whitewater. One rapid known as Sluice Box is 14 miles of twists and turns, holes and haystacks, making it the longest commercially run rapid in the world. Besides whitewater adventure, we'll meet local prospectors, cook freshly caught salmon in our frying pans, and end up in the shadow of Denali, the Great One, which looms over our take-out at the historic town of Talkeetna in the heart of Gold Rush Alaska.

ITINERARY:

Day 1: Anchorage to Talkeetna; bush flight up canyon to put-in.

Day 2: Begin river trip to Prairie Creek.

Day 3: Prairie Creek layover.

Day 4: Back on river to Moose Creek.

Day 5: Running Sluice Box to Disappointment Creek.

Day 6: Down river to confluence with Susitna at Talkeetna; return.

MEDIUM

June-August

Adventure River Company

Alaska on Your Own (NA 14/15/16)

SELF-PROPELLED ADVENTURES — CLASS III

➤ *Canoe Admiralty Island (NA 14)*

➤ *Sea-kayak Hubbard Glacier (NA 15)*

➤ *Glacier Bay Kayak (NA 16)*

One of the best ways to see Alaska is to strike out on your own adventure— to practice some of the rugged individualism for which the state is known. We can help arrange this for you, providing itineraries, equipment, and transport. How about a canoe trip in the Admiralty Island National Monument Wilderness off southeastern Alaska, where brown bears and bald eagles easily outnumber people? This five-day package includes floatplane access to the remote regions of the large island and time for fishing, hiking, and boat instruction.

Or, you might like to learn sea-kayaking in the remote waters of Russell Fjord, past the electric blue ice of Hubbard Glacier. Finally, in Glacier Bay, we offer a trip by two-person folding Klepper kayak. This trip is without doubt the best way to see the still-pristine waters of the bay, justifiably famous for its fjords, forests, flora, and marine life, including the great blue whales. Seeing Alaska on your own can be a spiritual experience, an awakening of long-forgotten senses, a trip to the heart. Why not give it a try?

ITINERARY, Admiralty Island (NA 14):

Day 1: Juneau to Admiralty.

Days 2-4: Canoeing and camping.

Day 5: Flight to Juneau and return.

July-August

ITINERARY, Hubbard Glacier (NA 15):

Day 1: Glacier Bay Lodge, Yakutat; flight to Russell Fjord.

Days 2-6: Kayaking and camping.

Day 7: Return to Yakutat.

July-August

ITINERARY, Glacier Bay (NA 16):

Day 1: Juneau to Glacier Bay.

Days 2-3: Kayak and camping.

Day 4: Return flight to Juneau.

PREMIUM

June–August

Alaska Discovery

Tuolumne River (NA 27)

CHALLENGING
WHITEWATER—
CLASS III

- ➤ *California's wild and scenic prize*
- ➤ *Run Class V Clavey Falls*

The battle to save the Tuolumne is one of the classic tales of the river conservation movement, especially because in this case the river won. In 1984, the Tuolumne was declared a Wild and Scenic River and its place was secured among California's great river adventures. See for yourself what made "the T" worth the fight—its tough technical whitewater, golden canyonlands, historic mining sites, and remarkable isolation, plus Clavey Falls, a double-dare drop from flatwater to seething suds. Couple this on-river excitement with the campside pleasures of good food, including fresh meats and fruit salads, off-river hikes to secret pools and crystal falls, and time to contemplate and photograph the beauty, and you've got a whitewater winner. The Tuolumne, with its headwaters in Yosemite National Park, is runnable on trips of one, two, or three days' duration. The one-day is available only during the flush of spring snow-melt—a raucous 17-mile ride at blinding speeds through enormous drenching holes and towering waves. The more leisurely two- and three-day runs allow time for camping, hiking, and savoring the true wilderness flavor of "the T," the toast of California whitewater.

ITINERARY:

Day 1: Meet near Groveland, California; drive to river and begin trip.

Day 2 or Days 2-3: Down the river to Don Pedro Reservoir; take-out and return to Groveland.

MEDIUM

March–September

O.A.R.S.

The Rogue River (NA 36)

RAFTING/SCENIC—
CLASS III

- ➤ *Raft the rowdy Rogue*
- ➤ *Treasure trove of wildlife*

The rowdy reputation of the Rogue is well earned, its playfulness giving way to unpredictable fits of passion, thundering whitewater, and spirited swirls. Then it turns pretty, and a lovelier river would be hard to imagine: green-scented cedar and fir forest, narrow gorges of black basalt, and the crystalline cascades of side creeks. Our leisurely float down the Rogue allows plenty of time to savor its special charms, sight its osprey and deer, swim in its warm waters, and doze in its shady groves. Enjoy the respite, for rapids like Blossom Bar, Wildcat, Mule Creek Canyon and the all-but-unrunnable Rainie Falls are soon to come. One of the original Wild and Scenic Rivers, the Rogue is a perfect river for rafting so everyone can enjoy the thrills and chills of running one of the West's best.

ITINERARY:

Day 1: Put-in near Galice.

Days 2-4: On the Rogue.

Day 5: Return to Galice.

MEDIUM

June-September

O.A.R.S.

Hoover Wilderness Area (NA 38) ⋀⋀⋀⋀⋀⋀

LLAMA PACKING —
CLASS III

➤ *The beauty of Yosemite*

➤ *Hike among sagebrush and thistle*

California's High Sierra is a rough and ready landscape of lodgepole pine and red fir, arid desert, U-shaped glacial valleys, solitude and spectacle. The Hoover Wilderness is 42,800 acres of primitive countryside in the east-central part of the state, touching on Yosemite National Park at the Sierra Crest—some of the most remote and special acreage in the West. Here we hike for five days among the sagebrush and the thistle, the escarpments and the late summer snowfields, while South American llamas carry our cargo. Bobcats and coyote live here, as do mule deer, bear and an occasional mountain lion. The streams are choking with trout, while the high peak region—including Materhorn and Dunderber (over 11,000 feet)—host technical and amateur climbers. Wildflowers, birdlife, and other features are explained by well-versed guides, so our hike becomes a natural history course, a fishing vacation, a high country adventure, and an animal appreciation amusement all in one.

ITINERARY:

Days 1-5: Hiking.

MODERATE

August

Mama's Llamas

Main Fork of the Salmon (NA 43) 〰〰〰

RAFTING/SCENIC —
CLASS III

➤ *Pine forests and sandy beaches*

➤ *BIG river, BIG rapids, BIG wilderness*

"The river of no return," decided Lewis and Clark when they looked down its churning length and rerouted their expedition. We don't avoid a thing—not the big wilderness or the big canyon, not even the big rapids on the big river itself. For fifty kilometers we follow the Salmon as it cuts across Idaho's vast Primitive Area in the second deepest canyon in North America, a journey of drama and quietude, huge standing waves and lazy calms.

As if the river's own variety is not enough, there's human history aplenty— from the Shoshone campsites and petroglyphs to the abandoned gold mines coddled among the pines. Golden eagles glide above the river's moody course, and bighorn sheep, brown bear, cougar, and a few surprises lurk in the wilderness. Join us on a six-day journey through the largest undeveloped land area in the Lower Forty-eight, teeming with delights hydraulic, historic, and human.

ITINERARY:

Day 1: Salmon, Idaho, to put-in.

Days 2-5: On the river.

Day 6: End trip.

MEDIUM

May-September

Holiday River Expeditions

Desolation Canyon (NA 47)

RAFTING/SCENIC— CLASS III

> *Explore Butch Cassidy's cabin*
> *Big challenging rapids*

Desolation Canyon earned its name when John Wesley Powell first explored it in 1869 and has re-earned it over the years as settlers, trappers, and outlaws strove to eke out a living or lose a posse in its tortured mazes. Rock spires, arch formations and natural monuments rise high above sandy riverbanks, piñon and juniper slopes and the petroglyphs of the Anasazi. Where legend and landscape are so impressive, river running is a reflection: enjoy the introductory-level whitewater in paddle boats while a supply raft carries all the necessary camping gear down the river for a fun, family-oriented trip. Or choose a six-day oar option and relax in superb surroundings. Swim, fish, take pictures, and listen to the lore of Butch Cassidy and the Wild Bunch, Indian history, and the spectacular geologic record of the Green River.

ITINERARY:

Day 1: Meet in Green River, Utah, fly to Sand Wash for river trip.

Days 2-4 or 2-6: River trip.

Day 5 or 7: Return to Green River.

MODERATE

June-September

Sheri Griffith Expeditions

Cataract Canyon (NA 48)

CANYONLANDS RAFTING— CLASS III

> *Red cliffs and white water*
> *Big and challenging rapids*
> *Choice of oar or motor rigs*

The Colorado River cuts its fair share of canyons, including one with Class IV whitewater, the Cataract. Alongside the

Grand Canyon, Cataract may appear diminutive but only from a distance. From the bottom of a standing wave, looking up at its frothing crest twelve feet above, it's clear the Cataract holds some of the biggest and most challenging springtime whitewater in the country, with rapids like Mile Long and Little Niagara, Satan's Seat, and Satan's Gut.

While waves and holes provide the thrills, it's the grandeur of the red-rock gorges that lingers in the memory: abstract sandstone spires, razor sharp mesas, impressive monuments, and soaring cliffs. The trip begins in Moab, Utah, passes the confluence of the Colorado with the Green, then roars down to Lake Powell. Along the way there are side canyons to explore, sunny beaches to sprawl on, rapids to scout, and plenty of photographs to frame. Trip lengths of four, five, or six days are available, with the two shorter trips aboard larger motorized rafts. For the full wilderness experience, the six-day, oar-powered trip offers maximum time on the Colorado River in Cataract National Park.

ITINERARY:

Day 1: Meet near Moab, Utah; transport to put-in and begin river trip.

Following Days: On the river.

Last Day: End trip at Lake Powell; air transport to Moab.

MEDIUM

September

Sheri Griffith Expeditions

Pacific Quest (NA 49) ~~~

ACTIVE VARIETY PACKAGE— CLASS III

➤ *Hike the Na Pali Coast*

➤ *Snorkel emerald lagoons*

➤ *Worship Pele at Kilauea Volcano*

Sample the highlights of Hawaii's earthly paradise on this two-week trip through the island's natural wonders. We explore the hidden niches of Kauai, Maui, Hawaii, Molokai and Lanai, places so diverse in color, mood, and miracle that you wonder what keeps your feet on the igneous soil. We snorkel the coral reefs of Mahukona, climb along the rainbow cliffs of Waimea Canyon, hike through the bamboo forests and the rainbow-draped scenery of the Na Pali Coast, and camp in the cindery caldera of Maui's spectacular Haleakala Volcano.

On the Big Island we study the petroglyphs of Hawaii's Polynesian settlers and see the steaming dwelling of the fire goddess Pele at the summit of Kilauea, a volcano that has been erupting continuously since 1983. Chances are we can even see molten lava pouring into the ocean! But even paradise is more than just scenery, and our adventure includes a sail across the channel from Molokai, to Lahaina, the old whaling capital of Maui, and winding drives along the famous rugged coasts of Maui, Molokai, and the Big Island. All this in fourteen days, plus tropical nights and barbecue feasts on the beach. How can anyone resist?

ITINERARY:

Day 1: Meet Lihue, Kauai; beach-side camp.

Day 2: Na Pali.

Days 3-4: Waimea Canyon.

Days 5-6: Molokai.

Day 7: Sail to Lahaina.

Days 8-10: Maui.

Days 11-12: Volcanoes National Park, Hawaii.

Day 13: Mahukona diving and farewell luau.

Day 14: Midday flight to Honolulu and return.

MODERATE

Year-round

Pacific Quest

Northwest Dogsledding (NA 54)

CULTURE/NATURAL HISTORY—CLASS III

➤ *Falaise Lake*

➤ *Rare wood buffalo, moose, wolves, and more*

➤ *Numerous photo opportunities*

The call of the wild rings out over the frozen wastes of the Northwest Territories, and answering it in the terms it deserves is an adventure like no other. The inhabitants of this rugged land are the hunters, trappers,and traders of a far domain, many of whom are Chippewa or Cree Indians. For those willing to share in this timeless way of life, arrangements can be made to allow small groups of visitors to join an Indian guide on his established rounds, whispering over the trails on an oak toboggan behind teams of nine huskies.

We suggest two major destinations: the Tazin Highlands, in the heartland of caribou free-range on the tundra, with wolves, red fox, and other wintering creatures; or Wood Buffalo National Park, a wilderness of forest and prairie where wild bands of bison and wolf continue their ancient relationship. Visitors may bring snowshoes or cross-country skis but are encouraged to take an active role in making camp and harnessing dogs. In exchange, they can learn the art of driving a team, camp beneath the Northern Lights, and be serenaded by the eerie, lonesome howling of wolves—the call of the wild.

ITINERARY: Trips of 1-5 days by arrangement. Departures from Fort Smith, Northwest Territories, and Fort Chipewyan, Alberta.

PREMIUM

February-April, November-December

Great Slave Sledding Company

Northwest Safari (NA 60)

SAILING—CLASS II

➤ *Sail a 68-foot ship*

➤ *Whales and porpoises*

➤ *Totem poles and Indian culture*

The spectacular coastline of British Columbia provides an excellent setting for three different natural history cruises. You may choose to visit the majestic Queen Charlotte Islands, to see killer whales in Johnstone Strait or cruise the beautiful San Juan and Gulf islands. Our 68-foot yacht, the *Island Roamer,* navigates through coastal areas on one of the finest sailing adventures possible. You may choose to relax while we chart our course for some of the most outstanding scenery and wildlife in the world or get involved with the task of sailing by learning more about navigation, sail handling, knots, or other skills used aboard a sailing ship.

You can rely on our experienced crew to offer you a top-quality sailing adventure. Their knowledge of marine biology, whales, native Indian culture, birds, and ecology will make your trip as interesting and as educational as you wish. The crew is available to answer your questions on everything from how to trim a sail to why there's a hump on a humpback whale.

We anchor every night and make stops during the day. This allows ample opportunity for active individuals to engage in kayaking and fishing, and for the hardy individuals, snorkeling.

Orcas and Inside Passage

This trip will give you a unique opportunity to view one of the world's most exciting marine mammals in the world. The north end of Vancouver Island is one of the few places in the world where *Orcinus orca* (killer whales) can be seen every day. We will learn about the behavior of these active whales as we watch them forage for salmon, blow spouts, and breach (leap clear out of the water). By lowering an underwater microphone, we will hear the distinctive calls made by these marine mammals. Other wildlife seen in the area include Dall's porpoise, minke whales, harbor seals, and an abundant variety of birds including bald eagles.

We will have an opportunity to learn about the native Kwakiutl Indians. We visit the abandoned village of Mamalilculla to see totem poles and stop at the U'Mista Cultural Centre in Alert Bay to view an outstanding collection of potlatch masks and other artifacts.

Queen Charlotte Islands

Canada's newest national park in the Queen Charlotte Islands is an outstanding wilderness area with fascinating native

Indian history. Aboard our 68-foot sailboat *Island Roamer*, we will see abandoned Indian villages, an abundance of wildlife, and outstanding scenery. Our visits to the Haida villages of Tanu, Skedans, and Ninstints (Anthony Island) reveal the best examples of standing totem poles in the world, the remains of longhouses, and other artifacts showing the rich heritage of the Haida.

There will be many opportunities to view tufted puffins, peregrine falcons, rhinoceros auklets, eagles, and other of the tens of thousands of birds that nest on the Charlottes. We will also see Steller sea lions on their breeding beaches and hope to spot whales and porpoises. For those who enjoy fresh seafood, we will sample cod, halibut, abalone, scallops, and other shellfish. The forests of the Charlottes are among the few places where you can walk through unlogged stands of enormous Western red cedar, hemlock, and Sitka spruce trees.

A highlight of the trip will be our stop at Hot Springs Island to luxuriate in the steaming mineral pools. At the end of the trip we fly over the 130 islands of the archipelago to return to Sandspit.

San Juan and Gulf Islands

In September and early October, our choice is to cruise south and enjoy warm weather and the friendly cruising atmosphere of the San Juan and Gulf islands. We expect to see Dall's porpoise, harbor seals, sea lions and to have one or two encounters with the elusive killer and minke whales of this area. We will see eagles and a large variety of seabirds. Active participants will enjoy the frequent excursions ashore to hike and explore tidepools. These trips visit Victoria and Vancouver as well as picturesque coastal villages such as Friday Harbour, Roche Harbour and Chemainus.

These sailing trips depart from the popular Granville Island in central Vancouver. The trip meets at 10:00 a.m. at our dock, on the west side of Bridges Restaurant. Our crew will assist you in stowing your gear aboard the *Island Roamer* and then give you an orientation tour of the vessel. Before we cast off you may want to do a little shopping for charts for the trip, books or special food items.

When everyone is aboard the vessel we will depart Vancouver Harbour and set sail across the Strait of Georgia to the Gulf Islands. One of our first stops may be at Gabriola Island where we walk inland to view an Indian petroglyph site. Sailing south we may stop at the picturesque town of Chemainus, where colorful murals depicting historic scenes have been painted on buildings in town. Among the more popular stops are Pirates Cove with its interesting history and beautiful bay, Brethour Island, Sidney Spit, and Bedwell Bay.

On the final day of the trip we sail across to Vancouver Island. The highlight this day is a visit to Race Rocks to see the large herds of California and Steller's sea lions.

SAMPLE ITINERARY:

Day 1: Campbell River, B.C.; begin sail.

Days 2-5: Sailing.

Day 6: Victoria and return.

MEDIUM

Orcas and Inland Passage: *August.*

Queen Charlotte Islands: *May-July.*

San Juan and Gulf islands: *September-October.*

Bluewater Adventures

Adventure Sailing Escape (NA 64)

SAILING — CLASS II

➤ *Florida's Gulf Coast*
➤ *200 species of birds*
➤ *Incredible sailing and diving*

The romance of the islands of the Florida Gulf Coast is an anchor drop away on this week-long adventure in flotilla sailing. We sail 26-foot Commodores, especially built for stable cruising, through the small islands off Fort Myers for seven dawns and dusks in groups of up to six boats at a time. The boats are designed for four adults, and qualified sailors can captain their own craft for the entire duration of the trip. There's plenty of time to free sail, exploring tropical barrier islands inhabited only by gulls, pelicans, and man-of-war birds. Dolphins lace your bow, red snappers snap at your line, living shellfish color your snorkeling, and Gulf breezes fill your foresail.

ITINERARY:

Day 1: Fort Myers, Florida.

Days 2-5: Sailing.

Day 6: Fort Myers.

Day 7: Return.

MEDIUM

Year-round

Ft. Myers Yacht Charters

Grand Canyon Rafting (NA 76)

THE WHITEWATER CLASSIC—CLASS III

➤ *279 miles of timeless travel*

➤ *Lava Falls, Crystal, and other rapids*

This two-week run down the Colorado on regular-sized inflatable rafts is the trip of a lifetime, combining some of the world's most exciting whitewater with a journey of incredible beauty and geological richness. The Colorado is a marvelous paradox: an intense, adrenalin rush of a river in one of the most peaceful places on earth. And on this two-week trip down the canyon we have the time to explore the quiet side of the river as well as to come in close contact with the awesome big rapids.

We bask in the spectral beauty of Elves Chasm, the sensual pleasure of Havasu, the haunting timelessness of the Anasazi ruins. And for a dozen days of sunshine and excitement we ride the big waves and punch through amazing holes. In between, we have time to contemplate the geology: the Colorado cuts a course two billion years and a mile deep into the Earth's crust, exposing the rainbow colors of Marble Canyon, the dark foreboding rock of the inner gorge, and side canyons of rare beauty and peacefulness. The trip may be taken in either its Upper Half from Lee's Ferry to Phantom Ranch through Marble Canyon; its Lower Half from Phantom Ranch to Lake Mead; or the full course, a double-shot of thrills and wonderment.

ITINERARY:

Day 1: Launch at Lee's Ferry.

Days 2-4: Raft Marble Canyon.

Day 5: Reach Phantom Ranch; end Upper Half and begin Lower Half (Day 1).

Days 6-11 (Lower Half Days 2-7): Raft the Lower Grand.

Day 12 (Lower Half Day 8): Motor across Lake Mead to Pierce Ferry; transport to Las Vegas.

ITINERARY:

Upper Half/Lower Half:
5- and 12-day:

May-October

ITINERARY:

Lower Half/Upper Half:
6- and 13-day:

May-September

Deluxe Paddle Trips: *June-August.*
Please call for details.

MEDIUM

Outdoors Unlimited

Everglades Canoeing (NA 84)

CANOE/NATURAL
HISTORY—CLASS III

➤ *Discover bays, creeks, and channels by canoe*
➤ *Coastal flora and fauna*

"River of Grass" is the meaning of "Everglades," and it is this distinctive feature of the region that makes it an ecosystem unique in all the world. Hundreds of square miles of water filter slowly through saw-grass prairies into the sea, creating mangrove swamps that protect the land from violent Atlantic storms, a maze of narrow twisting channels and islands, and rocky tidal pools brimming over with unusual flora and fauna.

We paddle down these channels, explore mangrove forests, and beachcomb in tidal pools to sample the pacific quality of the Florida Everglades. The scenery changes daily as we canoe between our four campsites, photographing orchids and spectacular sunsets, fishing for dinners of snapper, and watching herons and egrets gracefully bend their long necks to feed. A layover day on a remote Gulf Coast island is relaxing and educational. The camping is often primitive, as we must dig our own latrines and carry our drinking water with us, but it is a primitive world we visit. To do the Everglades justice, and to do justice to ourselves, we acknowledge rather than combat its timelessness.

ITINERARY:

Day 1: Meet in Fort Myers, Florida, travel to Everglades.

Days 2-5: Canoeing.

Day 6: End canoeing; to Fort Myers and return.

MODERATE

February

Wilderness Southeast

Denali Climb (NA 93)

CLIMBING—CLASS V

➤ *Climb to North America's top*
➤ *Kahiltna Glacier*

An ascent up the west buttress of Denali, North America's highest point, is a peak experience indeed. Stand at the summit of the continent, 6,194 meters above sea level, while the mighty mass of McKinley spreads out its bulk from horizon to horizon. This is no slick packaged tour, for there is no easy way up. We spend nearly three weeks on the mountain, living and climbing in true expedition style as we set up a base camp at 7,000 feet on the tongue of Kahiltna Glacier, relay loads over the course of a week to the 14,000-foot level, and finally reach our high camp at 17,200 feet. Then we wait—for the crystal clear morning when the wind is still and the horizon line sharp and the snowy route to the summit firm. Our final push to the 20,320-foot apex makes the most of the mountaineering skills we have developed over the previous two weeks on Denali. Although previous climbing experience is helpful, it is not essential. Far more useful is the physical and mental health necessary to cope with the long days of glacier travel, moderate snow and ice climbing, and the possibility of poor weather delaying the summit attempt. All expenses on the expedition are covered, from departure from Talkeetna to our return nearly three weeks later.

ITINERARY:

Days 1-2: Talkeetna.

Day 3: Charter flight to Kahiltna Glacier; begin climb.

Days 4-21: On the mountain.

Day 22: Talkeetna.

Day 23: Return. Date of return to Talkeetna approximate.

MEDIUM

April-June

Genet Expeditions

Complete Grand Canyon (NA 95)

MOTORIZED RAFTING—
CLASS II

➤ *Full canyon in seven days*
➤ *Top-quality meals*
➤ *Comfort, safety, and family fun*

The name says it all: the Grand Canyon, the most impressive cut on the skin of the Earth, a living museum of geological forces. This is a trip you'll remember all of your life and not just for the scenery. Rapids like Hance, Hermit, Crystal, and the incomparable Lava Falls make the Grand Canyon the pinnacle of big water excitement the world over. And yet on this trip we raft the rapids in complete safety, with all the comforts of home, on a large, stable, motorized pontoon boat. This is also the only way to see the entire 279-mile length of the Grand Canyon in less than a week, with plenty of time left over to enjoy some quiet, private moments on the river—swimming, sunbathing, exploring tributaries and nurturing friendships.

When we enter the canyon at Lee's Ferry, we enter a time antecedent to human history. Once in Marble Canyon, the red-stained walls rise higher in tiers of rock ever more ancient. The river guides tick off their names one by one: Hermit Shale, Redwall Limestone, Bright Angel Shale, and finally the Great Unconformity—250 million years of no geological record whatsoever. These first few days are like the unfolding of a blossom, a visual manifestation of the earth's creation.

Then we head into the deepest strata of the inner canyon where the rock walls are older than the first stirrings of multicellular life on the planet. And here the river changes in character. The canyon narrows and we meet the big rapids: Horn Creek, Granite, Hermit, and finally Crystal—a narrow approach down a rapidly accelerating current into a boulder-choked chute, culminating in one of the largest hydraulic holes on any river in the world. After Crystal, the charms of the Grand Canyon begin to reveal themselves. We see cactus, juniper, and an occasional bighorn sheep or feral burro. A clear stream spills into the river down seventy-foot Deer Creek Falls; a side hike up the small Matkatamiba Creek leads to an open chamber of pools, ferns, and huge stone altars set in cathedral like serenity. Most impressive of all is Havasu Creek, with its aquamarine waters. Just nine miles up the creek is the village of

Supai where 300 Havasupai Indians make their home.

The awesome Lava Falls, the fastest navigable waters in America, mark the beginning of the end of the gorge and in terms of whitewater, the highlight of the trip. But we are in an unflippable boat and we sail through with much cheers and shouting—and still plenty of ice-cold drinks left on our raft to celebrate. In addition to cold drinks and fabulous food, we have with us on this "luxury ride" three trained crew members per boat, a trip geologist, and plenty of wine—not to mention the free T-shirt.

ITINERARY:

Day 1: Arrive Las Vegas; hotel.

Day 2: Transport to the river, begin trip.

Days 3-6: Down the Grand Canyon.

Day 7: Jet boat across Lake Mead; return transport to Las Vegas.

MEDIUM

April-September

SOBEK's White Water River Expeditions

Alsek River (NA 100) ▰◣◢◣◢◣

ADVANCED RAFTING— CLASS IV

➤ *Wild and scenic wonder*

➤ *Whitewater and wildlife*

➤ *Helicopter portage of Turnback Canyon*

Rafting the wilderness of the Alsek River is a journey undertaken only a handful of times in history. First run in 1961, the Alsek is one of the biggest rivers in the Northwest and perhaps the most spectacular Wild and Scenic River in the world. For most people it will be the biggest river they will ever float on; it's not an easy journey by any stretch of the imagination. Located at the ankle of Alaska, it gets spring runoff through the summer from the glaciers of the St. Elias Range, and along the way it picks up tremendous speed.

The trip begins in Haines, and from there we take a three-and-a-half hour drive over the Coastal Mountains into Yukon Territory, Canada, for put-in. For the first few days on the Alsek we ride the mighty currents, taking time to stop and hike the nearby glaciers and scout for mountain goats and grizzly bears. Then we spend a layover day at Lowell Glacier and climb up some 3,000 straightforward feet to Goatherd Mountain for spectacular views. Midway through our journey the Alsek picks up speed and the water becomes very powerful with lots of big waves and strong current piling up on the walls. Even so, we have time to look for grizzly bear, Alaska moose, mountain goat, beaver, wolf, muskrat, wolverine, mink, weasel, and Alaska red fox along with countless species of birds. The days are long, and there's plenty of time to relax, fish and explore tributary streams as well as ponder the incredible sky.

Then we come to Turnback Canyon. This narrow gorge, in places but 30 feet wide, has only been run by a select few kayakers—the bravest of the brave—and far more have been turned back by its roiling turmoil. We hike downriver to view this awesome spectacle—a five-mile canyon where the river is squeezed to just 30 feet wide in places; a boiling mass with tough 90-degree turns and chunks of ice. And then we ready our gear for a helicopter portage, a feature unique in the world of commercial river running. After a beautiful chopper ride, we rejoin the Alsek and soon reach the confluence with the Tatshenshini. Here the river jumps in volume and power, but it widens, too, and we float the final four days between calving glaciers and soaring peaks to take-out in Dry Bay. Along the way we can hike across a large glacier that has sprawled down its valley to within a few yards of the river's edge, and in Alsek Bay, we stop a while to see the Alsek and Grand Plateau glaciers alive and booming with calving bergs.

This is a river trip for those who want a genuine river adventure, with white-water to humble even the most jaded. But it's also a very special way to experience Alaska's pristine wilderness.

ITINERARY:

Day 1: Arrive Haines, Alaska.

Day 2: Drive to Kluane National Park, Yukon; begin river trip.

Days 3-7: Rafting the Alsek.

Day 8: Layover at Tweedsmuir.

Day 9: Helicopter portage; resume river trip.

Days 10-11: On river.

Day 12: Dry Bay and return.

PREMIUM

July-August

SOBEK

San Juan Islands (NA 102) ▲▲▲▲▲▲

SEA KAYAKING— CLASS III

➤ *San Juan charm*

➤ *Sleep under the stars*

Scattered like precious jades within the sheltered waters of Washington's coastal zone, the San Juans are a treasure, with natural abundance and scenic splendor to spare. Bald eagles swoop to scan the emerald waters; orcas dance and dine in the salmon-laced tides; scaups and scoters dive for fry near the forested isles. And sea kayakers meet them all, eye to eye and beam to beak. Even for the novice kayaker, these seagoing crafts are easy to handle from the first day onward. With small groups of no more than six sea-lovers under the guidance and tutelage of expert 'yakers, five days in the plentiful wonders of the San Juan will make a convert of the most devout desert-lover. Come find the plenty of life's fullest horn in these lush northern waters. Charter trips available.

ITINERARY:

Day 1: Ferry from Bellingham, Washington, to Gooseberry Point; begin trip.

Days 2-4: Sea kayaking in the San Juans.

Day 5: To Bellingham; sauna and return.

MEDIUM

March-October

Tide-Rip Tours

Riding and Rafting the Tetons (NA 110) 〰️

VARIETY PACKAGE— CLASS III

➤ *Grand Teton National Park*

➤ *Raft the Snake River*

➤ *Horseback riding in Wyoming's canyons*

Why choose just one way to explore Grand Teton National Park when you can travel through its majestic mountains by both horse and boat? In this trip, which takes us through the backcountry region near Jackson Hole, Wyoming, we travel through the mountains on horseback and then go down a whitewater river in a raft. With experts to guide us, we begin the trip by riding through the lush meadows and pine forests of the Snake River canyons where we look for herds of elk and bighorn sheep. At night, hearty meals around the campfire complete our hard-earned status as cowboys of the range. Then we switch gears and fish for cutthroat trout in the clear blue waters of Jackson Lake, keeping eyes open for the beaver, otter, osprey, and moose that enjoy the national park's protection. Finally we launch on the swift-flowing Snake itself, one of America's most popular river runs. The special two-day river trip includes all the highlights of great river runs: breathtaking scenery, abundant wildlife, whitewater thrills, and the isolation of a riverside camp. This is an ideal week-long wilderness vacation for the whole family, offering both daily variety and the uniform pleasures of a shared experience.

ITINERARY:

Day 1: Meet in Jackson, Wyoming; transport to trailhead and begin riding.

Days 2-3: Horseback riding.

Days 4-5: Jackson Lake fishing.

Day 6: Begin rafting the Snake River; camp.

Day 7: End rafting and return to Jackson.

MEDIUM

July-August

Parklands Expeditions

Banff by Horseback (NA 111)

HORSEBACK CARAVAN — CLASS II

➤ *Ride the scenic Canadian Rockies*
➤ *Firelit camps in bighorn country*

Imagine the perfect combination of mountain scenery, lakeshore serenity, and backcountry wildlife. Now imagine yourself gliding through all this atop a striding stallion! If it sounds too good to be true, then you haven't been horseback riding in Banff National Park in the Canadian province of Alberta. Banff has been called "the most beautiful parkland in the world," and when you take the full circle route into the Cascade Valley, where open grassy ridges climb to the glaciated flanks of the Canadian Rockies in every direction, you'll agree.

The Rockies here are dramatic and bold, with carpets of wildflowers and peaks of snow and ice. Immerse yourself in this scenery for even a moment and you'll begin to experience the timeless sense of wonder that comes with big mountains and vast meadows. Six full days of horseback riding, firelit camps in bighorn country, and robust Western-style food all add up to a memorable journey for photographers, fishermen, and families, from tenderfoots to grizzled seniors.

ITINERARY:

Day 1: Banff to trail head; begin ride.

Day 2: Stoney Creek camp.

Days 3-4: Flint Park camp.

Day 5: Mystic Valley.

Day 6: Early evening arrival in Banff and return.

MEDIUM

June-October

Warner and MacKenzie Guiding and Outfitting

The New River (NA 112)

RAFTING/WHITEWATER— CLASS III

➤ *Choose kayak or raft*

➤ *Side hikes and wild rapids*

From North Carolina's mountains to the green foothills of West Virginia, the ironically named New River—actually the oldest river on the continent—carves its way north. Along this age-old route, it has dug a thousand-foot gorge that whitewater enthusiasts call the Grand Canyon of the East. On our 48-mile rafting and kayaking trip, we thrill to some of the finest whitewater rapids in the East but also take time to explore old mining claims, hike among the waterfalls, and swim in calm, quiet pools. A day's training in kayaking begins the trip, and the first couple of days on the New are perfect for learning the skills necessary for negotiating the Lower Gorge, if you so desire.

ITINERARY:

Day 1: Meadow Creek, West Virginia; kayak orientation.

Days 2-4: New River.

Day 5: Take-out at Teays Landing, West Virginia

MEDIUM

April-November

Class VI River Runners

Colorado Mountain Sports (NA 114)

ACTIVE VARIETY PACKAGE—CLASS III

➤ *Paddle-raft the Arkansas*

➤ *Mountain biking, riding, and more*

➤ *Ranch-style accommodations*

For a week of quality sporting in a beautiful setting, consider this potpourri of action in Colorado's Sangre de Cristo Mountains. Based at a rustic but very comfortable 5,000-acre ranch in one of the most scenic ranges of the Rockies, we sample rock climbing, mountain biking, whitewater rafting, and horseback riding during a six-day stay.

During the day we explore the range on horseback and mountain bike, stopping to investigate some of its treasures: an old gold mine or Indian camp, or maybe an industrious community of beavers at an alpine pond teeming with trout. At night, after relaxing in a wood-fired sauna, we retire to Bear Basin Ranch's log cabins, lit by gas lights and warmed by a wood stove.

The last day of the trip finds us tackling the Arkansas River, one of the high mountain tributaries of the Mississippi. Here swift water fed by mountain snows spills downstream through rapids such as the Zoom Flume and Widow-Maker, rapids that rank the Arkansas among Colorado's best whitewater runs. From raw, wild mountain ridges to succulent smoked trout, this is a sporting week of quality.

ITINERARY:

Day 1: Colorado Springs to Bear Basin Ranch.

Days 2-3: Horseback riding.

Days 4-5: Mountain biking.

Day 6: Rafting the Arkansas; return to Colorado Springs.

MODERATE

May-September

Adventure Specialists

Brooks Range Adventures (NA 115) ~~~~~

VARIETY — CLASS IV

➤ *Gates of the arctic*

➤ *Dogsledding in style*

➤ *Northern Lights*

The Brooks Range is one of the last remote corners of wilderness remaining on this planet. With the encroachments of civilization only too evident in most of the continental United States, the arctic Alaska—in particular the 600-mile-long Brooks Range—still remains a vast rugged reservoir of nearly immeasurable wealth.

The Gates of the Arctic National Park lies within the heart of this majestic expanse, providing the wilderness traveler with millions of acres of pristine mountains, tundra, and river valleys to explore. It is here within a remote wilderness so vast that caribou still stream through silent valleys that you have that once-in-a-lifetime encounter with nature.

Because of the great variety of wildlife that populates this area, you are likely to see arctic animals such as moose, caribou, black bear, grizzly bear, sheep, wold, fox, lynx, wolverine, beaver, otter, and marten. You can observe a wide variety of birdlife as well as raptors such as golden eagles, gyrfalcons, several species of hawks and owls, and ravens. Among the other birds commonly seen are ptarmigan, grouse, sandhill cranes, geese, and a tremendous variety of migratory waterfowl and shorebirds.

The rivers and lake offer exciting opportunities for the spinning or fly fisherman. On previous trips, clients have made successful catches of arctic grayling, lake trout, northern pike, arctic char, chum salmon and sheefish. Special fishing trips can be arranged for small groups with sufficient prior notice.

Note: Trips of 5 to 21 days begin and end in Bettles, Alaska

PREMIUM

January-April, June-September

Brooks Range Wilderness

Alaska Wildland Safari (NA 118) ▲▲▲▲▲

EASY VARIETY
PACKAGE — CLASS I

➤ *Raft the Kenai and Nenana Rivers*

➤ *Cruise the Kenai Fjords*

➤ *See the wildlife of Denali*

The biggest state demands an ambitious itinerary, one that at least acknowledges the diversity and scale of Alaska's magnificence. The Alaska Wildland Safari is just such a trip, traversing a wide range of exciting wilderness, from the rocky seacoast and tidewater glaciers of Kenai Fjords to the upland tundra and high mountains of Denali. We'll hike and raft and cruise through some of the most beautiful scenery in the world, with a good chance of seeing the most memorable of Alaska's wildlife. And all this adventure is packed into just ten days.

We begin with a two-day rafting trip on the scenic Kenai River in south central Alaska. This segment takes us through the heart of the National Wildlife Refuge, where we watch for animal and birdlife under the long summer sun. We camp out on beautiful Skilak Lake and have time to hike on nearby trails, watching for bald eagles and brown bears.

Then it's on to the Kenai Fjords National Park, close enough to Valdez to have escaped most of the oil spill. Here we take a full-day cruise along some of Alaska's most beautiful coastline. Here dark, pewter-gray cliffs soar abruptly from the water's edge and blue-iced tidewater glaciers spill down to sculpted bays. Dusky green spruce trees cling to toeholds on the steep slopes and thousands of kittiwakes nesting on the cliffs burst into the air at the sound of our boat. We see colonies of nesting seabirds here, harbor seals on the icebergs drifting by our boat, and sea otters, puffins, and perhaps some porpoises escorting the boat down the river.

Finally, we drive to Denali National Park, home of North America's highest peak, Mount McKinley, where we'll stay in rustic cabins with hot tubs and showers. Weather permitting, we will be able to see "The Great One," one of the grand sights of the planet, a snow-covered mountain that rises higher from foot to summit than any other on earth. But this is also a country of painted mountains, high, dry tundra, wildflowers, and spruce, aspen, and cottonwood trees. We explore it on foot as well as on a short rafting trip through the famous Nenana River Canyon.

After four days of hiking, biking, rafting, and photographing, we end our safari on an afternoon train ride to Anchorage aboard the world-famous Alaska Railroad.

ITINERARY:

Day 1: Kenai Airport to river cabins.

Days 2-3: Raft Kenai River.

Day 4: Hiking Skilak Lake.

Day 5: Cruise Kenai Fjords.

Day 6: Drive to Talkeetna Mountains.

Day 7: Raft Nenana River.

Days 8-9: Denali National Park.

Day 10: Afternoon train to Anchorage.

PREMIUM

June-September

Alaska Wildland Safari

Rivers of Dinosaur (NA 120) ∿∿∿∿∿

RAFTING—CLASS III

➤ *The rapids of Green and Yampa rivers*

➤ *Utah's great red canyon and slickrock scenery*

➤ *Pre-Columbian ruins*

Lodore Canyon thrust John Wesley Powell into his first real whitewater on the 1869 expedition. His adventure lives on in the rapids he named Disaster Falls, Triplet Falls, and Hell's Half-Mile. This 44-mile stretch of the Green River begins at the ''Gates of Lodore'' where the river enters the canyon. At the confluence of the Yampa River we round Steamboat Rock and enter Whirlpool Canyon, which is highlighted by small rapids and a beautiful stream at Jones Hole. The last day we run the rapids of Split Mountain Gorge. This trip has rapids every day!

The Yampa River is at its finest when there is high water with fast current and good whitewater every day. It is famous for Warm Springs Rapid, a major rapid that ranks with Cataract and Grand Canyon's largest. Though fast, the Yampa is also serene and beautiful with towering sheer walls. Forty-six miles of this 71-mile trip are on the Yampa River and 25 miles are on the Green River through Whirlpool

and Split Mountain gorges (same as the lower half of the Lodore Canyon trip).

ITINERARY: (4- or 5-day):

Day 1: Vernal, Utah, to put-in.

Days 2-3 or 2-4: On the river.

Day 4 or 5: Vernal and return.

MEDIUM

Lodore: *May-September*

Yampa: *4-day: May-June; 5-day: June*

Holiday River Expeditions

Hawaii Cycle (NA 123) ▰▰▰▰▰▰

BICYCLING—CLASS III

➤ *A big pedal around the Big Island*

➤ *Volcanoes and black sand beaches*

➤ *Temples and historic sites*

The Big Island of Hawaii offers some of the world's most diverse backdrops for cycling. Lush tropical forests contrast with moonscape lava deserts. Colorful gardens sit beneath roaring waterfalls. Cacti abound on sprawling cattle ranches. Snowcapped mountains are viewed from beaches of white, green, and black sand, and active volcanoes sustain the legend of Pele, the goddess of fire.

Cycling begins in Hilo and then along the lush Hamakua Coast bounded by rugged cliffs and lava rock beaches, and continues through the rolling cowboy country of Parker Ranch. Downhill from the ranch, we enter a sun worshiper's paradise at Anaehoomalu Bay. On to Kailua-Kona on Kona Bay, then through coffee and macadamia nut country. The trip's last major stop is Volcanoes National Park where we spend a night perched on the rim of Kilauea Crater.

Our ride begins along the lush Hamakua Coast, with its wonderful vistas of rugged hills and lava rock beaches. Tropical rain forests and brilliantly colored flowers border the road. We cycle through fields of sugarcane, then enter the cattle country of Parker Ranch, one of the largest private ranches in the United States. Cycling from Hilo at sea level to Parker Ranch, we gain 2,500 feet. The next day we are rewarded with a ten-mile descent from 2,500 feet to the Kona Coast. The black lava fields are quite a contrast to the lush tropical forests along the Hamakua Coast. On Day 5 we cycle an easy 25 miles across the Mauna Kea lava flows to the resort town of Kailua-Kona. On Day 7 we continue south on the Kona Coast climbing to 1,500 feet then descend back to sea level through Hawaii's lush coffee country along Mauna Loa's western slopes.

The Kona Coast is of extraordinary historical significance as the place where Captain James Cook, the famed British explorer, was killed shortly after being received by the natives as a god. We explore this history at Captain Cook Monument, Kealakekua Bay and Pu'uhonua o Honaunau National Historic Park—the Place of Refuge. Here defeated warriors sought sanctuary after swimming the "den of sharks."

On the final days we roll through lush vegetation, vast areas of lava flows, and the world's largest macadamia nut grove. We descend along a spectacular stretch of the Ka'u Coast—the southernmost part of the island and of the United States. From lovely vistas of the Pacific, we cycle inland through a desert landscape of scrub brush and ferns to dramatic views of the Kilauea Crater in Hawaii Volcanoes National Park. There's plenty of time to explore this fascinating park that features miles of unique terrain, rugged coastline, groves of giant tree ferns, hardwood rain forest, and rare plant and birdlife. At last, it's a downhill

ride for 30 miles—a 4,000-foot elevation loss—to Hilo where we board our flight back to the mainland.

ITINERARY:

Day 1: Parker Ranch.

Day 2: Sheraton Royal Waikoloa.

Day 3: Rest.

Day 4: Kailua-Kona.

Day 5: Rest.

Day 6: Captain Cook.

Day 7: Volcanoes National Park.

Day 8: Rest.

Day 9: Return to Hilo.

MEDIUM

November-April

Backroads Bicycle

Haute Route Gaspesie (NA 126)

SKI/NATURAL HISTORY — CLASS III

➤ *Canada's best back-country skiing*

➤ *Comfortable 150-year-old manor as base*

➤ *Maple syrup camps*

For the Nordic or telemark skier who looks for more in a destination than just great backcountry skiing, Quebec's Gaspe Peninsula may be "paradise found." Winter snowstorms add healthily to the height of the peninsula's Chic-Choc Mountains, already among the province's highest. Skiable terrain ranges from open, undulating alpine meadows to steep, virgin colors. Snowy owls, herds of caribou, and stands of stunted spruce evoke childhood images of Canada—a vast, snowbound land of rock, tree, sky, and beast. As if to enhance this effect, snowfield runoff feeds legendary rivers like the Bonaventure and the Cascapedia, home of the Atlantic salmon, "the noble fish."

Our accommodations in the coastal town of Saint Anne des Monts are as civilized as the Chic-Chocs are wild. On a cliff overlooking the St. Lawrence Seaway is perched one of the most beautiful seigneuries in all Quebec. Its newly remodeled kitchen serves the best of Quebecois fare, with an emphasis on traditional breakfasts and seafood dinners. Afterward in the lounge, we unfold maps and plan the next day's pursuits from a selection of the region's treasures; limitless backcountry skiing both above and below treeline, canoeing on famous salmon streams, trips into backwoods maple syrup camps, seabird nesting colonies, traditional lumberjack cookeries, folk art, and wood-carving studios, and possibly enough other enticements to cause syncope from sheer enjoyment. Live the life of the *seigneur* each day unlocking new secrets of this matchless land, warm in the knowledge that "the habitant" endures in the kingdom of the Gaspesie.

ITINERARY:

Day 1: Mont Joli.

Day 2: Mont Albert.

Day 3: Mont Jacques Cartier.

Day 4: Forillon National Park.

Day 5: Mont Logan.

Day 6: Mont Jacques Cartier.

Day 7: Gaspesie.

Day 8: Return to Montreal.

PREMIUM

April

SOBEK Canada

Surf and Turf (NA 127)

RAFTING / HORSEPACKING—CLASS II

➤ *The best of Colorado*

➤ *Rafting the Arkansas*

➤ *Horseback riding in the Sangre de Cristos*

This famous combination of whitewater rafting on Colorado's Arkansas River and horseback riding into the Sangre de Cristo Mountains will delight anyone who likes action. We begin with three days on horseback, climbing switchbacks, crossing mountain meadows bright with alpine flowers, and camping by rushing creeks. It is an escape to a world where a horse is your trusted companion and the wilderness your pathway. It is important to understand how your horse thinks and how best to communicate with him whether you are guiding him over a rocky pass or simply resting beside a mountain stream. After camping in the mountain wilderness, we return to civilization to raft the best whitewater in Colorado and lodge in modern condos in the tiny western town of Westcliffe.

Our pack trips are suited for those people who have never ridden a horse as well as for the most experienced riders. The high mountain trails do not allow fast riding, and we acquaint you with all the ins and outs of handling your horse in any situation we may meet. No experience is required for the rafting. However, for both activities, participants should be in good health and moderately good physical condition. People of all ages take this trip. On portions of the trip, altitudes of 9,000 to 10,000 feet are reached.

ITINERARY:

Day 1: Meet in Colorado Springs. Riding the Rainbow Trail.

Days 2-3: Riding or fishing.

Days 4-5: Rafting on the Arkansas and Colorado rivers.

MEDIUM

May-September

Adventure Specialists

Rocky Mountain High (NA 131) ◣〜〜〜

RANCH/NATURAL
HISTORY—CLASS I

➤ *Hot-air ballooning*

➤ *Spruce log lodge*

➤ *Hiking, riding, and swimming*

Since the time of the earliest home-steaders, the Vista Verde Ranch and its pristine valley have remained undisturbed. Elk, deer, bear, fox, coyote, porcupine, beaver, golden and bald eagle and even the extraordinary greater sandhill crane roam this peaceful setting. Vista Verde is open year-round so that guests may enjoy the full range of seasonal activity. Summer days are pine scented, crisp and full of sunshine. Occasional afternoon showers bring rainbows and moisture for the multitude of wildflowers. Nights are cool and starry. September brings beauty unsurpassed, as the aspens turn gold against a backdrop of evergreen. Soon follows winter and Steamboat's famous champagne powder, ideal for ski-touring and snowshoeing.

Hot-air ballooning brings an added dimension in beauty and adventure. Our balloon pilots fly Raven balloons that carry three to eight passengers on an incredible 1½-hour journey over the countryside. Flights take off from the ranch at sunrise and float quietly down the Elk River Valley over the river and surrounding mountains, flanked by the majestic spendor of the Continental Divide and Mt. Zirkel Wilderness Area. This amazing experience is enhanced by a bird's-eye view of elk, deer, fox and other wildlife in their natural habitat. One can pick pinecones at treetop level or at 3,000 feet above the valley, see into the Wyoming and Utah mountain ranges.

ITINERARY:

Make your own schedule during a wonderful week at the ranch.

MEDIUM

Year-round

Vista Verde

Paddling in Paradise (NA 133) ◣〜〜〜

NATURAL HISTORY/SEA
TOURING—CLASS III

➤ *Instruction in sea kayaking*

➤ *Choose Molokai or the Big Island*

➤ *Swim, snorkel, or snooze*

Hawaii is America's own tropical paradise, with all the wonders that the words conjure up: warm, clear water, rustling palm trees, sandy beaches, living coral reefs, dramatic volcanoes and misty rain forests. Much of the state has succumbed to development but not all. And the best way to see the rest is by sea kayak. On a kayak, you can visit the parts of the coast inaccessible by road, slip soundlessly among the birds and marine life, explore pristine coastal beaches, and reach emerald bays where you may find the snorkel-dive of your dreams.

For the first-timer or for the experienced kayaker, this adventure will show you why sea kayaking is the fastest-growing sport in adventure travel. The Molokai itinerary visits Hawaii's highest waterfalls and tallest seacliffs. On the Big Island, choose either the Waipio or Miloli'i trips, both of which have time for village hikes and snorkel stops. Instruction from guides trained in natural history as well as in camp and kayak skills is included on all packages.

ITINERARY:

Day 1: Arrive Molokai, Kauai, or Hawaii; begin sea kayak.

Days 2-4 or 2-5: Sea kayaking, snorkeling, hiking, etc.; camping overnights.

Day 5 or 6: End kayak tour; return.

MODERATE

Waipio: *June-August*

Molokai: *June-September*

Miloli'i: *March-May, September-November*

Pacific Outdoors Adventures

The North Pole (NA 134)

BUSHPLANE ADVENTURE—
CLASS II

➤ *Land at the geologic North Pole*

➤ *Fly-over of magnetic North Pole*

➤ *Inuit community of Grise Fjord*

The Apex, the Zenith, the Apogee, Ultima Thule—this is it, the North Pole. This is a swift but serious expedition to the top of the world, where few have been since Robert Peary's disputed 1909 journey. Our eight-day adventure begins in Resolute Bay among the Queen Elizabeth Islands, Canada's northernmost territories. From here, we fly on to Lake Hazen near the tip of Ellesmere Island, where we savor the stillness and silence of the arctic world and wait for the ideal weather to make our polar flight. It's a 557-mile jump from camp to pole, a long and mind-blowing sky-cruise to the planet's pivot point, the axis of daily rotation. And here we land to spend an eternal hour where the sun stands still, sipping champagne and snapping photos.

Immediately following the Polar flight, we unwind with an overnight visit to Grise Fjord, a friendly Inuit village where we can dogsled, track seals, and sleep on caribou hides. Then we fly to where the compass skids to a stop— magnetic North, a short but exciting trip over the wildlife-rich islands of Canada's farthest reach. The best and most comfortable accommodations possible make this an exclusive but rugged trip. After an adventure like this, it's all downhill from the top!

ITINERARY:

Day 1: Montreal to Resolute.

Day 2: Flight to Ellesmere Island.

Day 3: Polar flight (if possible).

Day 4: Grise Fjord.

Day 5: Magnetic North; to Resolute.

Days 6-7: Free days in Resolute; arrival here depends on polar flight day.

Day 8: Midday return via Montreal.

PREMIUM

April

Worldwide Adventures

Grizzly Valley
(NA 135) ▲▲▲▲▲▲

NATURAL HISTORY
DISCOVERY—CLASS I

➤ *Pacific Coast bear sanctuary*
➤ *Unique valley ecosystem*
➤ *Explore by Zodiac and sailboat*

Khutzeymateen Valley—just as the name may defy pronunciation, the valley itself defies description. The word for this unique coastal bear sanctuary near Prince Rupert, British Columbia, comes from its Tsimshian Native American name, "valley of salmon and bears." And within the 150-square-mile valley there are fish and grizzlies a plenty.

This is a special opportunity to see the wildlife along the coast of the Khutzeymateen with an experienced wilderness biologist and bear expert. From the comfortable all-wood traditional 65-foot ketch, *Ocean Light*, we see bears who have come down to the valley from their winter dens to feed on the green grasses and roots beneath the dense forest canopy of mammoth Sitka spruce. And when the salmon begin their spawning run up the river, feast time really begins.

Here is the ecology of the Pacific Northwest in spades: black and grizzly bear, moose, seals, geese, ducks, and heron. And in the waters of Khutzeymateen Inlet we may also find halibut, salmon, prawns, and crabs to enliven our table. A short, four-day trip, this offers a rare chance to experience and study the wildlife of the Northwest at its most robust.

ITINERARY:

Day 1: Prince Rupert to dock; board *Ocean Light*.

Days 2-3: Coastal exploration.

Day 4: End sail and return to Prince Rupert.

PREMIUM

May-June

Worldwide Adventures

Copper River
(NA 200) ～～～～

RAFTING—CLASS II

➤ *Glaciated wilderness*
➤ *Historic copper mining towns*
➤ *Abundant wildlife*

Experience the wilderness of Alaska's Copper River, where peaks reach upward over 16,000 feet and glaciers pour down from the mountains to spill their ancient ice directly into the river's silty waters, where grizzly bears roam and bald eagles soar and harbor seals swim up river from their home in the Pacific Ocean.

This rugged and remote wilderness is consummate Alaska on a grandiose scale. Its mountains loom massive, its valleys and glaciers spread humblingly wide, and the Copper River itself runs awesomely. We'll travel this country in comfort by raft and eat hearty gourmet meals around the campfire. Our guides do the navigating and rowing, but the option for the whole group to paddle is available.

We will start our trip at the old railroad outpost town of Chitina on the Copper River. We'll float about 90 miles to the famed and historic Copper River Railroad's Million Dollar Bridge near the port town of Cordova. Along the way we'll remain at our camp at Miles Lake for an entire day of hiking, relaxing, and exploring around and on the Miles Glacier. The spectacular scenery, abundant wildlife, great salmon fishing, and occasional glimpses of Alaska's rich mining history make this trip one of Alaska's premier river adventures.

ITINERARY:

Day 0: Evening orientation in Anchorage.

Day 1: Anchorage to Chitina.

Days 2-5: Float Copper River to Miles Lake.

Day 6: Explore Miles Glacier.

Day 7: Cross Miles Lake, take-out, shuttle to Cordova, fly back to Anchorage.

Also available: 12-day trip, which combines this stretch of the Copper River with five days on the Chitina River.

MEDIUM

June-September

Osprey Expeditions

Hawaiian Cycling Double Delight (NA 201) ◤◣◤◣◤◣◤

CYCLING—CLASS III/IV

➤ *Year-round bicycle touring*

➤ *Cool tradewinds at our backs*

➤ *Dramatic tropical scenery*

Experience a unique view of Hawaii. With the smoothness and grace only a bicycle can provide, ease slowly and quietly into a dramatic showcase of Hawaii's magnificent scenery. Balmy Hawaiian weather changes very little with the seasons and is perfect year-round for departing the beaten path on a bicycle. This adventure is a 12-day, 11-night tour combining two islands: Hawaii and Maui, or Hawaii and Kauai.

Hawaii Highlights — We begin in lush tropical Hilo, home of the world's largest orchid industry. Our most dramatic highlight is Volcanoes National Park. Here we see the results of volcanic forces that formed the islands of Hawaii. Hike through the underground plumbing of now-quiet volcano vents. Ride through fern-filled forests on the eleven-mile crater rim road. If we are lucky, there may be another eruptive phase of Pu'u O'o. Part of Kilauea's curtain of fire, Pu'u O'o is Hawaii's newest volcano. Around South Point, the southernmost tip of the United States, we meander through the coffee lands and macadamia nut plantations toward ancient and sacred Hawaiian temples. The last days are spent riding in the Kona district, where we challenge a portion of the Ironman triathalon bicycle course and explore Kealakekua Bay, the scene of many triumphs and tragedies in Hawaiian history.

Kauai Keepsake — Leaving the bustling small town of Lihue, we travel quiet back roads through tall fields of sugarcane that spread in shining green waves to the mountain slopes, roll on the prehistoric salt ponds at Hanapepe, and visit the site of an 1817 attempted Russian invasion of Hawaii at Fort Elizabeth in Waimea. Turning inland, we skirt the rim of Kauai's famous "Grand Canyon of the Pacific", in Koke'e State Park. One of our favorite refreshers is a secluded swimming hole tucked in a fragrant ginger-lined grove. Our van retraces our route toward the north shore and world-renowned Hanalei Bay. At road's end we can hike to the first hidden beach along the Na Pali coast, where cliffs and chasmlike valleys allow access only by foot.

Maui Magic — We head out from Kahului along the sparsely populated and ruggedly beautiful northern coast of Maui. We follow the path of migratory humpback whales to our second overnight stay on the sunny leeward shore. The next day, we travel by van to the

10,023-foot summit of Mount Haleakala and Haleakala National Park. A hike into the volcanic crater takes us across the threshold into a wilderness environment of unique natural beauty. Next, to lush, somnolent Hana town. We roll past rock faces ribboned with waterfalls and gorges choked with tropical vegetation to linger two nights in Hana, the home of celebrity retreats. The end of the paved road brings us to the Seven Pools. Here, Palikea Stream winds through a series of ever-larger rock pools to meet the sea. Enjoy the warmth of sunbathing and swimming or take a cool hike through a bamboo forest to Waimoku Falls.

ITINERARY (Hawaii):

Day 1: Arrive Hilo.

Day 2: Chain of Craters Road.

Day 3: Volcanoes National Park.

Day 4: South Point and Pu'uhonua o Honaunau.

Days 5-6: Kona.

ITINERARY (Kauai):

Day 1: Arrive Lihue.

Days 2-4: Kokee State Park and Waimea Canyon.

Day 5: Na Pali coast.

Day 6: Return to Lihue.

ITINERARY (Maui):

Day 1: Arrive Kahului.

Day 2: West Maui coast.

Day 3-4: Haleakala National Park.

Day 5: Hana.

Day 6: Hana Highway return to Kahului.

MEDIUM
(includes interisland airfare)

Year-round

Island Bicycle Adventures

Boundary Waters Canoe Trip (NA 202)

CANOEING — CLASS III

➤ *Acres of icy, clearwater lakes*
➤ *Moose, otters, and bald eagles*
➤ *Superb fishing*

The Boundary Waters Canoe Area Wilderness is the largest canoeing wilderness in North America. It has over 1,500 clear water lakes accessible by paddle only and is in an area of well over one million acres. Today much of the wilderness is the same as the voyageurs and Indians found it.

You arrive at Gunflint, Minnesota, on a Sunday afternoon in time to enjoy a big dinner at our family-run lodge and to meet your fellow canoeists and your guide. That evening you review the trip plans and do the final repacking of your personal gear. After breakfast on Monday morning we head out with our guide for our first day of canoeing.

On this trip, we spend six days exploring a remote area of the wilderness. We usually encounter moose, beavers, eagles, loons, otters, and many more animals of the forest. There is fishing for several species of fish: walleye, northern, lake trout, and smallmouth bass. The whole trip is an adventure with new sights and different lakes each day. Arrive at your campsite each night to find tents pitched and campfires started with tasty meals soon to follow. It's lake canoeing and wilderness at its best.

Our package includes dinner, bunkhouse accommodations at our lodge, breakfast before and after your trip at Gunflint, complete outfitting for six days and five nights, all maps, paddling instruction, a guide, and a bull cook. Each group is limited to eight guests.

ITINERARY:

Day 1: Arrive Gunflint, Minnesota.

Days 2-6: Canoeing Boundary Waters Canoe Area Wilderness.

Day 7: Return to Gunflint.

MODERATE

June-September

Gunflint Northwoods Outfitters

Middle Fork of the American (NA 203)

WHITEWATER RAFTING—
CLASS IV

➤ *Class IV rapids*

➤ *Trout fishing*

➤ *Secluded sandy beaches*

The Middle Fork of the American River, first run commercially in 1982, provides one of California's truly exciting wilderness experiences. Stretches of whitewater assault the senses, while calmer sections allow us to enjoy the scenery, fishing, and abundant wildlife along its banks. For those who have previously rafted, are in good physical condition, and want a challenging river in addition to a wilderness experience, this adventure is the one for you.

During our two-day journey we will encounter some of the most unique and challenging rapids on the West Coast. Our first major obstacle is the infamous Tunnel Chute rapid, a man-made diversion chute blasted out by Nineteenth-century gold miners. After first carefully scouting this rapid, our boats navigate it one at a time, and the force of this 18-foot drop propels us through a picturesque and runnable

90-foot underground tunnel. At any water level, the "Chute" is a challenge, and portaging it is always an option, sometimes a necessity. From this point we float down through a secluded section of Class II rapids before setting up camp on a long, sandy beach.

Day 2 will see us exploring pristine side streams before making the mandatory and strenuous portage at Ruck-a-Chucky Falls. Our journey ends with a mad dash through a challenging section of Class IV rapids to our take-out.

The Middle Fork promises an unforgettable wilderness adventure, with some of the finest trout fishing available in the state. Due to the nature of the rapids and the portages, this trip should only be attempted by those in good physical condition. It is an adventure to long remember.

ITINERARY:

Day 1: Arrive Coloma, California, for put-in at Oxbow Bend.

Day 2: Take out at Greenwood Bridge.

MEDIUM

June-October

Adventure Connection

Around the World in 40 Days (NA 204)

CULTURAL ADVENTURE—
CLASS III

➤ *The ultimate Phileas Fogg adventure*

➤ *Worldwide cultural interaction*

➤ *Adventure on five continents*

You've always wanted to go around the world but never had the time? Imagine standing atop the Eiffel Tower in Paris;

climbing steps to the Kings Chamber of the Great Pyramid in Cairo; photographing lions, elephants, and giraffes in Kenya; glimpsing a sunset over the Taj Mahal and floating down the Ganges River in India; chatting with Tibetan refugees over "chang" barley beer in Kathmandu; relaxing in your own thatched hut on a tropical island in Thailand; bargain shopping in Hong Kong and visiting ancient Taoist temples in Taiwan. Set aside 40 days and the world is yours!

Mother Earth Adventures specializes in metaphysical adventure travel. The focus is holistic health, meeting spiritual beings, and connecting with the earth's natural beauty. Group leaders are trained in counseling and meditation. We make time for rituals, visits to power spots, and finding ways of joining our spirit with the spirit of the land, the people and the past.

The price for this around-the-world odyssey includes three-star hotels in the major cities, the best available accommodations in the country, all meals, domestic transportation, and guide service in each country.

ITINERARY:

Day 1: San Francisco to Paris.

Days 2-3: Paris.

Days 4-7: Cairo.

Days 8-13: Nairobi.

Days 14-15: Bombay.

Days 16-22: Delhi, Agra, and Jaipur.

Days 23-25: Kathmandu.

Days 26-32: Bangkok, Ko Samet.

Days 33-36: Hong Kong.

Days 37-39: Taipei, Chiayi.

Days 40: Return to San Francisco.

MEDIUM

March, October, December

Mother Earth Adventures

Alaska Stikine-LeConte Glacier Tour (NA 205)

SEA KAYAKING/WILDLIFE— CLASS III

> *Majestic icebergs*
> *Killer whales and playful seals*
> *Winding fjords*

Our sea kayaking adventure begins in the little town of Petersburg, on Mitkof Island, in central southeast Alaska. The town was founded because of its fine harbor, abundance of wildlife, and the ready supply of ice from nearby LeConte Glacier.

From Petersburg, we paddle the southern arm of LeConte Bay with its forest of western hemlock and western spruce, passing through winding fjords and hidden coves. At LeConte Glacier, the southernmost calving glacier in North America, we'll see cold, iridescent blue icebergs of mammoth proportions floating alongside our boats, along with the harbor seals, Dall's porpoises, and occasional killer whales. Eagles are everywhere, and bears stalk the riverbanks. Our journey continues south to the Stikine River Delta where we explore its many tributaries and continue to bask in the natural beauty before we have to leave this new, raw, breathtaking world as yet untouched by man.

The word "Alaska" is from the Aleut term "Alyeska" meaning "The Great Land." The southeast panhandle of Alaska is only a small part of it (7%), but it contains 27 million acres of primitive lands, ice fields, inland waterways (11,000 miles of shoreline), and abundant wildlife. It's also a prime bald eagle habitat with the highest density of eagles in North America. When John Muir explored the area in 1879, he called it "Yosemite of the North"—for him, the ultimate accolade.

ITINERARY:

Day 1: Arrive Petersburg, Alaska, from Seattle, Washington, for kayaking and safety orientation.

Day 2: Kayak Stikine River.

Days 3-5: LeConte Bay.

Days 6-7: Fredrick Sound and Mitkof Island.

Day 8: Return to Seattle.

MEDIUM

June-July

Outback Expeditions Inc.

Canyon Country Bike and Hike: The Grand Staircase (NA 206)

HIKING / MOUNTAIN BICYCLE TREK—CLASS IV

➤ *Petrified forests*

➤ *Pumas and bobcats*

➤ *Anasazi culture*

Between the pink cliffs of Bryce Canyon and the sheer walls of the Grand Canyon's north rim, an expansive geological staircase climbs skyward in rainbow pastels. Through this vast wilderness of remote forested mesas and colorful buttes flows the Paria River, whose waters, cutting unceasingly through layers of sedimentary rock, have formed some of the finest slot canyons in the world.

During the first five-day section of the trip, we mountain bike through the sinuous yet spacious backcountry of the upper Paria, which flows out of Bryce Canyon. On foot, we discover signs of elusive wildlife such as puma and bobcat, explore the artistry of rock sculpted by wind and water, and marvel at the relics of ancient forests delicately preserved in arroyos scattered with petrified wood.

On the second five-day section, after descending the Echo Cliffs and rumbling along dirt roads to the rim of the Grand Canyon, we climb from sagebrush valleys to groves of pinon to tall ponderosa pine forests following jeep trails into the Kaibab Mountains, where vestiges of the Anasazi culture proliferate. A hike through Buckskin Gulch and a cool dip in Lake Powell round out our adventure.

A support vehicle that meets us each night carries our camping gear, lots of fresh food, and plenty of ice cold drinks, allowing us to travel lightly throughout this rugged, arid terrain during the day and feast royally by campfire each starlit night.

ITINERARY:

Day 1: Meet in Page, bike to Paria.

Days 2-4: Hike and bike in the Paria-Hackberry.

Day 5: Bike to Page, end of first half of trip.

Day 6: Begin second half of trip, bike to Marble Canyon.

Day 7-9: Continue bike and hike trek.

Day 10: Bike to Lake Powell and back to Page.

MODERATE

April-July

Puma Expeditions

Kobuk River Valley and Great Sand Dunes (NA 207) ⚡⚡⚡

PADDLE RAFTING —
CLASS III/IV

➤ *Kobuk Valley National Park*

➤ *Southwestern Brook Range*

➤ *Kotzebue Basin*

Kobuk Valley National Park occupies a broad valley along the central Kobuk River in Kotzebue Basin in northwestern Alaska, some 25 miles north of the Arctic Circle. The park is approximately 350 miles west-northwest of Fairbanks and 75 miles east of Kotzebue. The villages of Ambler and Kiana lie on the park's western and eastern sides respectively. This region sits in a large basin, ringed on the north by the Baird Mountains of the Brooks Range and lined on the south by the Waring Mountains. The Great Kobuk Sand Dunes and the Little Kobuk Sand Dunes extend over some 25 square miles south of the Kobuk River. Inland Eskimos (Inupiak) maintain subsistence patterns that have existed for millennia.

We paddle and float the middle Kobuk River that flows from Ambler village along the southwest flank of the Brooks Range and visit adjacent areas in the Kobuk River Valley. Day hikes near Onion Portage Archaeological Site gives us opportunities to see a unique arctic woodlands cultural area of prehistoric significance. Treks into the Little and Great Kobuk Sand Dunes also expose us to some of the unusual diversity of the flora and fauna as well to as the dynamic geology of the Kobuk River Valley. A scheduled trip extension (Option B) allows party members to spend extra days exploring the Dunes and then continue paddling downriver to the village of Kiana. Here we can spend some extra evenings exploring or fishing.

ITINERARY:

Day 1: Meet in Fairbanks, Alaska, then fly to Ambler.

Days 2-9 or 2-14: Rafting/kayaking/hiking in Kobuk Valley.

Day 10 or 15: Fly from Ambler or Kiana to Kotzebue.

MEDIUM

July-August

Alaska Treks n̲ Voyages

Autumn Wildlife (NA 208) 〰〰〰

WILDLIFE/VARIETY —
CLASS II

➤ *Mountain goats, humpback whales, mink, and more*

➤ *Extensive photo opportunities*

In late autumn, Southeast Alaska's leaden skies brighten, air crisps, the whole pace of life changes. This is an ideal time to observe three dramatic species in the wild. Join us as we seek out humpback whale (Surprise! Not all humpbacks vacation in Hawaii every year!) and wintering trumpeter swans near Petersburg, and travel to North America's largest gathering of bald eagles in the Chilkat Valley.

The trumpeter is largest and rarest of the world's swans. While their numbers remain few in other states, they are thriving in Alaska where about 10,000 nest each summer. Most winter in remote parts of coastal British Columbia, but about 100 of these elegant birds regularly come to Blind Slough near Petersburg. The slough is easily accessible by roadway for swan viewing and photography.

We'll also take a charter boat from Petersburg in search of those hardy humpbacks who winter in Southeast Alaska. Humpbacks thrust their 45-ton bodies completely free of the water in an exuberant leap called a "breach." Main diet for these enormous creatures is tiny, shrimp-like krill, taken in great gulps of seawater.

From Petersburg, we'll board the Alaska Marine Highway, a ferry system that provides the only transportation link between the communities of Southeast Alaska other than aircraft. Our destination will be the community of Haines and the nearby 48,000-acre Alaska Chilkat Bald Eagle Preserve.

Between late October and January, up to 3,500 bald eagles come from throughout coastal Alaska and British Columbia to feast on a late salmon run in the Chilkat River. Their meeting place is so spectacular it has been named the Eagle Council Grounds.

Opportunities for observing and photographing eagles are unparalleled. Because the eagles are so preoccupied with the great feast nature has set before them, you will not need to use a blind. Each year the gathering attracts some of the best-known wildlife photographers and film crews from around the world.

Fresh snow may reveal the tracks of great brown bears who also come to the banquet table of the Chilkat River under cover of the night sky. Moose are sometimes visible in day or twilight hours. Mountain goats, black bears, wolves, lynx, coyotes, fox, martens, minks and a variety of birds also live in the area.

Throughout the trip, a professional wildlife photographer will offer hands-on field instruction and advice, and naturalists, biologists, and resource managers will further our understanding of these great creatures and their environment. We'll conclude with a day in Juneau, Alaska's picturesque capital city, to view and photograph the dramatic Mendenhall Glacier, visit the private King Bird Ranch, and see local galleries.

You'll find the weather surprisingly mild in this maritime climate, with temperatures ranging from the teens to the forties F. Bring layered clothing you would wear for any winter outing, and pack some rain gear for a passing warm front.

ITINERARY:

Day 1: Meet in Petersburg.

Days 2-5: View and photograph trumpeter swan by land and humpback whales by charter boat.

Day 6: Cruise Lynn Canal to Haines.

Days 7-9: Bald eagle photography along Chilkat River. Evening programs.

Day 10: Morning photography, afternoon cruise to Juneau.

Day 11: View and photograph Mendenhall Glacier, visit private King Bird Ranch and Juneau area galleries.

Day 12: Return home from Juneau.

PREMIUM

November

Alaska Up Close

Tlikakila River (NA 209)

KAYAKING/PADDLE RAFTING—CLASS III

➤ *Lake Clark National Park*

➤ *National Wild and Scenic River*

➤ *Chigmit Mountain*

This 3.6-million-acre park and preserve is located north of Iliamna Lake, 150 miles southwest of Anchorage. Lake Clark/Iliamna is a superlative area where the Alaskan and the Aleutian mountain ranges converge. These have been the Alaskan Alps. The region boasts a dazzling array of features including a jumble of glacier-carved peaks reaching up to 10,000 feet; three active steaming volcanoes from Mt. Spurr on the north to Redoubt and Iliamna volcanoes on the south; many alpine lakes ranging from 40-mile-long Lake Clark to shallow tundra ponds; deep U-shaped valleys with rushing streams and waterfalls.

Starting at Summit Lake near Lake Clark Pass, our voyage begins at the crest of the northern Aleutian Range, southwest of Anchorage. The Tlikakila River, a swift glacial stream with National Wild and Scenic River status, flows past hanging valley glaciers, amid waterfalls, deep forest, soaring rocky crags, and snowcapped peaks. This river offers an enjoyable paddle trip with superlative scenery reminiscent of the Swiss Alps. Two half-day hikes familiarize voyagers with geologic features of an active alpine glacier and afford the opportunity to observe wildlife such as moose, bears, wolves, and eagles in the lower reaches of the forested river valley. We paddle and float the entire length of this river from its glacial source to Lake Clark using inflatable kayaks and/or paddle rafts during our week-long trip.

ITINERARY:

Day 1: Meet in Anchorage, Alaska, then charter flight to Summit Lake.

Days 2-7: Tlikakila River Valley.

Day 8: Charter flight to Port Alsworth,then return to Anchorage, Alaska.

MEDIUM

June-August

Alaska Treks n̲ Voyages

Banff to Glacier Safari (NA 210) ∿∿∿

CYCLING/RAFTING—
CLASS III

➤ *Two countries and three national parks*

➤ *Active days and leisure nights*

➤ *Dramatic mountain views*

In this ultimate pedal and paddle adventure, we mix equal portions of mountain biking in Banff, Kootenay, and Glacier national parks with whitewater rafting on the White River and the North Fork of the Flathead. Escaping the swift pace of modern travel, this safari is a return to the opulent leisure of the Victorian-era African safari. We soak in hot springs, enjoy elegant meals, and sleep in comfortable tented accommodations.

In Canada's Banff National Park, we cycle the Bow Valley Parkway over the Vermillion Pass, track the Kootenay River through beautiful Marble Canyon, and climb Sinclair Pass for a descent to Radium Hot Springs. Wilderness rafting for three days is next on our agenda. We skim by the incredible scenery of White River Canyon, camping along its course. Shift gears again and we pedal the back roads of southern British Columbia which lead us through pine forests, quiet farmlands, and alongside the Kootenay River to the shores of Lake Koocanusa. Following the Flathead River, we enter the United States and cycle down Glacier National Park's western border. There's time for one more whitewater roller coaster ride down the North Fork of the Flathead River.

Our trip's grand finale is a spectacular bicycle ride on the Going to the Sun Road, carved from the cliffs of the Garden Wall. It is a long, gently graded climb with an exhilarating downhill run finishing at St. Mary's Lake.

ITINERARY:

Day 1: Meet Banff Train Station.

Day 2-3: Cycle Banff and Kootenay National Park.

Days 4-6: Whitewater rafting through White River Canyon.

Days 7-8: Cycle along Kootenay River.

Days 9-11: Enter United States and cycle Glacier National Park.

Day 12: Depart Kalispell, Montana.

MODERATE

June-August

Off The Deep End Travels

Yellowstone Safari (NA 211)

CYCLING/RAFTING/ HIKING—CLASS III

➤ *Explore America's first national park*

➤ *Chow down at a cowboy cookout*

➤ *Soak in boiling rivers*

This one-week adventure in Yellowstone National Park will strip away the insulation of urban living and leave you feeling exhilarated and wholly relaxed. Yellowstone's 2.3 million acres of wild grandeur are perfectly suited to leisurely self-paced cycling. Its magnificent wildlife, surrealistic landscapes, and sulfurous waterworks are best seen close up from a bike saddle, or while hiking, or from the vantage of a raft while floating the Yellowstone River.

We combine all three to add to your enjoyment and exploration of North America's first and finest national park. Our loop through this thermal wonderland conjures up a surrealistic array of fumaroles, geysers, and hot springs.

Among the delights: Old Faithful, Grand Prismatic Spring, Mammoth Hot Springs, Fountain Paint Pots, and the technicolor Grand Canyon of Yellowstone. We'll get close to all of these during short hikes. We'll soothe weary muscles in the natural hot waters and experience close encounters with elk, deer, buffalo, and moose. For added excitement we thrill to a bucking bronco whitewater trip through Gardiner Canyon on the Yellowstone River. Then we'll travel by horse-drawn covered wagon to an Old West cookout under the open skies. All together, it's a fantastic adventure.

ITINERARY:

Day 1: Arrive Jackson, Wyoming.

Day 2: Cycle to Lake Yellowstone.

Day 3: Cycle to Hayden Valley, Grand Canyon of Yellowstone and Tower Falls. Cookout.

Day 4: Cycle to Mammoth Hot Springs and raft down Gardiner Canyon.

Day 5: Cycle to Norris Geyser Basin and Madison.

Day 6: Cycle to Old Faithful Geyser Basin.

Day 7: Return from Jackson, Wyoming.

MODERATE

May-September

Off The Deep End Travels

OUTFITTERS DIRECTORY

Above The Clouds
P.O. Box 398
Worcester, MA 01601-0398
☎ (617) 799-4499
EU 23, EU 48

Adventure Connection
P.O. Box 475
Coloma, CA 95613
☎ (916) 626-7385
NA 203

Adventure Pakistan
Walji's Building
P.O. Box 1088
Islamabad, Pakistan
☎ (823) 963
AS 18, AS 127, AS 138, AS 139

Adventure River Company
4316 Kingston Dr.
Anchorage, AK
☎ (907) 337-9604
NA 10

Adventure Specialists
Bear Basin Ranch
Westcliffe, CO 81252
☎ (719) 783-2519
NA 114, NA 127

Afro Ventures, Ltd
P.O. Box 2339
Randburg 2125
Republic of South Africa
☎ (29) 7601
AF 28, AF 46

Alaska Discovery
396 South Franklin St.
Juneau, AK 99801
☎ (907) 586-1911
NA 14/15/16

Alaska River Expeditions
669 2nd Ave.
Salt Lake City, UT 84103
☎ (801) 322-0233
NA 3

George Fuller/SOBEK photo file

Alaska Treks n̲ Voyages
SUMMER ADDRESS:
P.O. Box 625
Seward, AK 99631
☎ (907) 224-3960
WINTER ADDRESS:
P.O. Box 89—Ikogmute
Russian Mission, AK 99657
NA 207, NA 209

Alaska Up Close
P.O. Box 32666
Juneau, AK 99803
☎ (907) 789-9544
NA 208

Alaska Wildland Safari
P.O. Box 259
Trout Lake, WA 98650
☎ (907) 595-1279
NA 118

Alpine Adventures
P.O. Box 124
Altrincham, Cheshire
England WA 141ZS
☎ (06) 10941-6058
EU 10

Alpine Guides
P.O. Box 20
Mt. Cook, New Zealand
☎ (05) 621-834
OC 46

Arctic Adventours
P.O. Box 164
N-8310 Kabelvag
Norway
☎ (088) 77-510
EU 200

Atalante
81, Grande-rue de la Croix Rousse
69 004 Lyon, France
☎ (33) 7839-6910
EU 54

Backroads Bicycle Tours
1516 Fifth St.
Berkeley, CA 94710-1713
☎ (415) 527-1555
NA 123, AS 13, AS 132

Barrier Reef Diving Services
P.O. Box 180
Airlie Beach
Queensland 4802, Australia
☎ (079) 466-204
OC 15

Bluewater Adventures
#202-1676 Duranleau Street
Vancouver, B.C.
Canada V6H 3S5
☎ (604) 684-4575
NA 60

Boojum Expeditions
2625 Garnet Ave.
San Diego, CA 92109
☎ (619) 581-3301
AS 141, AS 142

Brooks Range Wilderness
P.O. Box 48
Bettles, AK
☎ (907) 692-5312
NA 115

Class VI River Runners
P.O. Box 78
Lansing, WV 25862-0078
☎ (304) 574-0704
NA 112

Colors Of Asia
Jl. Wahid Haslyn 86
Jakarta, Indonesia 10340
☎ (62) 21-333-640
AS 158

SOBEK photo file

Coral Trekker Sailing Safari
P.O. Box 519
Airlie Beach, Whitsunday
Queensland, 4802, Australia
☎ (079) 467-197
OC 37

Costa Rica Expeditions
P.O. Box 6941
San Jose, Costa Rica
☎ (506) 22-0333
SA 27

Dvorak Expeditions
17921-B U.S. Hwy 285
Nathrop, CO 81236
☎ (719) 539-6851
OC 80

Eurotrek
Malzstrasse 17-21, Postfach
8036 Zurich, Switzerland
☎ (01) 462-0203
EU 42, EU 45

Exodus Expeditions
9 Weir Road, Balham
London SW12 OLT
England
☎ (01) 675-5550
EU 13, EU 25, AS 52, AS 114, AS 135

Explorandes
Av. Bolognefi, No. 159
Miraflores
Lima, Peru
☎ (46) 9889
SA 5, SA 39

Ft. Meyers Yacht Charters
R. R. 77, Box 105
Ft. Meyers, Fl 33908
☎ (813) 466-1800
NA 64

Genet Expeditions
P.O. Box 230861
Anchorage, AK 99523
☎ (907) 376-5120
NA 93

Go! Adventures
P.O. Box 5155
Cairns, Queensland 4870
Australia
☎ (070) 937-689
OC 76

Jim Slade/SOBEK photo file

Great Slave Sledding Company
P.O. Box 2882
Yellowknife, N.W.T.
Canada X1A 2R2
☎ (403) 873-8249
NA 54

Guide For All Seasons
P.O. Box 174
Calpine, CA 96124
☎ (916) 994-3613
AS 41, AS 42

Gunflint Northwoods Outfitters
Box 100 GT
Grand Marais, MN 55604
☎ (800) 328-3325
NA 202

Holiday River Expeditions
544 East 3900 South
Salt Lake City, UT 84107
☎ (801) 266-2087
NA 43, NA 120

Island Bicycle Adventures
569 Kapahulu Avenue
Honolulu, Hawaii 96815
☎ (808) 734-0700
NA 201

JOURNEYS International, Inc.
4011 Jackson Road
Ann Arbor, MI 48103
☎ (313) 665-4407
EC 8, AF 202, AS 205

Lihue Expeditions
Belgrano 262 OF. 104
San Isidro (1642)
Pcia. De Bs. As.
Argentina
☎ (541) 747-7689
SA 45

Liounis and Cortez Expeditions
117 Lomas Santa Fe Dr.
Solano Beach, CA 92075
☎ (619) 755-5136
AF 57

Mama's Llamas
P.O. Box 665
El Dorado, CA 95623
☎ (916) 622-2566
NA 38

Mother Earth Adventures
290 East Blithesdale Avenue
Mill Valley, CA 94941
☎ (415) 389-0306
NA 204

New Zealand Adventures
11701 Meridian Avenue N.
Seattle, WA 98133
☎ (206) 364-0160
OC 201

New Zealand Pedaltours
P.O. Box 49-039
Roskill South
Auckland, New Zealand
☎ (09) 3020-968
OC 69

Niugini Adventures
P.O. Box 550
Kundiawa, Simbu Province
Papua New Guinea
☎ 675-751-304
OC 1

O.A.R.S.
P.O. Box 67
Angels Camp, CA 95222
☎ (209) 736-4677
NA 27, NA 36

Odin Air
Reykjavik Airport
Iceland
☎ (354) 1-687063
EU 62

Off The Deep End Travels
P.O. Box 7511
Jackson, WY 83001
☎ (307) 733-8707
NA 210, NA 211

Osprey Expeditions
P.O. Box 209
Denali National Park, AK 99755
☎ (907) 683-2734
NA 200

Outback Expeditions, Inc.
Box 16343
Seattle, WA 98116
☎ (206) 932-7012
SA 200, NA 205

Outdoors Unlimited
P.O. Box 854
Lotus, CA 95651
☎ (916) 626-7668
NA 76

Overseas Adventure Travel
349 Broadway
Cambridge, MA 02139
☎ (617) 876-0533
AF 36, AF 55

Pacific Outdoors Adventures
2463 Kohio, Suite 2B
Honolulu, HI 96815
☎ (808) 924-8898
NA 133

Pacific Quest
P.O. Box 205
Haleiwai, HI 96712
☎ (808) 638-8338
NA 49

Parklands Expeditions
P.O. Box 3055
Jackson Hole, WY 83001
☎ (307) 543-2398
NA 110

Puma Expeditions
P.O. Box 215
Ojo Caliente, NM 87549
☎ (505) 583-2428
NA 206

Raging Thunder
88 Lake Street
P.O. Box 1109
Cairns, Queensland 4870
Australia
☎ (070) 514-911
OC 62, OC 77

Regal Excursions
P.O. Box 4325
Lazimpat
Kathmandu, Nepal
☎ (415) 040
AS 80, AS 88, AS 108, AS 136

Rioandes
Av. Sol, Edificio "San Jorge"
Psje. Grace S/N
Cuzco, Peru
☎ (51) 84-233-190
SA 8, SA 62

Sheri Griffith Expeditions
P.O. Box 1324
Moab, UT 84532
☎ (801) 259-8229
NA 46, NA 48

Slickrock Kayak Adventures
P.O. Box 1400
Moab, UT 84532
☎ (801) 259-6996
SA 65

SOBEK Canada
159 Main Street
Unionville, Ontario
Canada L3R 2GB
☎ (416) 479-2600
NA 126

SOBEK Expeditions
P.O. Box 1089
Angels Camp, CA 95222
☎ (800) 777-7939
☎ (209) 736-4524
EC 1, EC 2, EC 3, EC 4, EC 5, AF 9, AF 13,
AF 14, AF 26, AF 30, AF 35, AF 45, AF 48,
AF 50, AF 60, AF 65, SA 1, SA 3, SA 13,
SA 14, SA 28, SA 36, SA 37, SA 46, SA 50,
SA 61, SA 64, SA 66, SA 68, SA 69, SA 70,
SA 71, EU 14, EU 15, EU 53, EU 56 EU 57,
EU 58, EU 59, EU 61, OC 79, OC 83, AS 50,
AS 51, AS 77, AS 78, AS 129, AS 129,
AS 130, AS 153, AS 154, AS 156, AS 157,
AS 206, NA 1, NA 95, NA 100

SOBEK Expeditions Zambia
P.O. Box 60957
Livingstone, Zambia
☎ (321) 432
AF ½

Speed Travel
933 Pico Blvd.
Santa Monica, CA 90405
☎ (213) 450-3262
AS 159

Steve Currey Expeditions
Box 1547
Provo, UT 84603
☎ (800) 937-7238
AS 204

Tide-Rip Tours
P.O. Box 4143
Bellingham, WA 98227
☎ (206) 671-3804
NA 102

Transglobal B.V.
Singel 190
1016 AA Amsterdam
The Netherlands
☎ (20) 261-042
AF 22, AF 23

Trans Niugini Tours
P.O. Box 371
Mt. Hagen, Papau New Guinea
☎ 011-675-52-2438
OC 52, OC 53, OC 74

Trek Travel
Aydede Caddesi 10
Taksim Istanbul, Turkey
☎ (1) 155 1624
AS 124

Trezise Bush Guide Service
Laura, Queensland
Australia
☎ (070) 603-236
OC 35

Tropical
Turven Tropical Travel Services
Calle Real de Sabana Grande,
Edif. Union, Piso 1, #13
Chacaito, Caracas, Venezuala
☎ (717) 098
SA 57

United Touring International
400 Market St.
Suite 206
Philadelphia, PA 19107
☎ (215) 545-1355
AF 56

Vista Verde
P.O. Box 465
Steamboat Springs, CO 80477
☎ (303) 879-3858
NA 131

Voyages Maldives
2 Fareedhee Magu
Male 20-20, Maldives
AS 39

Warner & Mackenzie Guiding and Outfitting
P.O. Box 2280
Banff, Alberta
Canada T0L 0C0
☎ (403) 762-4551
NA 111

Wilderness Trails
61 Brompton Road
London SW3 1DP, England
☎ 01-589-0144
AF 67

Wilderness Southeast
711 Sandtown Rd.
Savannah, GA 31410
☎ (912) 897-5108
NA 84

Wild Life Adventure Tours
606 Akash Deep, 6th Fl.
Barakhamba Road
New Delhi, India
☎ (331) 2773
AS 109

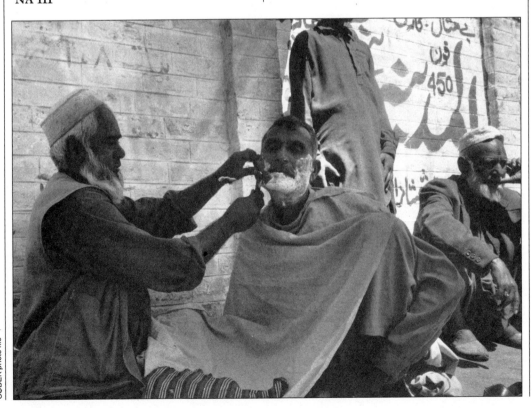

SOBEK photo file

World Expeditions
377 Sussex St., 3rd Floor
Sydney, NSW 2000
Australia
**AF 200, AF 201, OC 12, OC 16, OC 38,
OC 82, OC 200, AS 2, AS 3, AS 7, AS 8,
AS 12, AS 15, AS 27, AS 29, AS 31, AS 37,
AS 47, AS 49, AS 63, AS 85, AS 89, AS 94,
AS 95, AS 111, AS 201, AS 202, AS 203**

Worldwide Adventures
920 Yonge St., Ste. 747
Toronto, Ontario,
Canada M4W 3C7
☎ (416) 963-9163
NA 134, NA 135

SOBEK photo file

Other Books from John Muir Publications

Adventure Vacations: From Trekking in New Guinea to Swimming in Siberia, Richard Bangs (65-76-9) 256 pp. $17.95

Asia Through the Back Door, 3rd ed., Rick Steves and John Gottberg (65-48-3) 326 pp. $15.95

Being a Father: Family, Work, and Self, *Mothering* Magazine (65-69-6) 176 pp. $12.95

Buddhist America: Centers, Retreats, Practices, Don Morreale (28-94-X) 400 pp. $12.95

Bus Touring: Charter Vacations, U.S.A., Stuart Warren with Douglas Bloch (28-95-8) 168 pp. $9.95

California Public Gardens: A Visitor's Guide, Eric Sigg (65-56-4) 304 pp. $15.95 (Available 3/91)

Catholic America: Self-Renewal Centers and Retreats, Patricia Christian-Meyer (65-20-3) 325 pp. $13.95

Complete Guide to Bed & Breakfasts, Inns & Guesthouses, Pamela Lanier (65-43-2) 520 pp. $15.95

Costa Rica: A Natural Destination, Ree Strange Sheck (65-51-3) 280 pp. $15.95

Elderhostels: The Students' Choice, Mildred Hyman (65-28-9) 224 pp. $12.95

Environmental Vacations: Volunteer Projects to Save the Planet, Stephanie Ocko (65-78-5) 240 pp. $15.95 (Available 10/90)

Europe 101: History & Art for the Traveler, 4th ed., Rick Steves and Gene Openshaw (65-79-3) 372 pp. $15.95

Europe Through the Back Door, 9th ed., Rick Steves (65-42-4) 432 pp. $16.95

Floating Vacations: River, Lake, and Ocean Adventures, Michael White (65-32-7) 256 pp. $17.95

Gypsying After 40: A Guide to Adventure and Self-Discovery, Bob Harris (28-71-0) 264 pp. $12.95

The Heart of Jerusalem, Arlynn Nellhaus (28-79-6) 336 pp. $12.95

Indian America: A Traveler's Companion, Eagle/Walking Turtle (65-29-7) 424 pp. $16.95

The Indian Way: Learning to Communicate with Mother Earth, Gary McLain (Young Readers, 8 yrs. +) (65-73-4) 114 pp. $9.95

The Kids' Environment Book: What's Awry and Why, Anne Pedersen (10 yrs. +) (65-74-2) 192 pp. $12.95 (Available 1/91)

Mona Winks: Self-Guided Tours of Europe's Top Museums, Rick Steves and Gene Openshaw (28-85-0) 456 pp. $14.95

The On and Off the Road Cookbook, Carl Franz (28-27-3) 272 pp. $8.50

Paintbrushes and Pistols: How the Taos Artists Sold the West, Schwarz and Taggett (65-65-3) 280 pp. $17.95

The People's Guide to Mexico, Carl Franz (65-60-2) 608 pp. $17.95

The People's Guide to RV Camping in Mexico, Carl Franz with Steve Rogers (28-91-5) 320 pp. $13.95

Preconception: A Woman's Guide to Preparing for Pregnancy and Parenthood, Brenda E. Aikey-Keller (65-44-0) 232 pp. $14.95

Rads, Ergs, and Cheeseburgers: The Kids' Guide to Energy and the Environment, Bill Yanda (8 yrs. +) (65-75-0) 108 pp. $12.95 (Available 2/91)

Ranch Vacations: The Complete Guide to Guest and Resort, Fly-Fishing, and Cross-Country Skiing Ranches, Eugene Kilgore (65-30-0) 392 pp. $18.95

Schooling at Home: Parents, Kids, and Learning, *Mothering* Magazine (65-52-1) 264 pp. $14.95

The Shopper's Guide to Art and Crafts in the Hawaiian Islands, Arnold Schuchter (65-61-0) 256 pp. $12.95 (Available 11/90)

The Shopper's Guide to Mexico, Steve Rogers and Tina Rosa (28-90-7) 224 pp. $9.95

Ski Tech's Guide to Equipment, Skiwear, and Accessories, edited by Bill Tanler (65-45-9) 144 pp. $11.95

Ski Tech's Guide to Maintenance and Repair, edited by Bill Tanler (65-46-7) 144 pp. $11.95

Teens: A Fresh Look, *Mothering* Magazine (65-54-8) 240 pp. $14.95

A Traveler's Guide to Asian Culture, Kevin Chambers (65-14-9) 224 pp. $13.95

Traveler's Guide to Healing Centers and Retreats in North America, Martine Rudee and Jonathan Blease (65-15-7) 240 pp. $11.95

Understanding Europeans, Stuart Miller (65-77-7) 272 pp. $14.95

Undiscovered Islands of the Caribbean, Burl Willes (65-55-6) 232 pp. $14.95

Undiscovered Islands of the Mediterranean, Linda Lancione Moyer and Burl Willes (65-53-X) 232 pp. $14.95

A Viewer's Guide to Art: A Glossary of Gods, People, and Creatures, Shaw and Warren (65-66-1) 152 pp. $9.95 (Available 3/91)

22 Days Series
These pocket-size itineraries (4½" x 8") are a refreshing departure from ordinary guidebooks. Each offers 22 flexible daily itineraries that can be used to get the most out of vacations of any length. Included are not only "must see" attractions but also little-known villages and hidden "jewels" as well as valuable general information.
22 Days Around the World, Roger Rapoport and Burl Willes (65-31-9) 200 pp. $9.95
22 Days Around the Great Lakes, Arnold Schuchter (65-62-9) 176 pp. $9.95 (Available 1/91)
22 Days in Alaska, Pamela Lanier (28-68-0) 128 pp. $7.95

22 Days in the American Southwest, 2nd ed., Richard Harris (28-88-5) 176 pp. $9.95

22 Days in Asia, Roger Rapoport and Burl Willes (65-17-3) 136 pp. $7.95

22 Days in Australia, 3rd ed., John Gottberg (65-40-8) 148 pp. $7.95

22 Days in California, 2nd ed., Roger Rapoport (65-64-5) 176 pp. $9.95

22 Days in China, Gaylon Duke and Zenia Victor (28-72-9) 144 pp. $7.95

22 Days in Europe, 5th ed., Rick Steves (65-63-7) 192 pp. $9.95

22 Days in Florida, Richard Harris (65-27-0) 136 pp. $7.95

22 Days in France, Rick Steves (65-07-6) 154 pp. $7.95

22 Days in Germany, Austria & Switzerland, 3rd ed., Rick Steves (65-39-4) 136 pp. $7.95

22 Days in Great Britain, 3rd ed., Rick Steves (65-38-6) 144 pp. $7.95

22 Days in Hawaii, 2nd ed., Arnold Schuchter (65-50-5) 144 pp. $7.95

22 Days in India, Anurag Mathur (28-87-7) 136 pp. $7.95

22 Days in Japan, David Old (28-73-7) 136 pp. $7.95

22 Days in Mexico, 2nd ed., Steve Rogers and Tina Rosa (65-41-6) 128 pp. $7.95

22 Days in New England, Anne Wright (28-96-6) 128 pp. $7.95

22 Days in New Zealand, Arnold Schuchter (28-86-9) 136 pp. $7.95

22 Days in Norway, Denmark & Sweden, Rick Steves (28-83-4) 136 pp. $7.95

22 Days in the Pacific Northwest, Richard Harris (28-97-4) 136 pp. $7.95

22 Days in the Rockies, Roger Rapoport (65-68-8) 176 pp. $9.95

22 Days in Spain & Portugal, 3rd ed., Rick Steves (65-06-8) 136 pp. $7.95

22 Days in Texas, Richard Harris (65-47-5) 176 pp. $9.95 (Available 11/90)

22 Days in Thailand, Derk Richardson (65-57-2) 176 pp. $9.95

22 Days in the West Indies, Cyndy & Sam Morreale (28-74-5) 136 pp. $7.95

"Kidding Around" Travel Guides for Children
Written for kids eight years of age and older. Generously illustrated in two colors with imaginative characters and images. An adventure to read and a treasure to keep.

Kidding Around Atlanta, Anne Pedersen (65-35-1) 64 pp. $9.95

Kidding Around Boston, Helen Byers (65-36-X) 64 pp. $9.95

Kidding Around Chicago, Lauren Davis (65-70-X) 64 pp. $9.95

Kidding Around the Hawaiian Islands, Sarah Lovett (65-37-8) 64 pp. $9.95

Kidding Around London, Sarah Lovett (65-24-6) 64 pp. $9.95

Kidding Around Los Angeles, Judy Cash (65-34-3) 64 pp. $9.95

Kidding Around the National Parks of the Southwest, Sarah Lovett 108 pp. $12.95

Kidding Around New York City, Sarah Lovett (65-33-5) 64 pp. $9.95

Kidding Around Philadelphia, Rebecca Clay (65-71-8) 64 pp. $9.95

Kidding Around San Francisco, Rosemary Zibart (65-23-8) 64 pp. $9.95

Kidding Around Washington, D.C., Anne Pedersen (65-25-4) 64 pp. $9.95

Automotive Repair Manuals
How to Keep Your VW Alive (65-80-7) 440 pp. $19.95
How to Keep Your Subaru Alive (65-11-4) 480 pp. $19.95
How to Keep Your Toyota Pickup Alive (28-81-3) 392 pp. $19.95
How to Keep Your Datsun/Nissan Alive (28-65-6) 544 pp. $19.95

Other Automotive Books
The Greaseless Guide to Car Care Confidence: Take the Terror Out of Talking to Your Mechanic, Mary Jackson (65-19-X) 224 pp. $14.95

Off-Road Emergency Repair & Survival, James Ristow (65-26-2) 160 pp. $9.95

Ordering Information
If you cannot find our books in your local bookstore, you can order directly from us. Please check the "Available" date above. If you send us money for a book not yet available, we will hold your money until we can ship you the book. Your books will be sent to you via UPS (for U.S. destinations). UPS will not deliver to a P.O. Box; please give us a street address. Include $2.75 for the first item ordered and $.50 for each additional item to cover shipping and handling costs. For airmail within the U.S., enclose $4.00. All foreign orders will be shipped surface rate; please enclose $3.00 for the first item and $1.00 for each additional item. Please inquire about foreign aimail rates.

Method of Payment
Your order may be paid by check, money order, or credit card. We cannot be responsible for cash sent through the mail. All payments must be made in U.S. dollars drawn on a U.S. bank. Canadian postal money orders in U.S. dollars are acceptable. For VISA, MasterCard, or American Express orders, include your card number, expiration date, and your signature, or call (800) 888-7504. Books ordered on American Express cards can be shipped only to the billing address of the cardholder. Sorry, no C.O.D.'s. Residents of sunny New Mexico, add 5.625% tax to the total.

Address all orders and inquiries to:
John Muir Publications
P.O. Box 613
Santa Fe, NM 87504
(505) 982-4078
(800) 888-7504